This Book Is for You If . . .

- You are interested in beginning a spiritual practice rooted in Jewish tradition.
- You want to enhance a Jewish practice you already perform.
- You are looking for information on how to perform Jewish rituals.
- You are interested in the variety of ways Jewish rituals are performed.
- You are looking for spiritual inspiration.
- You are a liberal Jew who is curious as to how other liberal Jews have made a place for traditional rituals in their lives.
- You have left Jewish practice and are seeking a way back in through ritual.
- You are not Jewish but are interested in the background of Jewish ritual.

Contributors

Nina Beth Cardin
Debra Nussbaum Cohen
Ruth M. Gais
Daniel Judson
Mark Kligman
Haviva Ner-David
Kerry M. Olitzky
Mark Sameth
Andrew Vogel

Rituals & Practices

Upon Rising and Going to Bed
Covering the Head
Blessings throughout the Day
Daily Prayer
Tefillin
Tallit and *Tallit Katan*
Talmud Torah
The Continuum of Kashrut
Mikvah
Entering Shabbat

A Handbook for
Personal Spiritual Renewal

The Rituals &
Practices of a
Jewish Life

EDITED BY
Rabbi Kerry M. Olitzky and Rabbi Daniel Judson

FOREWORD BY
Vanessa L. Ochs

ILLUSTRATIONS BY
Joel Moskowitz

The Rituals & Practices of a Jewish Life:
A Handbook for Personal Spiritual Renewal

© 2002 by Kerry M. Olitzky and Daniel Judson
Illustrations © 2002 by Joel Moskowitz from the Hebrew Blessings series

Library of Congress Cataloging-in-Publication Data
The rituals and practices of a Jewish life : a handbook for personal spiri-
tual renewal / [edited] by Daniel Judson and Kerry M. Olitzky ; foreword
by Vanessa Ochs.
        p.   cm.
Includes bibliographical references.
ISBN 1-58023-169-1
1. Judaism—Customs and practices. 2. Jewish way of life. I. Judson,
Daniel. II. Olitzky, Kerry M.
BM700 .R46 2002
296.7—dc21
                                                    2002005154

Page 231 constitutes a continuation of this copyright page.

10   9   8   7   6   5   4   3   2   1

Manufactured in the United States of America

Published by Jewish Lights Publishing
A Division of LongHill Partners, Inc.
Sunset Farm Offices, Route 4, P.O. Box 237
Woodstock, VT 05091
Tel: (802) 457-4000   Fax: (802) 457-4004
www.jewishlights.com

For Joyce Cohen, *z"l*
—*DJ*

For Jesse Michael Olitzky,
in honor of his election as
international president of
United Synagogue Youth.
—*KMO*

Contents

Foreword

VANESSA L. OCHS

People are familiar enough with Jewish holiday and special occasion practices. We're known for praying for forgiveness for our sins, blowing the shofar, lighting Sabbath and holiday candles, casting bread crumbs on the water, and hunting out the leavened products in our homes and replacing them with matzo. People expect we'll be standing under a wedding canopy and breaking a glass, circumcising a baby boy, celebrating a bat mitzvah, and saying Kaddish.

It's the daily rituals and practices of Judaism that are less well-known to non-Jews; some of them—like the ritual bath and the *tallit katan,* worn under the clothing—are unfamiliar and even exotic to many Jews as well.

Jews have the possibility of performing hundreds of rituals and practices on a regular day and of marking life's much smaller, daily milestones, as mundane as putting on a brand new pair of socks or tucking a child in at night with a bedtime prayer. There are the ritual practices for opening our eyes in the morning, getting out of bed, and getting dressed. There is a ritual for going to the bathroom, a ritual for before we have our toast and coffee, and a ritual for after we've eaten. There is a ritual for walking out our front door, another for boarding the train to work, and another for opening up a letter or e-mail and reading good or bad news. There is a ritual to mark sundown each Friday as the Sabbath begins and each Saturday at the Sabbath's close. There is a ritual to mark the end of menstruation every month.

In the land of Jewish, there is, in fact, no moment that goes by when there is not *some* formal Jewish way to behave, interact, mark, respond, bless, or reflect. Nothing—even making love. Even speaking the right words *before* you make love has its own Jewish way.

Some of these practices are governed by laws that originate in the Torah and get more explicitly and intricately spelled out in rabbinic literature and contemporary codes of Jewish law. Others are cherished customs, *minhagim* (as they are called), that have emerged out of communities, become venerated, and are performed with the same care and seriousness as the text-bound laws, and with much tenderness. For liberal Jews, commandedness that is of divine or communal origin is not the rationale for engaging in these practices. Most likely it is instead the intuition that doing these practices opens the door to a life of greater purpose, greater moral depth, greater joy, and greater commitment to others. They open the way for transcendence.

To my mind, these daily rituals and practices are intensely poetic expressions of being Jewish, and while they are bound by intricate rules and social conventions that vary from one community to another, they also represent the most spiritually creative ways in which we are blessed to weave Jewish lives. These practices transform us as individuals and also take us out of our aloneness and connect us to the Jewish people.

Anthropologist Barbara Kirshenblatt-Gimblett refers to this rich Jewish way of living, a way of life perfused by ritual practices, as "the performance of hundreds of precepts."[1] She explains that in such a way of life, "through ritual elaboration, small and large, the most commonplace acts become deliberate and conscious activities. . . . The createdness of the universe is brought to consciousness again and again."[2] Each performance of a Jewish practice generates the potential of acknowledging that God created this world and that God is actively present in one's life and in all that happens. "The performance of precepts thus ritualizes and invests with meaning activities that would otherwise be habituated, taken for granted, or considered trivial."[3] This means that an encounter with the Divine doesn't just happen when the rabbi shows up, when you enter the synagogue, or when it's Yom Kippur. It means that holiness is a nonstop and continual way of being in which you are in charge. It means that you are engaging in holy behaviors and holy choices no matter where you are or what you're doing. Religion isn't just part of your life, something you do when it's appropriate, conventional, or when it feels right because you're so moved or because you're feeling virtuous. Religion is your whole life, and it's not separable from your private or professional life. It's your whole identity; it's reality itself, and in a cosmic sense it's more true than the facts of mundane reality.

In such a life, every activity is governed by religious rules, teachings, and wisdom about how to perform the practice with sacred intent, even when it gets done day after day. In such a life, "How do I live in God's image?", "How do I bring God into my life?", and "How do I make this life holy?" are not abstract questions with touchy-feely answers. An outsider might see such a life, so filled with proscribed activities and words, to be oppressive, robbing people of their free will, creativity, and spontaneity. Such a critique is certainly understandable: any practice that becomes rote risks becoming rigid and taken for granted. However, one could equally see being born into this Jewish way of being as an incredible blessing: here is a disciplined life that does not just go with the flow. It places values of holiness, community, family, justice, and righteousness above all else, and it supports the pursuit of a life filled with meaning, not as a nice and thoughtful private indulgence but as a sacred obligation, a covenant held by an entire people, one that begins with a good deal of training and requires a lifetime of disciplined, habitual performance.

There was a time when many Jews considered a daily life richly filled with Jewish practices to be the exclusive province of what we call "religious Jews" or "observant Jews"—people who, since birth,

lead lives that are altogether governed by Jewish laws that are carried
out rigorously and, seemingly, "to the letter of the law" by everyone
in their family and their community. People live this way because they
are brought up to do so. Unless a rebellious spirit or a complicating
circumstance leads them to distance themselves from this life, they do
not generally question their personal endorsement of this way of
being human.

In recent generations this is no longer the case. Many Jews who
were not born into families that observe the daily Jewish practices are
now paying attention to the spiritual beauty of those practices. They
have decided to learn about them, try them out, and perhaps adapt
them for their own lives and their own families. They are seeing
Jewish tradition as the treasury of not only the traditional "perform-
ers" but of all of us.

Once it seemed to be an all-or-nothing thing: you were born
keeping the Sabbath, keeping kosher, or wearing a *kipah,* and that's
what you did. Religious sensibilities have changed. Now a Jew who
is unfamiliar with Sabbath practices, for example, and unconnected
to an observing community might say, "You know, I'd like to bring a
little Sabbath practice into my week. I won't worry about getting it
all 'right,' and I won't worry if regular Sabbath observers will accept
what I do as legitimate. I'll light candles this week and see how it
goes." Many Jews who are born into religious practices are also self-
consciously reflecting upon the meaning of their practices in their
lives today and are revitalizing their stance toward them. This is not
a sign of rebellion or critique, but of spiritual hunger and intellectual
integrity. In addition to studying the practices in depth, they are rigorously considering the sociological, psychological, and spiritual
ways in which these practices give shape to their lives.[4] The reflection
doesn't endanger the practice, it deepens it.

Perhaps you are turning to Jewish tradition in order to try out a
new practice and, if it feels right, to embrace it as your own. You
might be learning this practice according to the guidelines suggested
by a particular Jewish community in which you feel at home, or you
might be encountering it alone, unbound by the conventions of a par-

ticular group. Perhaps you are reconsidering a Jewish practice you encountered in your childhood—one that may have once seemed oppressive, alienating, or just unfathomably strange. Now you are approaching it with a fresh and open adult consciousness. Perhaps you are revisiting a practice you've attached yourself to all your life, but now, equipped with deeper understandings of the practice's meaning and inspired to engage in a more nuanced appropriation of the practice, you are ready to encounter a richer spiritual experience in your own ritual "backyard."

Whether you are a first-time explorer, a returnee, or a "reencounterer," you are blessed to be living in a time when so many are engaging in spiritual exploration by reclaiming Jewish practices. You are supported by the "outreach" arms of many of the Jewish movements that stand ready with teachers and volunteers offering classes and workshops to introduce or deepen Jewish practice. You are also supported by this book, which strives to be there with you as a spiritual guide and teacher, with multiple strategies, in your quest to find yourself in the rich (and intricate, complicated, and sometimes daunting) Jewish traditions. Most of the contributors to this book are people, perhaps like yourself, who have come back to Jewish ritual in a serious way as adults or young adults. Most consider their involvement with Jewish practices as a journey, a process of individual discovery on a well-trodden path. Each speaks out of a unique experience; each is aware that when you take a Jewish practice into your life and let its meanings unfold, you will be moved and surprised by the depth of the experience.

In experiencing a new practice, or experiencing an old practice in a distinctively new way, you are probably moving outside your comfort zone. That's an impressive thing to do, because it expresses your willingness to expand the range of who you are. As anthropologists would say, what we do daily in our own culture—the ways we eat, dress, celebrate, mourn, and mark time—seem like the only natural and logical ways to handle our human needs and be human beings. It's the efficient way, the gracious way, the meaningful way, the way that holds our world together and tells us who we are.

Whatever the dimensions of your spiritual ambition—from creating an entirely kosher kitchen to trying to start each day with a small prayer—I am impressed, for I know that it is daunting to change your old habits or haphazard ways and to substitute new or unfamiliar ways of being human.

For many reasons, beginnings are hard. There are the people you live with, family and friends, who might stand in your way, consciously or unconsciously bollixing up your efforts to engage in a spiritual discipline. They may be afraid that this ritual practice you are taking on means that you have now "become religious" (whatever that means to them!) and that you will no longer be like you used to be. What if you won't eat in their house anymore, or go out to restaurants? What if you won't go to ball games on Saturday with them? What if you start preferring to spend your Friday nights with only Sabbath observers? What if you start treating these important people in your life as if they aren't very good or very authentic Jews?

Their fears are grounded in some reality, and you may need to assure the people who know and love you that it's true: a new practice you are taking on may indeed require some adjustments on your part and even theirs. However, you're still you, and your relationship shouldn't be threatened.

There will be other people who will say that if you don't plan on doing the ritual the "right way" (however they mean that—either exactly the way they do it or the way they imagine "really religious" people practice it), then you might as well not even bother.

You, yourself, might pose no resistance to taking on the new Jewish practices. You might be the kind of determined and focused person who decides that you will start exercising every day for the sake of your health. Having made the decision, you buy the right sneakers and the right exercise clothes; you join a gym, learn how to use the weight machines, elliptical trainer, and the Stairmaster; and you show up at 6:30 A.M. every day before work, with your work clothes packed in a hanging carrying case. You know that you will have to start slowly and build up stamina. You know that you will have good days and bad, and that you will have to be your own cheerleader. You know "no pain, no gain." You know that there are experts in exercise physiology you will want to consult, and you know how to spot people who are enough steps ahead of you who can give you pointers, both physical and psychic. You will take pleasure in seeing familiar faces in the gym, and you will enjoy cheering each other on and bantering in the locker room.

If this is your style, and if you choose to adapt a morning prayer ritual, for instance, you might go about it in the very same manner: making the commitment, mustering up your motivations, getting the right equipment and skills, showing up each day no matter what, dealing with distractions and setbacks in a graceful and mature manner, and finding teachers to guide you and partners who are fellow travelers.

Is taking on a new physical, health-related discipline comparable to a new spiritual regime? I believe it is. When you choose to exercise daily, you are affirming a belief (whether it's true or false) that there is a link between exercise and good health and that you can choose to have a longer and healthier life by exercising. There is a moral dimension, too, in your choice to exercise, for in doing so you are choosing life for yourself, and, by consequence, you are sharing the gift of your extended life with the people who love you. There is guilt, too: skip a day of exercise, and you get to beat up on yourself for having failed yourself and your loved ones.

This model may not fit your personality. You may not be the kind of person who commits to a lifestyle change and then pursues it gung ho. That's where I fit in: I always doubt that I'm making the right decision. I get bored or distracted. I feel too awkward in the face of the pros to even show up. I feel silly. I give up.

If this is your profile, if you resist change even when you want to make change, then you will find other strategies through which to grow into the Jewish ritual practices that beckon you. You might praise yourself extravagantly for just getting your toes wet in a ritual and not berate yourself for not venturing in more wholeheartedly. You might choose not to worry at all about being consistent, lighting Sabbath candles one week but not the next; eliminating chores and household work on the Sabbath but doing craft projects with your children that you could never otherwise get to do. You might choose to be in the presence of people who are practicing the ritual, without actually doing it yourself until you are comfortable with it. You might choose to give yourself all the time you need. If it takes a year to pick out the tallit you think you'd be comfortable wearing, and then another full year before you pull it out of its bag and wrap it around your shoulders, then that's fine. That's your time line. If you think you need a group of your friends to jump-start you into the ritual, you'll organize your supporters. A friend of mine made her Rosh Chodesh (new moon) group wake up early one Sunday morning— bribed with the promise of mimosas!—to hike down to a river for a ceremony that would get her to put on her tallit for the first time. It worked! These are all praiseworthy strategies.

You may have yet a different profile. You may have been raised in a home in which various Jewish rituals were practiced, and you may be intimately familiar with them. However, your experience may not have been a positive one, and you may associate many unhappy memories with these rituals. My mother, who is an artist, hated the strict Sabbath observances of her childhood because that was the day her beloved pen and paper were forbidden to her. Only as an adult has she been able to find some joy in keeping the Sabbath, and by conventional standards it's a quirky Shabbat, but she keeps it with rigor. After going to Saturday morning services and visiting with her friends at the kiddush, she and my dad always go out to Pierre's, their favorite restaurant, for lunch.

You may have rejected the Jewish practices of your childhood because they were forced upon you in a way that gave you little choice but to rebel and reject them. You may have seen the rituals as signs of being an insider in a group you didn't really want to be part of. You may have seen the ritual behaviors as merely exterior signs of piety or conformity. Without ever having been exposed to the many-layered meanings of the practices and the various ways one could experience them spiritually, you hardly saw them as attractive. Or, quite simply, perhaps you never had the right teachers who could lovingly explain what a practice was all about, who could give you compelling reasons to work at it, and who could show you how they had found strategies to make the ritual work in their lives.

Despite my own reluctance toward ritual change, I have nevertheless adapted Jewish ritual practices that were new to me in my adult life. In each case I'm glad I worked through the familial, social, and logistical complications and psychic discomforts. Some of the new practices were my own idea, and others were instigated by family members who either quietly lured the rest of us into their practice or consciously asked us for our support and championed our participation. It means that I have slowly adapted myself to practices that were new to me, and that eventually I found ways to start making the practices my own, to bring them into my comfort zone. In many cases, it's the new practices I've adopted—more than the old, habitual ones—that bring me more deeply into a feeling of the Divine Presence. In the long run, these practices have begun to feel as if they really are my own, and they are some of the richest experiences of being a Jew and of being human that I have.

The daily or weekly Jewish practices are harder to start keeping than are the more dramatic rituals of birth, coming of age, marriage, death, or even the holidays. The dramatic rituals emerge at special occasions, when there is an urge to mark what's happening in the correct Jewish way, or to observe it as Jews do. In the dramatic rituals, of which a wedding is one, there is real work that needs to be done, and there's usually a ritual expert on hand, typically a rabbi, who not only knows the rules and regulations but also has the confidence and experience in the ritual to be able to execute it with the right aura. In this case, two separate people and their families need to be brought together, committing themselves and binding their souls in the eyes of God and Israel forever. The drama is "Will it happen? Will it all work out?" If you are the groom, and a rabbi tells you to say some unfamiliar Hebrew words and put a ring on your bride's finger, and if you believe you are really married and so does everyone else, then it may not really matter if you were ever fully comfortable with the ritual. The ritual did its work, and you probably celebrate that there was a venerable cultural script to get you through this "crisis." The daily rituals don't do such "work" or solve problems in such an obvious, clear, and dramatic way. You can resolve the matter of "What's for dinner?" without keeping kosher; you can pass a lovely Saturday without the disciplines of Shabbat; and, without going to the *mikvah,* you can find other strategies that sustain your marriage or celebrate the monthly renewal of a woman's body.

Although the daily practices add value to life, in most cases we have managed without them. Taking on a new daily or regular practice, like Shabbat or the *mikvah,* allows us to transform our lives on whatever scale and at whatever pace we choose. A new ritual practice is a bold statement, allowing us to say, even if it's just to ourselves, "I want my everyday life to be different. I want to bring being Jewish into my life, not just at weddings and funerals, but in waking up and having breakfast and making love. I want to enact Jewish rituals in the minidramas of many moments of life. I want that ritual to blossom into my life. I want to feel at each moment that I am connected to other Jews, past and present, in my own life and around the world, who are sanctifying life in these kinds of ways. I want to know what it's like to feel the Divine Presence enriching, directing, and being present in my everyday life."

Acknowledgments

We are indebted to Stuart and Antoinette Matlins for their support of this project. We are particularly appreciative of the time that Stuart Matlins, publisher of Jewish Lights, took to edit this volume because the reclaiming of Jewish ritual is a subject dear to his heart. We also thank the many staff members of Jewish Lights Publishing who, with great care and compassion, gently moved this project along. In particular, we thank Emily Wichland and Martha McKinney.

We would like to thank two members of Dan's congregation, Anne Strickland and Hannah Orden, who read the chapters with great care and insight. Their comments were invaluable in improving and enhancing the manuscript.

We want to acknowledge the keen eye and pen of Vanessa L. Ochs for writing the foreword and serving as constructive critic for material in this book.

We also thank the many people who contributed their own personal stories for this volume, some of which we unfortunately were unable to include. While their specific words may not be included in total, their thoughts and ideas certainly helped to frame this volume. In particular, we appreciate the efforts of Daniel

Brenner, Leon Morris, Peter Ochs, David Horowitz, Elyse Goldstein, and Rachel Sabath.

The initial idea for the approach for this project, as with most good ideas in his life, came from Dan's wife, Sandy Falk.

We thank our families—Sandy Falk and Naftali Falk-Judson, and Sheryl, Avi, and Jesse Olitzky—for helping us to find a rhythm for Jewish living in our lives and in theirs, knowing that the ultimate goal is to connect us to God and to one another in the process.

We must acknowledge the Almighty One, whose vision brought us together years ago as student and teacher and now once again as colleagues and friends.

RABBI DANIEL JUDSON
RABBI KERRY ("SHIA") M. OLITZKY

Introduction

There are many options for Jewish living and just as many entry points. As a result, it may be difficult for some liberal Jews to find the right fit in the world of ritual practice. The challenge is to find a way to get in sync with the rhythm of Jewish living. How do you know where to begin, or what to do first? What feels right and does not compromise what you know about the world? It may seem an overwhelming, even forbidding, prospect, but it does not have to be. This volume is designed to provide you with access and options. It is divided into ten chapters. Each chapter focuses on a specific ritual practice or set of practices along a continuum of observance. They include personal testimony and basic how-to. Try them on to see what fits, what works, and what brings you closer to God and thus closer to yourself. The specific rituals and the pattern of rituals that have been chosen for inclusion in this volume keep those goals in mind. They are designed to enrich your spiritual life. Adopt a new ritual practice into your daily routine, progressively increasing practices throughout the year. This book will show you how to do so.

Some readers may come to these pages with little or no background in Jewish ritual practice. That's OK. This book provides guidance and background to help those who are new to ritual practice. Others may already have started on their personal path to Jewish renewal through ritual. Still others may come to this book having long understood the importance of using ritual as part of a daily spiritual discipline. If you encounter a practice in this volume that you have already added to your spiritual routine, or if it is something that you have carried with you since childhood, there is still a wealth of material in the book to help you deepen the meaning of that ritual. We provide suggestions for alternative ways of performing the rituals, background on their historical development, and descriptions of the variety of ways they are presently practiced.

Some people think that Jewish ritual is an all-or-nothing proposition. Others believe that there is only a monolithic approach to Jewish ritual, that it has to be done in a certain way. Although it is true that there are established rules and regulations, there is a great deal of flexibility, as well the opportunity for personal and creative expression. Everyone has to start somewhere, someplace. The taking on of Jewish ritual evolves over time in uneven stages. This volume takes into consideration that notion of uneven development as part of the dynamic of one's personal religious life and gives you the opportunity to stop, reflect on certain things, and then move forward.

It is never too late to take on Jewish ritual practice. It is not important *when* you start; it is only important *that* you start.

וארשתיך לי לעולם, וארשתיך לי בצדק
ובמשפט ובחסד וברחמים: וארשתיך
לי באמונה, וידעת את-יהוה:

Tefillin

RABBI KERRY M. OLITZKY

THE BASICS OF USING TEFILLIN

Phylacteries. Black leather boxes. "Laying tefillin." Wrapping the straps. These are words that refer to the admittedly peculiar Jewish practice of literally binding oneself with the word of God by wrapping a black leather strap—attached to a specially made matching leather prayer box—around one's arm and hand. A separate strap with a slightly larger box is wrapped around one's forehead—straps left dangling on the side, draped around the neck, hanging down in front. This is what is referred to by the general term *tefillin,* a Hebrew word that emerges from the root word for prayer. In these boxes are contained essential Jewish prayer texts, taken from the Torah, teachings that bind us to the Divine. By literally binding God's word to our arm and hand, we give unique concrete expression to the abstract notion of inviting the Divine into our lives for inspiration and guidance. Laying tefillin is the way we begin each day, it is part of the morning prayers and serves as a foundation for the hours that follow.

My Great-grandfather's Tefillin

I am not one of those people who has laid tefillin since I was thirteen (the age when one traditionally begins laying tefillin). In fact, I had never even seen tefillin until my grandfather died. Cleaning out his apartment, I found a small, embroidered bag with what seemed to be an ancient pair of tefillin nestled inside. It turns out that they had belonged to my great-grandfather, who had tucked them in his shirt as he fled Russia. I never knew my great-grandfather, but now suddenly I had a connection to him. Hesitantly, I tried on his tefillin, mostly from a desire to connect to him rather than to God. Little did I know the powerful spiritual effect it would have on me.

At the time, I was a serious classical pianist, and I had a habit of absent-mindedly doing finger exercises whenever I had to sit still for more than two minutes at a stretch. My spirituality had always expressed itself through my fingers. Prayer was a relatively new avenue of expression for me. I was far more comfortable reaching out to God by playing a Brahms Rhapsody or a Chopin Prelude than the thrice-daily fixed liturgy of observant Jews.

I shall never forget the first time I put on my great-grandfather's tefillin. After binding the straps around my arm seven times, I placed the other one around my head, then circled my middle finger three times as I recited the traditional verse from Hosea: "I will betroth you to me forever, I will betroth you to me in righteousness, and in justice and in kindness, and in mercy. I will betroth you to me with faith and you will know God." It was an amazing tactile experience for me. The straps felt like a wedding ring; I was getting married to God!

What became even more incredible was that as I sat trying to absorb the experience, my fingers unconsciously started going through their exercises—but I couldn't move them! They were bound together by the tefillin straps. When I looked down at my hand to figure out why I couldn't move my fingers, I saw the pattern of the straps spelling out God's name, Shaddai, across the back of my hand (as they are intended to do). Ironically, I couldn't move my fingers, because God's name was constricting them. Perhaps this was a true expression of "accepting the yoke of the sovereignty of heaven." Yet that very constriction was there because I had placed it there myself, consciously and freely. Part of my "marriage" with God was the fact that I was not always going to be free to act on my personal desires.

Since that first experience, tefillin has become a strong influence on me. Sometimes when I daven (pray), I even sit and play the piano with my tefillin on. I find this to be a beautiful way to connect with God through my senses. It keeps me from making prayer too cerebral and allows me to "touch" my relationship with God in a deeper and more meaningful way.

RABBI SHOSHANA GELFAND

A PHYSICAL REMINDER

The practice of putting on tefillin is a concrete response to the instruction from the Torah to "bind them as a sign upon your hand and they shall be a reminder between your eyes." Tefillin are a reminder of our responsibilities to God in appreciation for setting us free from Egyptian slavery. Tefillin are wrapped around the arm to remind one of "God's outstretched arm" and God's "mighty hand," metaphors used in the Torah to describe God saving Israel from the Egyptians. By recalling God's power in saving Israel from Egypt, we daily remind ourselves of God's power to save us from spiritual and physical enslavement.

MY OWN EXPERIENCE

Although the practice of putting on tefillin has been part of the (solely) male Jewish experience for many generations, this was admittedly not a constant part of my life. My traditional grandfathers used them daily—and were even buried with them. My own father used tefillin as a young adult, but I have no recollection of ever seeing him join the other men of his generation in early morning prayers—not the occasional Sunday morning or even shiva (mourning) minyan. My parents abandoned traditional Judaism and its practices at the same time that they left Pittsburgh's close-knit Jewish community for the wilds of central Florida—and Reform Judaism—in the 1960s; tefillin was therefore one of the many practices they left behind. The use of tefillin was not discussed in my religious school, and since there were no daily services, there was no place for them in the local synagogue that shaped my youth. (They are never used on Shabbat and holidays.) However, there was a lone pair sitting in the museum case that adorns the sanctuary lobby, which I longingly observed each time I entered that sacred precinct on Friday evening when we went to services. I wondered what they really contained, why they inspired generations of my ancestors, and why they were carefully crafted by hand by skilled scribes learned in the art of Hebrew calligraphy. Tefillin also never found their way into the synagogue youth group and its creative services that claimed some of my attention and where I first found a small spark to ignite my early spiritual expression.

During my first extended trip to Israel, I experimented with a great deal of traditional Jewish practice, including a year of study at sixteen. It was then that I purchased my first pair of tefillin. I did not want to borrow anyone else's or wait until someone finished before putting on my own during that year—even though I only did so occasionally: holidays with a Conservative rabbi; an extended Shabbat at a Lubavitch yeshiva; *hashkamah minyan* (early morning prayer service) at the Western Wall. However, the tefillin I purchased remained for many years in the satin-lined, velvet-covered bag in which they were purchased. Even when I attended rabbinical school, they did not see the light of day. There they were not merely ignored; they were considered an anathema by my teachers and consequently by most of my fellow students. The very time I thought I would finally be able to use them proved to be a disappointment, because their use was frowned upon by nearly all of my teachers. As a result, I mentally excused myself from putting them on, citing the many reasons that I had been taught for not using them. They were primitive, out of touch, reminiscent of the Orthodoxy that kept us behind and isolated from the rest of the world.

The years passed, and although my daily spiritual practices continued to grow, tefillin still remained a practice that was foreign to me. Refusing to be dismayed by my own inherited feelings about tefillin, I purchased a pair for each of my sons for their bar mitzvah—gifts brought back from annual trips to Israel. I wanted them to have this ritual opportunity that had passed me by in my youth. Something deeply embedded in my soul yearned for expression through tefillin, although I knew not how to articulate it and did not realize that I could give it voice simply by putting them on. Instead, like so many other things we do as parents, I tried to express myself somewhat vicariously through my children. Purchasing two exquisitely crafted pairs of tefillin in Israel, as I had done in my own youth, seemed to add spiritual significance to the gift. Then my boys, prompted by their involvement in our local synagogue youth group and the conventions and trips in which they participated, got up early each day in order to put on tefillin before starting their day at school. There was no internal debate, no one there to question their motives or practice.

Instead of rushing off to my office as had been my pattern, I lingered more and more each day, reflecting on the powerful spiritual discipline that had claimed the attention of these two otherwise rebellious teenagers. Sleepily, they would lovingly wrap these leather straps around their young and innocent arms and heads as inoculation for the world they were to face. I pretended to walk past them for different reasons each day, but the real reason remained the same: I was taken by the expression on their faces that accompanied their daily practice. Tefillin helped to center the roller-coaster ride of adolescence that they endured each day. Perhaps it might do the same for me, although my roller coaster was most certainly not adolescence. Then one morning—I can't explain the specificity behind it—as part of my own reclamation process of traditional Jewish ritual, having slowly shaken off the socialization in which I had been professionally trained, I added the practice of tefillin to my daily morning routine.

It was awkward at first. I knew the rules and the "how to" of the technique of wrapping; I knew the laws and the texts, but they had become somewhat irrelevant. I knew that routines take time to develop and I had to work out my own. Like new physical exercises that are peculiar at first, the fluidity of this practice was slow in coming, so I worked at it each day, carefully binding myself in the leather straps and prayer boxes, concentrating and focusing, avoiding the distractions of the emerging day. In some ways, these first days of laying tefillin were among the most honest ritual practices in which I have ever engaged, because I did not take it for granted. The practice of tefillin demanded my attention, for it did not come naturally or easily. I could not "double task" or do it half-heartedly. After all, I was attempting to make contact with the Divine.

After my morning prayers are finished and I remove the tefillin, telltale signs of the practice are left behind: reddened skin indentations on my arm and forehead and a messy head of hair. These are not disconcerting, however. Rather, I find these signs comforting as I look in the mirror and finish the process of readying myself for the day. I am proud of these marks and I sometimes look for them on others as I encounter them on my way to work. In a physical way, I have reminded myself of God's presence in my life, the nearness of the Divine and the inspiration and guidance that I constantly seek.

BROAD STROKES OF OBSERVANCE

Tefillin are worn each morning (except for Shabbat and holidays) and during the afternoon on Tisha B'Av. With a special blessing, they are put on at the very beginning of the morning prayer service and kept on through its conclusion, except on days when the additional prayers (called *Musaf*) are said. Then they are taken off earlier in the service, before *Musaf* begins. First comes a meditation to get us focused on the task. Then the arm is placed through the loop of the tefillin. We pause and say a blessing before wrapping the arm. We temporarily wrap the remaining length of strap around the hand and pause so that we can place the head tefillin where it belongs. We pause once again for a second blessing, much like the first. Then, as we unwrap the loosely wrapped hand and then wrap it again carefully, we recite the familiar words from the prophet Hosea. It is one complete sequence of rituals, done without interruption.

Tefillin are wrapped around one's weaker arm. Therefore, right-handed people wrap them around the left arm, and left-handed people wrap them around the right arm. While the manner in which they are wrapped differs slightly in some communities (e.g., some wind clockwise, others wind counterclockwise), the straps of the tefillin symbolically spell out a name of God (*Shaddai,* or Almighty; *shaddaim* means "breasts," so this name emphasizes the nurturing aspect of God).

Each tefillin contains four excerpts from the Torah, although there are two different systems regarding the order and placement of these Torah texts. In the tefillin for the arm, all four sections are written together on one piece of specially prepared parchment, written by hand with special ink. On the head tefillin, the excerpts are written on four separate pieces of parchment and separated into sections.

THE LOVE OF GOD

One of the four texts in the tefillin is the well-known prayer called the *Shema,* which contains within it the commandment to wear tefillin. The Rabbis of the Talmud say that one who says the *Shema* without wearing tefillin is a liar. Because the *Shema* includes the commandment for tefillin and the essence of wearing tefillin and saying the *Shema* is the same—to recognize God's power—if you did one without the other you would be inconsistent, and thus a liar.

"Pay attention, Israel! Adonai is our God, Adonai alone. You should love Adonai your God with all your heart, with all your soul, and with all your substance. Take to heart these instructions with which I charge you this day. Impress them on your children. Recite them when you stay at home and when you are away, when you lie down and when you get up. *Bind them as a sign on your hand and let them serve as a symbol on your forehead,* inscribe them on the doorposts of your house and on your gates" (Deut. 6:4–9).

FOLLOWING GOD'S INSTRUCTIONS FOR YOUR LIFE

Another of the four texts is the second paragraph of the *Shema*. These verses do not use the word *tefillin*, rather they literally say "to wear symbols between your eyes." Jewish tradition has always taken the word *totafot*, "symbols," to refer to tefillin. However, Jewish practice is to wear the tefillin on the forehead and not exactly between the eyes, as the Torah suggests. The Rabbis of the Talmud discuss this point and come to the conclusion that between the eyes is too small an area; the Torah must mean the place where one can make a bald spot, that is, the forehead.

"If you obey the instructions that I give you today, loving Adonai your God and serving God with all your heart and soul, I will grant the rain for your land in season, the early rain and the late. You will gather in your new grain, wine and oil—I will also provide grass in the fields for your cattle. Thus, you will eat your full. Take care not to be lured away to serve other gods and bow to them. For God's anger will flare up against you, and God will shut up the skies so that there will be no rain and the ground will not yield its produce; and you will soon perish from the good land that God is assigning to you. Therefore impress my words on your very heart; *bind them as a sign on your hand and let them serve as a symbol on your forehead*, and teach them to your children—reciting them when you stay at home and when you are away, when you lie down and when you get up; and inscribe them on the doorposts of your house and on your gates—to the end that you and your children may endure, in the land that Adonai promised to your ancestors to assign to them, as long as there is a heaven over the earth" (Deut. 11:13–21).

THE ORIGIN OF TEFILLIN

It is not clear what factors converged to help create the specific look to the ritual as we know it, but it most probably emerged from a mimicry (and adaptation) of the look of ancient rulers who wrapped jewelry (snakelike and probably of idols) around their arms and head. With the wrapping of tefillin, Jews became kings of a sort, controlling their internal lives even when they had no control over the external reality of their lives.

TIED UP IN KNOTS

Rabbi Elimelekh of Lizhensk, a Hasidic rabbi, suggests that the word *tefillin* is itself important to its meaning. *Tefillin* comes from the word *tefillah*, meaning "prayer." The word *tefillah* is in turn derived from the word *patal,* which means "knotted," because through prayer one "knots" or binds oneself to God. This idea is suggested by the knot of the tefillin on the arm, the function of which is to "knot" the individual with God.

THE VARIETY OF APPROACHES

Reform Judaism was the only branch of Judaism that generally rejected tefillin. This was part of the dismissal of many rituals and practices that the early Reformers labeled as primitive. Moreover, in Reform's attempt to align its practices with American religion, it rejected many of the special rituals that once identified Jews as Jews and instead opted for those practices that brought us closer in form to Protestants. Once Reform Judaism was transplanted from Germany to America, the goals of its organizers were to create an American Judaism, a Jewish religion that shared much in common with other American religions and contained few rituals that separated it. However, Jews in our generation are comfortable as Americans and are now looking to reclaim many of the rituals and practices of the past. They are therefore embracing the practice of putting on tefillin with newfound enthusiasm, unfettered by the approach of previous generations of Reformers. As new spiritual disciplines are being explored, those historically indigenous to Judaism are being affirmed anew.

What do you do when the ritual does not quite fit your other sensibilities, when your commitment to being a vegan or a vegetarian extends to not wearing animal skins or using products tested on animals? Tefillin are made from leather, and this may be out of step for someone who is eco-conscious. Some Jews who are "eco-kosher" have challenged the idea of leather tefillin and have made them from synthetic materials instead.

Some women have taken on the obligation of putting on tefillin, something from which they have been exempt, according to a traditional understanding of the obligations of Jewish women. Others have said that tefillin are a male ritual and have opted not to adopt them in their religious lives. Some have taken this notion one step further and designed tefillin for themselves that they believe reflect their sensibilities as women and as Jews. Even though the leather does not offend them, the "maleness" does.

One Woman's Approach

During rabbinical school, I tried wearing tefillin for a time, but I was put off by the look of them. I wanted to bind the words within them to my head and hand, but the square, black, leather boxes and straps were repellent to me. For a long time, I gave up on the idea of doing this mitzvah. Lately, however, I felt a very strong desire to take on this mitzvah and decided that I would change the look in order to make that possible. I decided that I would take the parchments from my "regular" tefillin and put them into different holders. The basic mitzvah would remain—putting God's words, written as prescribed, on my head and arm—but the technology of attaching those words to myself would change.

I therefore commissioned the same women who made my soft, rather feminine, tallit to make similarly soft cloth pouches to contain the parchments from my old set of tefillin. They had never done so but were more than willing to work with me. These white pouches are attached by a ribbon to my *kipah* and to a wristband. On them are embroidered, in gold, the letters *ayin* (on the head) and *dalet* (on the wrist) for the two enlarged letters of the *Shema*. (The letter *ayin* in the word *shema* and the letter *dalet* in the word *echad* are enlarged. You can see this by looking at the passage in a Hebrew version of the Torah.) These letters spell the word *eid,* which means "witness," and so one becomes a witness for God when reciting the *Shema.* In addition, according to *gematria* (Jewish numerology), the letter *ayin* equals seventy and *dalet* equals four, which equals the value of the word *ve-anveihu,* "and I will glorify [God]." This word hints at the merit of doing beautiful mitzvot:

"This is my God and I will glorify [God] [*Zeh Eili ve-anveihu*]" (Ex. 15:2). Rabbi Yishma'el says: "And is it possible for flesh and blood to add glory to his Creator? It simply means: I shall be beautiful before him in the *mitzvot* that I shall do [with] a beautiful *lulav,* a beautiful sukkah, beautiful *tzitzit,* and beautiful [tefillin]" (*Mekhilta d'Rabbi Yishma'el* on Ex. 15:2).

Doing the mitzvot beautifully, a concept called *hiddur mitzvah,* is what the word *ve-anveihu* is taken to mean, for how else could we glorify God but through beautiful mitzvot? The colors of white and gold that I chose are meant to hearken back to the priesthood and the Temple, where the priests wore white and the utensils were trimmed with gold.

Having taken on this mitzvah and used these tefillin daily for months, I am glad I took this step. When I touch my tefillin while saying the *Shema* (a practice directed by Jewish tradition), I can feel the texts weave their way inside me in a manner I was not able to feel with the traditional boxes. I also feel the letters *ayin* and *dalet* embroidered on the cloth as I touch the tefillin; this helps to remind me that my faith is an open door (*delet* means "door" and is similar to the name of the letter *dalet*) to spiritual development and gives me insight (*ayin* means "eye") to help me live my life. The oval shape reminds me of my own belly when I was nine months pregnant: an oval with something holy and pure inside. (Note that the Talmud, *Megillah* 24b, says that the wearing of round tefillin are dangerous and of no religious value. Rashi comments that this does not mean tefillin shaped like an egg; thus, he implicitly affirms the possibility of oval-shaped tefillin.)

Nonetheless, I confess to a feeling of failure. I wish I could have done this mitzvah in the way everyone else does it, and eventually I hope to be able to wear black, square tefillin. I did not do this as a dilettante or simply to be creative for creativity's sake but because, at this stage in my personal and spiritual development, it was the only way I was going to be able to practice this mitzvah on a regular basis. Having changed only the technology of attaching God's words to my hand and head, I embrace this mitzvah and this way of doing it in joy and love.

RABBI JUDITH ABRAMS

SO, *NU*, ARE YOU JEWISH?

Chabad (Lubavitch) Hasidim are known for many things. Perhaps they are best known for their uniquely visible approach to outreach, particularly in big cities and on college campuses. Because they understand that there is intrinsic value in taking on Jewish ritual, their mitzvah mobiles are found each day with their force of passionate men and zealous young boys inviting male passersby into their synagogue-on-wheels to put on tefillin—but only after you have responded affirmatively to their question, "Are you Jewish?" Then they take you inside these mobile homes and campers and trucks and quickly move you through the process of putting on tefillin, hoping that from that experience, you might want to add it to your daily routine.

The Conservative movement, spearheaded by its Men's Clubs, recently dedicated a particular Sunday morning to a "worldwide wrap," encouraging people in synagogues around the country to celebrate the practice of putting on tefillin by inviting them to do so, particularly those who had never done so before. They understand the power of a community at prayer and the enhancement of a ritual when doing it with others.

WHERE AM I TODAY AND WHERE AM I PLANNING ON BEING TOMORROW?

I get up each morning, get dressed, and then put on my tallit and tefillin before finishing my morning routine and rushing off to work. Sometimes I get up a little earlier, stow my tallit and tefillin in my briefcase, and make a stop at a neighborhood synagogue or one near my office for morning prayers. I also keep a set in my office, particularly helpful in the winter when I often get to my office before the sun has risen. As personal as the practice of tefillin is for me, I often yearn for a greater sense of community. Maybe it also makes me feel better when I join with others in a practice that makes me feel like a disciplined Jew. I get particular joy when helping a new person who has joined us, awkwardly struggling with the practice, not wanting to ask for help or appear that he does not know what he is doing when he is a "master of the universe" in every other aspect of his life.

Thus I gain a significant measure of my spirituality through my discipline. In an odd sort of way, it is a feeling similar to the one I get after forcing myself to use the treadmill each evening, knowing that I will feel good at the end of my workout, even if I have dreamed up lots of reasons not to do it in the first place.

Unlike the many things that I have taught my children, with tefillin it is really they who have taught me. Now that I have taken on the discipline along with them, there is much more to teach. Perhaps I can take the time now to prepare for my grandchildren!

Tefillin often means getting up a little earlier in the morning. It means postponing my breakfast, my first read of the *New York Times,* or my first early-morning listen to CNN. The world will just have to wait a little longer before I am ready to face it.

Tefillin at the Airport

The first time I saw tefillin was in my kindergarten Sunday school class. A small group of men who had just participated in a morning prayer service passed through our classroom, a converted social hall, on their way from the service to breakfast. They seemed funny to me, these strange black boxes and straps. I remember thinking of the *shel rosh,* or head tefillin, as a tiny top hat worn too far on the front of their heads. Those men with tefillin looked as strange to me as unicorns set loose in the small synagogue in which we studied.

I knew for a long time that I wanted to wear tefillin. I liked that this was a ritual akin to no other religious tradition but my own. Unlike prayer or candles, dietary laws or blessings before food, it was distinctively Jewish. Seeing ancient tefillin from the Dead Sea sects in museum display cases, I knew that this was a religious act consistently performed for generations but still rather unfamiliar to me. Putting them on was something I made a point of learning during the semester of my junior year in college that I spent in Jerusalem. They mystified me. Since my senior year in college, I haven't missed a single day in my life of putting them on.

Although there is a great deal of ritual observance about which I am lax, tefillin, and specifically the commitment it engenders, is an act of spiritual discipline that has become part of who I am. I don't want to give a false impression. The act of putting on the tefillin certainly does not mean that I experience this as a spiritual high each morning of my life. In the context of contemporary discussions about spirituality, I have to say that this act fills me with neither a sense of contemplativeness nor one of calm. Tefillin does, however, speak to a different kind of spirituality—a spirituality of commitment and discipline. That there is something I must do whether I feel like it or not, whether I am at home or away, even en route, is a source of spiritual satisfaction, if not always in the actual performance of the mitzvah, then certainly in the reflection of my having done this on such a regular basis for such an extended period of time.

For me, tefillin unabashedly affirms the physicality of the Jewish mitzvah system. It affirms that our bodies are the primary way we have of serving God. To embrace the physical is not to deny the spiritual but to give the spiritual a concrete way of expressing itself. Our minds are only one part of our bodies. Mitzvot are largely not about thought, but rather about action. The mitzvah comes alive through the mouth, the arms, and the legs. Our eyes, our ears, and our reproductive systems are all used in the service of God. Tefillin reminds us of this. It binds our bodies to the Torah in a way that symbolically attempts to make them one.

Although I am completely supportive of transcending gender roles in the performance of mitzvot, and certainly tefillin among these, there is, in my own thinking, something particularly masculine about the physicality of tefillin. This is a mitzvah bound on a bare arm, with the tefillin for the arm tied tightly around the muscle. It feels like an affirmation of using my strength, body and soul, for redemptive purposes. It reminds me of God's outstretched arm.

My own adoption of tefillin as an important religious practice in my life is a kind of opposite experience to that of my grandfather's. My grandfather had put tefillin on every day of his life until his mid-twenties. While in a medical residency far from his childhood home, he failed to put on tefillin one morning in his rush to reach the hospital. Having seen that for the first time in his life he refrained from putting them on and nothing terrible happened to him, he never put them on again. In my twenties, at approximately the same age at which my grandfather stopped putting them on, I began to embrace tefillin as an important act of religious commitment. What for my grandfather was a burden, for me became a privilege. What for him was an imposed superstitious and perfunctory act, for me was a freely chosen connection with a tradition to which I desperately desired to connect. For my grandfather, Judaism was an organic part of his life. For me, and for many of my generation, Judaism is one choice among many with which we are inundated.

I have had the experience many times of putting on my tefillin in random gates at airports around the world. From Heathrow to Frankfurt, in Bombay and in Paris, I have been faced with situations where the only opportunity for me to put on my tefillin for morning prayers was during brief layovers in these strange cities. On international flights, boarding a plane in one city and transferring in another, it is easy to lose a day in transit. When the beginning of days is marked by laying tefillin, such a loss represents more than just the burden and disorientation of travel. In my search for that empty gate in which I can pray with tefillin, in trying to minimize my own self-consciousness, I affirm my commitment to this act and to its underlying symbolic meanings. In the strange public space necessarily turned private, I assert what this act of love requires of me.

RABBI LEON MORRIS

WHERE TO START AND HOW TO CONTINUE

For me, tefillin is an important part of my daily spiritual routine. It connects me with God, through Jewish tradition, in a way that nothing else does. The only way to start is to start. Putting on tefillin in a minyan is a community bonding experience. It is also a personal time, a time to initiate my dialogue with the Divine each morning, temporarily disrupted by my hours of sleep, however few they may be.

As with most other ritual practices, people have to find a "way in" to tefillin. Here are a few entry points, ways to get started, and even more ways to keep going.

Because wrapping tefillin takes some motor skills, we suggest that you practice even before you integrate it into your prayer life. The best way to learn is by observing someone else. (Just make sure that the one you observe knows what he or she is doing!)

Borrow a pair from someone else before you figure out what to buy for yourself. They come in a variety of styles and price ranges. Often local synagogues have extra pairs (those that have been donated or forgotten). If you have a pair that has been sitting in a bedroom closet or chest of drawers since your bar mitzvah, start with this pair, but don't be surprised if the straps are a little thin and a little short. You may have grown a little since then!

Some people find it easy to start once a week before taking on tefillin on a daily basis. Start with Sunday morning. Take in a local minyan service at the synagogue or begin in the privacy of your own home. Most Sunday mornings are less rushed than a workday weekday. This will give you some time to concentrate and practice wrapping. After a while, you'll get to know when you have wrapped it too tight (it cuts off circulation to your fingers!) or too loose (it slides off your bicep before you have even finished your prayers). Then do it also on the days when you are less rushed in the morning. In the summer, for example, we find that Friday mornings are less hectic than the rest of the days of the week. Add the days as you feel comfortable.

Take the tefillin in your hands. Get used to the way they feel and how they look. Whether old or new, they all have their own distinctive fragrance, which mixes over time with your own. That's how they become truly yours.

If they are wrapped tight around the cover, carefully unwrap them. Then remove the protective cover and gently take them out.

Start with a meditation to help your *kavanah*. Use the words that emerge from your heart. Others are included in most prayer

books. (Look for it among its first few pages.) This is one of our
favorites, penned by Rabbi Rami Shapiro:

"I welcome this morning in peace; opening my heart to wonder
and feeling the presence of God around and within me. I reach out
and connect with all those who lift their souls in prayer, adding my
voice to theirs in a choir of peace and healing."

Wrap slowly and deliberately. Pay attention to the details of
what you are doing. Observe every aspect, as if you were watching
someone else. Although the process will become easier over time, you
never want it to become routine.

It's a three-step process. The tefillin is initially wrapped on the
arm, then the head, and then the middle and ring fingers (no coincidence) and hand are wrapped. The first two steps are preceded by a
blessing. The third is accompanied by a text from the biblical Book of
Hosea (see below).

Here is a traditional meditation for wrapping tefillin with interpretations by Rabbi Shefa Gold and Rabbi Goldie Milgram. This
meditation emphasizes the growing relationship between the individual and God.

> *V'eirastikh li l'olam,* I betroth you to me forever.
> (We are in this together.)
> *V'eirastikh li b'tzedek,* I will betroth you to me equitably
> (We will share the challenges.)
> *U'v'mishpat,* and with impeccability
> (I will stay with you to get it right.)
> *U'v'chesed,* and with lovingkindness
> (I will care for you.)
> *U'v'rakhamim,* and with compassion.
> (I want to hear your pain, your joy to strive to
>   understand.)
> *V'eirastikh li b'emunah,* I will betroth you to me in faith
> (I will be there for you.)
> *V'yahdaht et Adonai,* so that you will know God.
> (So that you will experience what is possible only through
>   relationship.)

Now sit quietly with your tefillin wrapped around your arm and placed on your head. Don't rush to continue with your daily morning prayers. Reflect instead on the connection you are making with God and the sacred commandments. There will be time enough for dialogue with the Divine.

EASY STEPS

1. Roll up your sleeve (if you have one) on your weaker arm (that's the one you *don't* write with) to just above your bicep. Remember to take off any jewelry on this arm (watches and bracelets, in particular).

2. Unwrap the straps for the hand tefillin. Place the tefillin box on the bicep of your upper arm. Make sure that the leather knot protrudes on the side closest to your shoulder. The knot should be placed on the top of your biceps muscle, on the side closest to your body, to be close to your heart. Once everything is in place, before you begin wrapping, recite this blessing: *Barukh ata Adonai Elohenu melekh ha-olam asher kidshanu bemitzvotav vetzivanu lehaniach tefillin.* (Praised are You, Adonai our God, Sovereign of the universe, who has made us holy with *mitzvot* and instructed us to wrap tefillin.)

3. Pull on the strap to make sure that the tefillin is bound tightly to your arm. Try to keep it tight while you are wrapping the rest of the strap. (Some people wrap the strap once around the tefillin box to keep it in place.)

4. With the finished (black) side facing out, wind the strap four times, then three times, around your arm between your elbow and wrist. (Most people

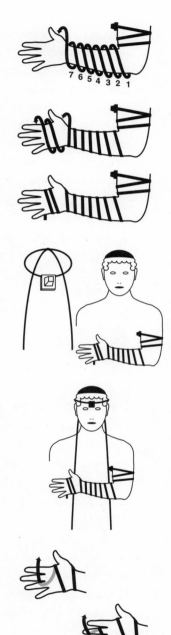

wind the strap counterclockwise, toward their bodies. Some follow the Sephardic tradition of winding the strap clockwise.)

5. Following the seventh wind, bring the strap around the outside of your hand to your palm and wrap the rest of it around the middle of your palm. Tuck the end of the strap underneath just to hold it temporarily in place while you put on the head tefillin.

6. Unwrap the head tefillin. Hold the box and place it on top of your head just above your hairline (even if your hair is no longer where it used to be!), centered between your eyes. The knot should be on the back of your head, near the nape of your neck. Bring the straps forward to hang down over your chest. Say this blessing: *Barukh ata Adonai Elohenu melekh ha-olam asher kidshanu bemitzvotav vetzivanu al mitzvat tefillin.* (Praised are You, Adonai our God, Sovereign of the universe, who has made us holy with mitzvot and instructed us concerning the mitzvah of tefillin.)

7. Unwrap the part of the strap previously coiled around your hand. Wrap the strap three times around your middle finger, once around the lower part of that finger, once around its middle, and once joining the two straps. This

forms the Hebrew letter *dalet*, the second letter in Shaddai (Almighty God). Then reflect on this verse while saying it aloud: *Ve'ayrastikh li l'olam ve'ayrastikh li betzedek u'mishpat u'vchesed u'vrachamim ve'ayrastikh li be'emunah veyda'at et Adonai.* (I will betroth you to Me forever. I will betroth you to Me with righteousness, with justice, with kindness, and with compassion. I will betroth you to Me with faithfulness, and you shall know God [Hos. 2:21].)

8.   Bring the remainder of the strap under your ring finger and over the outside of the hand, forming a V. Then wind the strap once again around the middle of the palm, forming the Hebrew letter *shin,* the first letter of Shaddai (Almighty God).

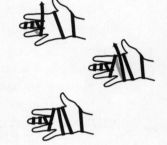

FOLLOWING ARE TWO OF THE TEXTS THAT
ARE IN THE TEFILLIN.

Exodus 13:1–10

Adonai spoke further to Moses, "Consecrate to Me every firstborn; human and animal, the first issue of every womb among the Israelites is Mine." And Moses said to the people, "Remember this day, on which you went free from Egypt, the house of bondage, how God freed you from it with a mighty hand: no leavened bread will be eaten. You go free on this day, in the month of Spring. So, when Adonai has brought you into the land of the Canaanites, the Hittites, the Amorites, the Hivites, and the Jebusites, which God swore to your ancestors to give you, a land flowing with milk and honey, you shall observe in this month the following practice: Seven days you will eat unleavened bread, and on the seventh day there should be a festival of God. Throughout the seven days unleavened bread should be eaten; no leavened bread should be found with you, and no leaven should be found in all your territory. And you shall explain to your offspring on that day, 'It is because of what God did for me when I went free from Egypt.' Thus, this will serve you as a sign on your hand and as a reminder on your forehead—in order that the teaching of Adonai may be in your mouth—that with a mighty hand God freed you from Egypt. You should keep this institution at its set time from year to year."

Exodus 13:11–16
And when Adonai brought you into the land of the Canaanites, as God swore to you and to your ancestors, and has given it to you, you will set apart for God every first issue of the womb: every male firstling that your cattle drop will be God's. But every firstling ass you will redeem with a sheep; if you do not redeem it, you must break its neck. And you must redeem every firstborn male among your children. And when, in time to come, your offspring asks you, "What does this mean?' you shall say to your child, "It was with a mighty hand that God brought us out from Egypt, the house of bondage. When Pharaoh stubbornly refused to let us go, God slew every firstborn in the land of Egypt, the firstborn of both human and animal. Therefore I sacrifice to God every first male issue of the womb, but redeem every firstborn among my sons." Thus, *it should be as a sign upon your hand and as a symbol on your forehead that with a mighty hand God led us out of Egypt.*

RECOMMENDED READING

Bailey, Stephen. *Kashrut, Tefillin, Tzitzit: Studies in the Purpose and Meaning of Symbolic Mitzvot Inspired by the Commentaries of Rabbi Samson Raphael Hirsch*. Northvale, N.J.: Jason Aronson, 2000.

Emanuel, Moshe. *Tefillin: The Inside Story.* Southfield, Mich. Targum Press, 1996.

Greenbaum, Nathan Avraham, ed. *Tefilin: A Chassidic Discourse.* Jerusalem: Breslov Research Institute, 1989.

Kaplan, Aryeh. *Tefillin.* New York: Orthodox Union, 1996.

Ner-David, Haviva. *Life on the Fringes: A Feminist Journey toward Rabbinic Ordination.* Needham, Mass.: JFL Books, 2000.

Sandberg, Martin. *Tefillin.* New York: United Synagogue of Conservative Judaism, 1992.

2

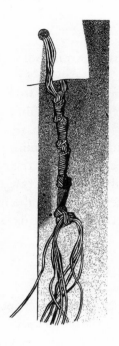

Tallit and *Tallit Katan*

HAVIVA NER-DAVID

THE BASICS OF WEARING A TALLIT

The Torah is succinct and rather direct about the instruction to wear a garment with fringes upon it: "You shall make for yourself fringes *(tzitzit)* on the four corners of your clothing with which you cover yourself" (Deut. 22:12). The fulfillment of this commandment to wear *tzitzit* takes two forms today: the wearing of a *tallit katan* (a small, four-cornered, fringed undergarment) and the wearing of a *tallit gadol* (prayer shawl) during morning prayers over one's clothing. The *tallit katan* is put on in the morning and worn all day. Generally it is worn under other clothes; some let the *tzitzit* hang out from underneath whatever they are wearing. Some people choose to wear it over their other clothes.

The *tallit gadol* is the more familiar form of the tallit. The *tallit gadol* is traditionally worn during morning prayers on weekdays, Sabbaths, and holidays. It is also worn throughout Yom Kippur. Some people cover their heads with the tallit during the recitation of the *Amidah* prayer (the prayer that forms the core of each prayer service). This allows the individual to withdraw from the congregation in personal prayer even as he or she is in the midst of it. The tallit is generally worn by the service leader during afternoon and evening services as well.

FROM THE TORAH

The Torah explains this instruction in detail: "Speak to the Israelites and tell them they should make fringes on the corners of their garments for generations; they should place a twisted thread of blue on the corner fringes. It will be to you as fringes, and when you see it, you will remember all of the instructions of God and you will do them. You will not follow after your heart and after your eyes by which you are seduced. Thus you shall be reminded to do all My mitzvot and be holy to your God" (Num. 15:38–40).

MY OWN EXPERIENCE

Deciding to take on this ritual practice was not easy or simple for me. I grew up in a modern Orthodox home in New York, where only men wore a *tallit gadol* and/or a *tallit katan*. It would have been totally out of the question for a woman to do so. In fact, I simply assumed that according to Jewish law, it was forbidden for a woman to wear a tallit, large or small, something that I would later find out was not the entire truth.

As a woman I felt excluded from doing what my brothers and the other men were doing, and I had the overwhelming feeling that I was being left out of Jewish life. This feeling of discontent led me to initially run away from Judaism. I resented being marginalized, feeling like a cheerleader at a football game where only the men could really play the game.

During the second semester of my first year of college, I realized that living without a serious connection to Judaism felt so empty to me. I began to see the beauty in the mitzvot and the depth that committing to a Jewish ritual life can bring to one's life.

When I began my return to a ritually observant Judaism, I began praying regularly. This meant, among other things, reciting the *Shema* prayer. When I began to recite this prayer regularly again, it bothered me terribly to recite the verse from Numbers 15:38–40, which is part of this prayer that is recited twice a day. I felt that I couldn't continue to recite this prayer, in which we say that God directed us to wear *tzitzit*, if I did not perform this ritual for myself.

My First Real Tallit

In the Reform congregation in which I was raised, tallitot were only permitted during a bar mitzvah—and that was after a long battle in the synagogue's ritual committee. For those few who chose to wear them for that special service, there was one specific rule to be followed: no formal presentation, no opportunity for a child to be given a tallit worn by a father or grandfather. The possibility of girls wearing tallitot was not even on the radar screen of this congregation. This tallit was small, more like a scarf than anything else. Then, after the bar mitzvah, it was hidden away because men were not encouraged to wear them as part of a regular ritual practice. So my tallit was closeted away like those of everyone else.

When I traveled to Israel for the first time at age sixteen, even before going to sleep that first night, almost right off the plane, I headed into the traditional neighborhood of Meah Shearim to buy my first real tallit. I wanted to make sure that I had the right tallit for my first Shabbat in Israel, and the small one that I had brought with me just did not seem to resonate with the land or what I had intended to experience there. Being in Israel seemed to be an indication that I had long since outgrown the tallit of my bar mitzvah. The new tallit felt enormous on my young, still-growing body, and I fumbled quite considerably when I tried to wrap myself in it. As the elderly shopkeeper gently helped me to put it on just right, I questioned him about its size, thinking that he just wanted to sell me the more expensive—larger—one. He replied, "Don't worry. It's supposed to be big. That way, you'll have many years to grow into it." Little did I know what he really meant. I thought he was talking about the size of my not-yet-mature adolescent body. It took me years to realize that he was talking about the size of my spirit. He was right; some thirty-five years later, it is still big on me and I am still growing into it. So as I put on my tallit each morning, I think about the challenge this anonymous teacher presented to me many years ago, that I continue to carry in its folds.

RABBI KERRY M. OLITZKY

As part of my journey to reclaim this ritual, I began an in-depth study of the laws of *tzitzit*. That's when I discovered that women are not forbidden to do this ritual practice. They may not be obligated to wear a tallit, small or large, but they are also not prohibited from it. Even the great medieval philosopher Maimonides, in his collection on Jewish law called the *Mishneh Torah,* wrote that women may wear *tzitzit* if they so desire (*Hilkhot Tzitzit* 3:9). Following this discovery, I decided to try wearing a *tallit katan.*

When I first began wearing one, I wore the kind that men wear: a kind of cornered T-shirt without seams. However, I discovered that I did not feel comfortable in the standard form of *tzitzit,* neither physically nor emotionally. I found that those *tzitzit* rode up on me and were constantly coming out of the collars of my shirts and dresses. Moreover, they were not made with the figure or clothing of a woman in mind. I simply felt that I was wearing a garment that was not really meant for me. So I commissioned a seamstress friend, also a *tallit katan*-wearer, to design a more appropriate camisole-like *tallit katan* for my daughters and me.

Even with my flowered camisole *tallit katan,* I still often feel shy about wearing it. Although I don't hide the fact that I wear a *tallit katan* and I am open about it, I try not to advertise it all the time.

THE LOST BUT REFOUND (PERHAPS) BLUE THREAD

Part of the mitzvah of *tzitzit* is to wear a string of *tekhelet* (blue thread) among your fringes. *Tekhelet* is a type of blue dye that comes from a snail. The knowledge of how to make the particular color was, however, lost after the talmudic period (approximately 600 C.E.). Recently, after much research and scuba diving, two men who live in a suburb of Jerusalem claim to have rediscovered the secret—a snail that produces the dye once used for *tekhelet*. They have started an organization, P'til Tekhelet, which distributes *tzitzit* fringes with *tekhelet*, along with information about *tekhelet* and how they rediscovered it.

Making the Decision to Wear a *Tallit Katan*

Because I am a Reform rabbi, the decision to wear a *tallit katan* is a particularly personal one for me. For Orthodox boys, it is a regular part of their clothing. They receive it when they are young, much like they make the transition from soft toddler shoes to those that can take the rough play of young children. Unlike wearing ritual outer garments, or making other publicly visible decisions of a similar nature (even if not of a ritual nature, such as when I decided to grow a beard), my decision was known by few people: my wife and my kids. That's about it. There is a certain sense of modesty that I feel about it, even as I share some of the rationale for this decision. People see my covered head. They see the clothes that I wear, but they do not see what I wear beneath my clothing. With the *tallit gadol* I make a very public statement about my faith. With the *tallit katan* I make a very private one.

As styles beckon me from the pages of fashion magazines, trying to persuade me to become the person pictured in its pages, the *tallit katan* reminds me that the only person I should strive to become is one who is committed to the mitzvot symbolized by its fringes. It warms me in a way, and as I place this special garment over my body, I am able to shelter my spirit from the cold.

RABBI KERRY M. OLITZKY

Why I Wear *Tzitzit*

I can remember vividly the first time I saw someone who loved *tzitzit*. I was in eighth grade studying at the community Hebrew high school in St. Louis, Missouri. I was studying with the principal's son. He taught us how to tie our own *tzitzit,* and he was doing it with such love and care that I was profoundly moved by it. At the time, I was just recovering from a lukewarm bar mitzvah experience and an even less pleasant afternoon Hebrew school experience. I was a ready vessel, waiting for that one lesson that would provide me with the spirit and enthusiasm I needed to continue my Jewish education and further my spiritual quest. This class on tying *tzitzit* would be that lesson.

I still have that pair of *tzitzit* that I tied, and I have worn *tzitzit* daily since then. At first, as a non-Orthodox Jew, I wore them tucked in so as not to give the impression that I was something I am not. As I grew and learned more, I realized that I had as much right to wear *tzitzit* as proudly as my Orthodox brothers.

I can remember praying once in the synagogue when we came to the third paragraph of the *Shema:* "And you shall see them [the *tzitzit*]." It may sound silly, but this phrase bothered me. After all, I couldn't see them. I had them hidden away for fear of misrepresenting them and myself. I had to struggle with what it meant to be commanded at all. I had to struggle with what it meant to wear, outwardly, those fringes that reminded me and binded me to those commandments. Since then, I have proudly worn my *tzitzit* out for all to see, but, most important, for me to see as well.

DAVID PASKIN

WHAT I FEEL AND WHAT I REMEMBER ABOUT WEARING A TALLIT

A midrash, a story in the Talmud (*Menachot* 44a), vividly illustrates the power of the tallit. There was a man who was very scrupulous in wearing his *tzitzit*. Once he went to visit a famous prostitute, but before he got into bed with her, his *tzitzit* fringes slapped him in the face, and as a result he did not sleep with her. In the end, the prostitute was so impressed with his piety and self-control that she converted to Judaism and married him. The Talmud is telling us that *tzitzit* can at least metaphorically slap us in the face when we are about to transgress. By putting on my *tzitzit* each morning, I take a personal step to ensure that I will be reminded throughout the day of my personal covenant with God. It is renewing, in a very intimate way, the covenant each morning afresh.

The *tzitzit* that I wear beneath my clothing serve to remind me all day long of the mitzvot, the sacred obligations that I have to fulfill, but they also remind me of the holiness of my body. According to the tradition, each person is a world unto him- or herself. When a person dies, a world is lost. This does not refer only to a person's spirit; it refers also to a person's physical body. When the Torah says that each person is created in the image of God, this does not mean that God looks like a human being. What it means is that each person is holy, both physically and metaphysically. Our bodies and our spirits are holy. By wearing a holy garment next to my skin, I am reminded of this notion. I feel, in a very physical way, that I was created in the image of God.

For me, a big part of this mitzvah is also wearing my *tzitzit* in the form of a *tallit gadol* (prayer shawl) each morning when I say my prayers. My *tallit gadol* enhances *kavanah,* or focused, meditative concentration. I can simply pull the *tallit gadol* over my head and block out the many things that distract me. With a *tallit gadol,* I can be in a synagogue full of people or at home while my four children are rushing around in the morning getting ready for school, yet I feel that I am standing alone before God.

However, my *tallit gadol* does not always function as a vehicle to block others out. At times I use it to bring others closer to me. For example, in traditional synagogues, during the priestly benediction, while the descendants of the sons of Aaron say a blessing over the congregation at the end of the *Amidah,* it is customary to pull one's tallit over one's head in order to avoid looking directly at the priests. As a child, I remember hiding under my father's tallit during this prayer; so I feel a sentimental warmth as I cover my four children and myself, listening to the *kohanim* (descendants of ancient Jewish priests) pray for peace and wholeness for the entire congregation.

Enriching My Soul by Wearing *Tzitzit*

My maternal grandmother, her parents, and all her family were Orthodox Jews from Baltimore. As a young child, my grandmother became deaf from spinal meningitis, and her mother died from cancer. She and her younger brothers were sent to Georgia, where my grandmother went to the Georgia School for the Deaf. As she grew up, functioning as a deaf person in the Jewish community became increasingly difficult because no synagogue had services that were sign language-interpreted. At the time, the only sign language-interpreted services were at the local Episcopal church, and most of the deaf community, regardless of religion, went there for services. My grandmother met and married my grandfather, a deaf Christian man, and they attended the Episcopal services together. As far as I know, my grandmother never converted and she maintained some Jewish practices such as lighting Shabbat candles, but she raised her daughters—my mother and her sister—in the Episcopal church. My mother converted to Catholicism after marrying my father, a Polish Catholic. I was raised in the Catholic church along with my siblings.

At about the same time that I became dissatisfied with the Catholic church and started attending Protestant churches, I discovered the Bible. As I was studying, I learned that Jewish lineage was passed through the mother, which then made me realize, to my utter amazement, that I was Jewish, according to traditional Jewish law.

It was difficult, but I decided to try to teach myself. I read numerous books about Jewish life. I read the Torah carefully, trying to absorb as much of its wisdom as I could understand. At some point during my study, I discovered my Jewish self. This was no longer about the simple ancestry of my grandmother; it was about my Jewish soul becoming inextricably connected to Jewish life.

However, I had no Jewish community. Elie Wiesel once remarked, "A Jew alone cannot be a Jew."

When I moved to Boston four years ago, I was finally able to live in a Jewish community. I joined a local Reform synagogue and made a formal return to Judaism, ready for a Jewish practice that truly bound me to the rest of the Jewish world. I wanted a way to continually remind myself of the Jewish identity from which I had been disconnected for so long. I decided to wear a *tallit katan* as a constant reminder of God's commandments, bound as a Jew to God's covenant. Wearing *tzitzit* is just one more soul-enriching step on my path home.

FRANKIE SNYDER

Proudly Wearing the Tallit

I actually chose to buy and wear my tallit exactly a week before I received the diagnosis of multiple sclerosis, as though it were planned to help comfort me when times got rough later on in the illness.

Once I was wearing it, it felt like an outward sign of the affirmation of my newly discovered faith and belief in God, toward which I had been working for a number of years. The simultaneous discovery of my illness and my return to Judaism resulted in the celebration of wearing a tallit with pride.

The fact that I chose to wear a black-and-cream-colored tallit is significant, too. Sometimes I feel that men who wear a blue-and-white-striped "scarf" do not revere their tallit in the same way that I revere mine. So as not to make my gesture casual or copying a man's, some of whom seem to take theirs for granted from bar mitzvah onward, I had to make mine look different, symbolic of my decision to state who I am, a statement of the woman in me.

It felt good and suitable from the outset. The reaction from other women in the Reform synagogue and visiting members from other synagogue movements is sometimes one of suspicion. A small group of us who wear tallit sit together, and perhaps we pose a threat; we are possibly labeled as cranks.

The ritual of touching the Torah scroll as it is carried around came much later, and it was harder; perhaps it had something to do with getting in touch with my own holiness. I am not able to make this gesture with my tallit every week.

I am still relatively new to wearing the tallit and I feel very emotional about it. If I am moved by the feeling of prayer or a human touch in the synagogue and I cry, my tears are caught and held on the tallit, and it feels all right to allow them to accumulate there.

SUE LEVIN[1]

Feeling Armed by God by Wearing a *Tallit Katan*

Every morning, as I am getting dressed, I put on my *tallit katan,* just as my father, a Reform rabbi, does. It is neither the first nor the last article of clothing I put on, but it is the most important. This garment is the only item I wear that is so privately Jewish. It keeps me Jewishly bound throughout the day. While it reminds me that God watches me at all times, it also helps to remind me that I have an obligation to work toward performing mitzvot throughout the day. To me, the *tallit katan* is part of the uniform of deed-doers and commandment-followers. No other piece of clothing makes such a demand on me.

Although my *tallit katan* is a much more private garment than my yarmulke, I made the choice to wear it much later. Halfway through high school, I grew attracted to it. I thought that by wearing it, I could enhance my daily relationship with God. Just as wearing the *tallit katan* became a routine part of my daily activities, so did the process that surrounds it. As I recite the appropriate blessing for putting it on, I am made mindful of the obligation that I take on as a result—my part of the covenantal relationship.

As I start out each morning, I am sometimes afraid of what I might encounter, so I imagine my *tallit katan* as a bullet-proof vest of sorts that protects me from harm on the outside as well as whatever evil may lurk on the inside.

AVI OLITZKY

THE ORIGINS OF TALLIT

The tallit is a rectangular-shaped piece of linen, wool, or silk (and now, sometimes polyester, but not a blend of linen and wool—called *shatnez*—which is traditionally prohibited), with special fringes called *tzitzit* on each of its four corners. While the tallit has taken on its own special significance, its original purpose was simply to hold the *tzitziot* (plural of *tzitzit*). And the purpose of the *tzitzit*—kind of like a string around the finger to remind us of things—is to remind us of God and God's guidance for our lives transmitted in the form of the commandments. As Rabbi Irwin Kula and Vanessa L. Ochs remind us, "Wrapped in the tallit, its fringes dangling from each of its four corners, we remember our sacred missions—to fix the world, to seek justice, and to pursue peace—and we feel protected by the many memories woven within its threads."[2]

Some scholars contend that there is a relationship between the *tallit katan* and the *kipah*. Once the tallit became an undergarment and thereby became smaller, years after tefillin were no longer worn all day long (as is suspected by many scholars), then it became popular for men to cover their head, as an outward acknowledgement of God and the individual's relationship to the Divine. The tallit may have resembled the *abbayeh* (blanket) still worn by the Bedouin for protection from the weather. A tallit of finer quality was probably similar to the Roman pallium; in this form, it was worn by the wealthy and more distinguished rabbis and scholars. (Such distinctions today are often expressed through the *atarah*, the embroidered collar of the *tallit gadol*.) As part of the attempt throughout Jewish history to look more like their non-Jewish neighbors, and once the *tallit katan* became an undergarment, the *tallit gadol* became a religious garment for prayer.

Judges wore tallitot as part of their professional garb, and the ancients wore them when visiting the sick because Jewish tradition contends that the Divine Presence rests at the head of a sick person.

HOW THE *TZITZIT* ARE USED DURING PRAYER AND AT OTHER TIMES

At various times during the service, the *tzitzit* are used. Just prior to reciting the *Shema,* we gather together the four *tzitziot* and hold them, using them to cover our eyes during the recitation. Some people suggest that it symbolically helps us to focus on the unity of God, as well as giving us a special awareness of this prayer that helps us to concentrate on its words. It is customary to kiss the *tzitzit* during the recitation of Numbers 15:37–41, when the word *tzitzit* is mentioned as part of the *Shema* prayer.

We also use the *tzitzit* as a way of kissing the Torah during its procession around the synagogue before and after its reading. It is also a Sephardic custom (that has made its way into the Ashkenazi community) to take the *tzitzit* and raise them toward the Torah when it is raised after its public reading. When you are called up for an *aliyah* (the blessing before and after the Torah reading), it is customary to take the fringes and touch the section of the scroll about to be read, kiss the *tzitzit*, and then recite the blessing before the reading. This procedure is repeated after the reading and before the second blessing.

Traditionally, men are buried in their tallit with a *tzitzit* cut to make it ritually unfit. The tallit follows an individual from birth to death; it is often used to wrap a baby during the ritual of *brit milah* (circumcision) for boys and baby namings for girls, and it is often draped across the casket during a funeral. Rabbi Adin Steinsaltz says that it offers a kind of divine protection for the unsafe journey the individual may face.

The tallit is sometimes used as a *chuppah* (marriage canopy). It is worn by those carrying the Torah scrolls during the Torah procession in the synagogue before and after its reading, as well as on Simchat Torah. It is used to cover children during the last *aliyah* (which is for children) on Simchat Torah.

THE VARIETY OF APPROACHES TO WEARING THE *TALLIT GADOL*

In some traditional communities, even young boys wear the *tallit katan*, but only married men wear the *tallit gadol* for prayer. This custom probably emerged in response to the juxtaposition of Deuteronomy 22:12 (which instructs us to wear *tzitzit*) and the verse that follows

1, 13, 613—INTERPRETING THE WAY *TZITZIT* ARE WOUND

There are various interpretations of the particular way in which the *tzitzit* are wound. One interpretation is that each set of windings corresponds to one of the four letters in God's unpronounceable Hebrew name (YHVH). Another interpretation employs *gematria*. According to this interpretation, the first three windings spell God's name, and the last set of windings is equivalent in value to the Hebrew word for "one" *(echad)*. Thus, the *tzitzit* communicate the foundation of Jewish theology, which is also expressed in the *Shema* prayer (the extended version of which contains the instruction for *tzitzit*): God is one. In another interpretation of this aspect of the ritual, the windings can be understood to reflect the thirteen attributes of God as articulated by the medieval philosopher and theologian Maimonides and set in poetic verse in the *Yigdal* hymn (generally sung at the end of the Friday evening Sabbath service). One final interpretation combines knots and strands in order to get 613, the traditional reckoning of the number of God-given commandments. Thus, looking at the *tzitzit* reminds us of the obligation we have to the covenant and to these instructions.

"If a man takes a wife . . ." (Deut. 22:13). Generally, in traditional circles, boys who become bar mitzvah (at age thirteen) are eligible to wear a tallit.

In liberal Jewish circles, tallitot are worn by boys and girls after they have become bar and bat mitzvah. While it is traditional to wear the tallit during morning prayer every day, the custom for many men and women is to wear it exclusively on Shabbat morning.

A growing number of Jews are now making their own tallitot. Some have chosen to do this for their child's bar or bat mitzvah; others want to add their own creativity to the garments in which they are going to pray. From a number of Judaica catalogues, you can purchase a blank tallit that is ready to be worn, and you can paint your own design on it. You can also make your own tallit from scratch. For a tallit to be valid under Jewish law, it only has to be a four-cornered garment, and the *tzitzit* have to be tied in a certain way.

Wearing a Tallit

Some months after my family joined the local Reform synagogue, I took a Hebrew class for adults. I enjoyed learning to read in Hebrew, and I was surprised at how much more the service meant to me when I could actually read the prayers in Hebrew. I felt a new connection to Jews of every era and every place. It was more profound than I could have predicted.

In the spring, my class was asked to lead a Shabbat morning service. I was a nervous wreck! The morning our class was leading services, there was no dealing with me at home. My husband, Joe, knew enough not to ask me what our four daughters should wear to temple, or to suggest that we stop at the bank or the post office or drugstore on the way. He was right not to add any stress to my life. We all knew that if we made one false move, the whole delicate balance of this Shabbat would collapse!

Just before we left the house for services, Joe took me aside and handed me a package. I opened it. It was a tallit! Joe thought it would be special for me to wear one on this very special Shabbat. We had never discussed it before, so this was a complete surprise to me.

I opened my *siddur* (prayer book) to the page with the blessing for wearing a tallit: "Praise Adonai, O my soul. . . . You wrap yourself in light as with a garment." And as I wrapped myself in this garment for the first time, I felt a relationship to God and to the Jewish people that was as warm and comforting as the precious cloth itself.

To me, ritual is like a handle—something we can grab when what we really need to hold on to seems too elusive. Some rituals are built into our lives in ways that often have no beginning; they are just things we have always done. Others come into our lives, and in a moment they become part of us. After a while they have a way of taking on meaning unto themselves. Just the act of doing them is comforting.

When I first wrapped myself in a tallit that special Shabbat, I knew something very important had happened. The ritual of saying the blessing and then wrapping myself in a tallit has become my handle. Now each Shabbat morning, I wrap myself in that tallit that Joe gave me. It is a symbol of his love, support, and understanding, and it is also a symbol of God's warm embrace.

SANDY SLAVET

Wrapped

I got my first tallit for my bar mitzvah along with a three-piece suit. It was at least a decade later that I needed either one again. Tallitot are not sold at Filene's Basement, and I could always borrow one, so I didn't get another until I was thirty-two years old. For the first time in my life, I engaged in a daily regimen of study and prayer, and I wanted something full-sized, not the narrow acrylic variety made available for communal use.

I went shopping for a simple white tallit with blue stripes—a grown-up version of the last one I'd owned. The salesman picked it out with the impatient familiarity of a man dispensing bowling shoes. "Did you ever play tennis?" he asked me. "You put it on just like serving a tennis ball, grab the edge and bring it right past your ear. There, that fits you fine." And it did. I had my adult tallit, which I expect to have for the rest of my life.

I pray. The tallit wraps perfectly around me in prayer—exposed, vulnerable, grateful, exhilarated, awed, helpless, distraught, and joyous. These feelings might arise at any moment in my day, but here they are different, felt as a Jew in prayer connected to other Jews in prayer next to me, around the world and backwards and forwards through time. For me, prayer is a portal to connection.

Although I don't need my tallit to pray, it does help. After the blessing, all wrapped up, eyes closed, I breathe slowly. I feel the material on my hands, cheeks, and forehead; I feel the warmth of my body and smell the tiny space around my head and torso draped in cloth. I feel the cloth containing all of me—struggles and potential, disappointments and aspirations, all of what God understands of me. Wrapped up that way in my tallit, I feel closer to understanding it myself.

STEVEN LEWIS

WHERE AM I TODAY AND WHERE AM I PLANNING ON BEING TOMORROW?

I am glad to be part of an ever growing circle of men and women who have chosen to wear the *tallit katan* and use the *tallit gadol* in prayer.

It is a controversial step that may not be right for all women or even all men. For those of us who have made the choice to wear a *tallit katan,* this mitzvah speaks in a very intimate way—as a strong pull, or a fulfillment of a personal need.

WHERE TO START AND HOW TO CONTINUE

Start with a *tallit gadol.* If you have one, even from your youth, then start with it. Run your hands over its surface. Rub each *tzitzit* between your fingers. Bring it to your nose and breathe deeply, taking in the years of its journey. (Each tallit develops a particular fragrance that offers comfort and familiarly to its wearer.) If fixed morning prayers have already become part of your spiritual practice (without tallit), then take a few moments to prepare for prayer by putting on the tallit. Once you are comfortable with it on your shoulders, follow the steps for the blessings below. Some people like to take quite some time quietly preparing for prayer, wrapped in their tallit.

Particularly if you have a large tallit, you might even want to wrap yourself in it with the one you love: a child, your spouse, a partner. Bring them within the sheltering presence of the Divine.

Some people see the tallit as a mystical symbol, representing the *sefirot* (God's emanations). As you put on the tallit, visualize the colors of the *sefirot* enveloping you in thin strips of divine light, wrapping you in a ten-colored rainbow. Visualize this rainbow tallit absorbing these energies and draping you in them.

Use the moments that you are wrapped in your tallit as an opportunity to prepare yourself for the day ahead and all that you may encounter. As you wrap yourself in your tallit, consider saying these words of Rabbi Diane Cohen: "God of Israel, as You covered Moshe Rabbenu with Your cloud of glory at Sinai, so that he might prepare to sit in Your Presence and learn Your Torah, so may You cover me as I wrap myself in my tallit this day, prepared to sit in Your Presence and learn Your Torah. May my heart be open to Your lessons and my feet be swift to do Your will."[3]

EASY STEPS TO WEARING THE TALLIT

The *tallit katan* is simply slipped over the head, after the following blessing is said: *Barukh ata Adonai Elohenu melekh ha-olam asher kidshanu bemitzvotav vetzivanu al mitzvat tzitzit.* (Praised are You, Adonai our God, Sovereign of the universe, who has made us holy with mitzvot and instructed us concerning *tzitzit.*)

The *tallit gadol* has a slightly more elaborate process. Hold the *tallit gadol* in front of you, taking its embroidered neckband *(atarah)* in your hands. Pause a moment to meditate on the meaning of this ritual act. You may want to consider these words: "I am about to wrap myself in the tallit in order to fulfill the instruction of my Creator. As it is written in the Torah, 'They shall make fringes for themselves on the corners of their garments throughout the generations.'"

Then say this blessing: *Barukh ata Adonai Elohenu melekh ha-olam asher kidshanu bemitzvotav vetzivanu lehitatef batzitzit.* (Praised are You, Adonai our God, Sovereign of the universe, who has made us holy with mitzvot and instructed us to wrap ourselves in fringes.)

Often people kiss either side of the *atarah* before putting on the tallit. Then, much like you would put on a scarf, crisscross your hands and place the tallit around your shoulders, coming around from the side, rather than over your head. If it is a large tallit, take each of the front corners and drape them over your shoulders.

After you have put on your tallit, you may want to add these words of the psalmist to help focus this spiritual act even further: "How precious is your lovingkindness, O God. Humans find refuge in Your presence. They will be satisfied in the abundance of Your House. You will cause them to drink from the river of Your delight. With You is the fountain of life. In Your light do we see light. Bestow Your lovingkindness on them that know You, and Your righteousness to those who are upright in heart" (Ps. 36:8–11).

Others prefer this selection from Psalms: "Let all my being praise Adonai, who is clothed in splendor and majesty, wrapped in light like a robe, unfolding the heavens like a tent" (Ps. 104:1–2).

RECOMMENDED READING

Cayam, Aviva. "Fringe Benefits, Women and *Tzitzit.*" In *Jewish Legal Writings by Women,* edited by Micah D. Halpern and Chana Safrai. Jerusalem: Urim Publications, 1998.

Kula, Irwin, and Vanessa L. Ochs. *The Book of Sacred Jewish Practices: CLAL's Guide to Holiday and Everyday Rituals and Blessings.* Woodstock, Vt.: Jewish Lights Publishing, 2001.

Ner-David, Haviva. *Life on the Fringes: A Feminist Journey toward Traditional Rabbinic Ordination.* Needham, Mass.: JFL Books, 2000.

3

The Broad Spectrum of Kashrut

RABBI MARK SAMETH

THE BASICS: IS IT KOSHER?

Kashrut is a spiritual dietary discipline that guides me in all that I eat, a system that makes me mindful of what I am doing. The word *kashrut* means, simply, "propriety" or "fitness." Kosher food means food that is "proper" or "fit" for consumption. According to the Torah, that means the following: One may not eat blood. One may not eat any animal that has been torn by a wild beast or that has died a natural death. One may eat only animals that chew their cud and have cloven hoofs—hence, the well-known prohibition against pork. Certain animal fats, as well as the sciatic nerve, must be removed.

Only fish which have both fins and scales are permitted; shellfish are not. Some birds are forbidden. With the exception of four kinds of locusts, insects and other swarming things are forbidden. It is forbidden to slaughter a mother animal and her young on the same day. One may not boil an animal in its mother's milk. One must chase a mother bird away before taking her eggs.

That, essentially, is what the Torah has to say about kashrut. Over time, the Rabbis extended the laws of kashrut to further ensure humane slaughter (which is called *shechitah*); to prohibit the consumption of all milk and meat, including fowl, at the same meal, and to require separate dishes and utensils for milk and meat. They also determined that foods such as fruits, vegetables, grains, fish, and eggs, which are neither milk nor meat, are neutral (called *pareve*) and may be eaten with either meat or dairy products.

Today, there are individual rabbis (and groups of rabbis, often called a community board, or *vaad*) who certify kosher meat. Processed foods may or may not be kosher. Those which carry a stamp of approval, or *hekhsher,* on the package—a symbol such as a K, a K or a U inside a circle, or a K inside the Hebrew letter *kaf*—are all certified kosher by these individual rabbis or local community boards of rabbis.

MY OWN JOURNEY: FROM SAUSAGE PIZZA TO PLUCKING THE SINEWS

In *Remembrance of Things Past,* Marcel Proust wrote the following: "Once I had recognized the taste of the crumb of madeleine soaked in her decoction of lime flowers which my aunt used to give me . . . immediately the old gray house upon the street, where her room was, rose up like the scenery of a theater." For Proust it was a madeleine pastry. For others it's chicken pot pie or *cholent*—a food so bound up with one's past that the mere taste of it, smell of it, or even mention of it produces a response so visceral that the experience is more akin to time travel than recollection. It is food that evokes nostalgic memories and leaves one awash in warm feelings of well-being.

For me that food has always been sausage pizza—not today's strip-mall version with cardboard crusts and precut toppings, but the drooping, dripping slices of my youth, with their gnarly nuggets of oregano-flecked meat. The sausage pizza we had every other Sunday night at Albanese's, as my brother and sister and I chased each other around the table and my parents made small talk with the parents of the kids who had also made the trek from New Rochelle to Eastchester—because who wouldn't travel a few extra miles, even on a school night, for the best handmade sausage pizza in probably the whole world?

To say, then, that kashrut was not on my radar screen does not even begin to capture the enormity of the chasm that existed between me and the ancient dietary code of my people. On the contrary: it is the aroma of *treyf* (non-kosher food) that still permeates my warmest memories of childhood. For when my family wasn't at Albanese's, we were in Larchmont at Tung Hoy, having bacon-wrapped jumbo shrimp. On special occasions such as birthdays and anniversaries, we'd head back to Brooklyn to Lundy's, where in my preadolescence my father initiated me into the secret art of lobster eating: how to find the hidden meat in the "red chicken," how to crack open the claws to suck out the juice. I'd still put that one up against any rite of passage anyone could find anywhere.

As a young adult, I could only agree with the humorist Fran Leibowitz when she cited linguine with clam sauce as one of the top ten reasons to live. So it was much more than merely odd when I later found myself sitting in a restaurant on the Upper West Side of Manhattan, picking the visible pieces of pork out of a bowl of Cuban-style black bean soup. I was in the process of developing a spiritual dietary discipline; at the time, however, I don't think it had yet occurred to me that the words *spiritual, dietary,* and *discipline* had anything whatsoever to do with one another. The thought that eating veal parmesan could have a deleterious effect on my inner spiritual life would have been beyond me—had I even stopped to consider that I might have an inner spiritual life.

One night, however, searching with some friends for yet another new cuisine, I ended up at an Argentinean restaurant and ordered the mixed grill. That was the beginning of a great change. What arrived at the table that night was a little hibachi, upon which was still cooking some poor animal's heart, brains, and other internal organs. It's not as if I'd never eaten internal organs before. I'd grown up on liver (broiled and chopped), and tongue, while not a personal favorite, was always on the table alongside the pastrami and the corned beef. Nevertheless, there was something different about slicing into that heart. It was as if I suddenly realized that eating meat really meant eating flesh, that eating liver was eating a *liver* and that eating tongue was eating a *tongue*.

It was not that I had suddenly had a philosophical problem with the human consumption of animal flesh, a flash of insight that eating meat is morally wrong. It certainly wasn't that I remembered some prohibitory Jewish teaching or tradition. It was simply an intuition that there were boundaries across which one should not allow oneself to pass, and that the slice of bloody heart on my fork was one of them. I had ordered the mixed grill because I'd never had it before and it sounded interesting. All at once that seemed the most insufficient of reasons.

KASHRUT IN THE BIBLE

The Torah does not require us to maintain a vegetarian diet, but it does hold vegetarianism as the ideal. In the Garden of Eden, God tells the first humans, "Here, I give you all plants that bear seeds that are upon the face of the earth, and all trees in which there is tree fruit that bears seeds, for you shall they be for eating" (Gen. 1:29).[1]

According to the Torah, not only were humans intended to be herbivores, but so were animals: "And also for all the living things of the earth, for all the fowl of the heavens, for all that crawls about upon the earth in which there is living being—all green plants for eating; it was so" (Gen. 1:30).

Permission to eat meat would come ten generations later. After the Flood, when only Noah and his family were left of the generation that had "gone to ruin" (Gen. 6:12), a concession was made. "All things crawling about that live, for you shall they be for eating, as with the green plants, I now give you all" (Gen. 9:3).

The concession, however, is not unconditional permission. There is one important proviso: "However: flesh with its life, its blood, you are not to eat!" (Gen. 9:4).

That was the last time I ever tasted heart, brains, or liver. For a time I even swore off red meat altogether. However, as is often the case with peak experiences, as time passed the impact of the experience faded, and so did my resolve. In retrospect, I found it unreasonable to not eat beef but still eat chicken; to not eat brains but still eat wings. OK, I'd been grossed out! Nevertheless, that couldn't rationally justify a wholesale change in my diet. Nor did I have a tradition or community to support the decision I'd come to so abruptly. So in time I was back to eating red meat again.

Something had changed, however. My consciousness had been stimulated. I had become, for the first time, mindful of my diet.

Sometime later I gave up shellfish. For years I'd ignored public health warnings that raw clams expose one to the risk of hepatitis, yet now I found that I was finally able to give them up. There was nothing moral, ethical, or aesthetic in my decision to quit eating mollusks. In no way did I equate eating crustaceans with eating the heart or brain of a previously conscious being. It was purely a health issue. However, it was only because I had had the experience of taking control of my diet, of making decisions to limit my omnivorousness, that I was able to protect myself by finally removing potentially dangerous shellfish from my diet.

I had made the connection between eating and health. Taste was no longer the only factor. Where once I had been rather mindless, I was now quite thoughtful. I was surprised that it had taken me so long to come to this quite reasonable decision: I wanted to take better care of my body.

The next step came much later. My spiritual searching had led me to a small but growing progressive Conservative synagogue on Manhattan's Upper West Side, Congregation B'nai Jeshurun, and to its first small congregational retreat. One night I was seated at dinner next to a woman who, I had noticed, carried herself with uncommon balance and grace. At dinner she told me of her years of living in Israel; her spiritual searching that had led her to this community; and, as the food was being served, of her decades of vegetarianism. Her diet was deeply rooted in Jewish spiritual practices of which I had only recently heard: *tzaar baalei chayim* (not to inflict suffering on animals), and *bal tashchit* (not to wantonly destroy).

AGAINST NEEDLESS SUFFERING

Tzaar baalei chayim. The prohibition of causing needless suffering to any living creature derives from such teachings in the Torah as (1) the injunction not to plow with a weak animal yoked to a strong one, as the weaker one will wear itself out trying to keep up (Deut. 22:10); (2) the prohibition of muzzling an ox while it is threshing grain, instead allowing it to eat at will (Deut. 25:4); (3) the requirement that one rest one's animals on Shabbat (Ex. 23:10); (4) the requirement that one chase a mother bird from the nest before one gathers her eggs or her chicks, so that she should not have to witness their removal (Deut. 22:6–7); and (5) the prohibition of slaughtering a mother animal and her young on the same day (Lev. 22:28).

Although my late-arriving interest in Judaism had left me with much to learn about ritual, prayer, and meditation, the values it championed seemed to already lie within me, waiting to be identified, elevated, and expressed. My dining companion's passing comments found a place of deep resonance in me. By the next meal, I had begun picking pieces of chicken out of the chicken soup.

Although the camp at which the retreat took place served strictly kosher food, it wasn't the laws of kashrut that were suddenly speak-

AGAINST NEEDLESS WASTE

Bal tashchit. The prohibition of wanton destruction or wastefulness derives from Deuteronomy 20:19, which reads: "When you besiege a town for many days, waging war against it, to seize it: You are not to bring ruin on its trees, by swinging away [with] an ax against them, for from them you eat, them you are not to cut down—for are the trees of the field human beings, [able] to come against you in a siege?"

From this, the Rabbis deduced a number of teachings against wanton destruction and in favor of conservation. "A palm tree," they wrote, "producing even one *kab* of fruit may not be cut down."[2] Regarding the consumption of meat, we are cautioned, "One should not eat meat unless one has a special craving for it." Nor, it is stated on the same page, should a parent "accustom one's child to flesh."[3]

ing to me. Rather, it was a desire to connect with the inner values of this Jewish community of spirit. In this very poised, intelligent, and spiritual woman, I had my first role model. I liked the idea of being as mindful as she. I liked the thought that I could do more than admire her compassion and sensitivity from a distance; I could share in them as well. I was, at the time, already not eating red meat or shellfish, so I had only to let go of chicken and fish.

I wondered if I could take this further. The tradition of not wearing leather shoes on Yom Kippur had me considering if it might be possible to remove leather products from my everyday life. Shoes and belts were the only items for which I really needed to find functional leather substitutes. It took a bit of poking around in those pre-Internet days, but after a while I was able to find a few places to go. (There are many more today.) It was not as difficult as I had imagined it might be.

I wish I could say that at this point I'd already reached a deep level of compassion toward all living beings. Strangely enough, I didn't experience it that way. Once I stopped eating meat and wearing hides, I did begin to find those practices revolting. I suppose that marked a certain deepening of compassion. More interesting to me, however, was how irritated I could still become by certain people.

Rather than transforming me into the model of compassion that I imagined a vegetarian and nonleather-wearing person to be, my practice set up a new standard of compassion against which to measure myself. If you can go through all this trouble to find cruelty-free footwear, I would muse, how can you not be kinder to this person on the phone who only wants to spend a few moments telling you the benefits of switching long-distance carriers?

REVERENCE FOR LIFE

The dietary laws are spread throughout the Torah. There is no one section to which one can turn to look them up. They include the following: the prohibition of eating *trefah* (in Yiddish, *treyf*)—flesh torn by beasts in the field (Ex. 22:30); the prohibition of slaughtering a mother animal and her young on the same day (Lev. 22:28); the injunction to chase the mother bird away before one takes her eggs (Deut. 22:6–7); the prohibition of eating any *nevelah*—anything that has died a natural death (Deut. 14:21); the prohibition of boiling a kid in its mother's milk (which appears three times in the Torah—Ex. 23:19, 34:26, and Deut. 14:21).

All of the foregoing share a concern for the feelings of and respect for all living creatures. Many have commented on the nature of these prohibitions. Maimonides, for instance, saw the prohibition of killing a mother animal and her young on the same day as a precautionary measure, in order to avoid slaughtering the baby in front of its mother. In these cases, he believed, animals feel very great pain, and there is no difference in this regard between humans and other animals.[4]

Of the law to chase the mother bird away, Maimonides wrote: "If the Law takes into consideration these pains of the soul in the case of beast and birds, what will be the case with regard to the individuals of the human species as a whole?"[5] By keeping us sensitive to the feelings *even of birds*, these laws, in the words of Rabbi Samuel Dresner, have as their purpose "the teaching of reverence for life."[6] It is not yet the ideal of vegetarianism, but it is an important movement in that direction.

THE NEXT STEPS: COMPASSION FOR OTHERS AND COMPASSION FOR SELF, INNER SPIRITUAL JOURNEYING AND OUTER SPIRITUAL CONNECTING

Through vegetarianism my diet now reflected overall the Jewish values that had become so much a part of my life. Nevertheless, there were some not necessarily vegetarian peculiarities of Jewish dietary law, some outer dimensions of kashrut, that I had yet to assimilate. Although I was no longer eating meat, we did sometimes have meat in the house. Thus the issue of separating milk from meat, of maintaining two sets of dishes and being conscious of cutlery and cooking utensils, required attention.

A vegetarian might not be so particular about whether a knife had ever been used to cut meat. A kosher vegetarian would want to know and would then avoid using a "meat" (fleishig) knife for a "dairy" (milchig) meal. A vegetarian might or might not take a moment before and after a meal to express gratitude, but a kosher vegetarian, operating within the Jewish universe with its tradition of blessings over food, certainly would.

Jewish dietary practice is expressed through specific forms. These forms are sometimes denigrated by Jews and others as "mere" ritual, or "meaningless" ritual, as if they were disconnected from the important task of cultivating goodness. (Some time before her death about seventy years ago, my great-grandmother, Toni Sameth, is said to have proclaimed: "My pots and pans are going to heaven, but I'm going the other way!") My experience has been that the self-discipline required by the kashrut system can be its most difficult but most transformative level.

My decision to stop eating meat and to stop wearing leather would not and could not be enough. I needed constant reminders of my Jewish spiritual discipline throughout the course of each day, opportunities to reflect on my reasons for choosing to take on these stringencies in the first place.

RABBINIC KASHRUT

When people use the term *kosher,* they usually mean "rabbinic kashrut"—a system that begins with the Torah but then expands upon it. The Torah says that in slaughtering an animal or a bird, one must "pour out its blood, and cover it with the dust" (Lev. 17:13), but it is not explicit about how that should be done. The Torah prohibits the eating of *trefah,* flesh that has been torn (Ex. 22:30), but it is silent about whether the prohibition should apply to internal injuries.

An entire tractate of Talmud is given over to consideration of such questions. Who may be a slaughterer? What are proper and improper acts of slaughter? What should one do if one finds a live fetus in the uterus of a slaughtered animal? Which animals may not be cooked in milk? Because rennet, the curdling agent used to make cheese, comes from the stomach of a calf, is it a meat product? All of these questions are taken up by the Rabbis in the tractate *Chullin.*[7]

Two important categories of concern, both rooted in the Torah, emerge from the Rabbis' deliberations. The first is known as *tzaar baalei chayim*—the prohibition of causing needless suffering to any living creature. The second is *bal tashchit*—the prohibition of wanton destruction. In addition, the Rabbis often establish a *siyag ha-Torah*—literally a "fence around the Torah"—an extra, prophylactic measure to ensure that the prohibition is not transgressed. (This is where the requirement of separate dishes comes from.)

It is certainly possible to be a mindless vegetarian, in precisely the same way that it is possible to be a mindless carnivore. Just as one can forget in eating a burger that one is eating flesh, one can forget in eating tofu that one is not eating flesh. After a while, whatever you do is just whatever you do. However, the kashrut system requires that one always be mindful of what one is doing. How was this knife used before? What part of the biosphere brought forth the food we are about to eat? How many of us have just eaten together? (The blessing after a meal changes if one dines alone, with two others, or in a group of ten or more.) Have I been inadvertently wasteful in my preparation or consumption of this meal? Has any person or animal been overworked or otherwise cruelly treated in the effort to bring this food to my table?

In addition, by taking on these specific dietary practices and intoning specific words of gratitude, I connect myself to a community—deeply rooted in the spiritual history of the world, widely scattered even now over the face of the globe—for whom these issues have long been defining ones. In locating my diet within the system of kashrut, I am not only taking on a spiritual practice, I am taking on the spiritual practice of a particular people. That connection is, by definition, self-transcending.

Jewish dietary practice is so peculiar that it is inevitably noticed in whatever host culture it appears. For instance, because the requirement to remove the sciatic nerve is so unusual, in China Jews came to be known as followers of the *Tiao Jin Jiao,* the "Sinew-Plucking Religion." Locating my dietary practice within the kashrut system now connected me, among other realities and concerns, to the *Tiao Jin Jiao.* I quite like that.

PLUCKING THE SINEW

The first dietary restriction intended specifically for the Israelites is described in the story of Jacob. An angel wrestles with him all night—dislocating his thigh at the hip socket—changes his name to Israel, and blesses him before departing. "Therefore the Israelites do not eat the sinew that is on the socket of the thigh until this day, for he had touched the socket of Jacob's thigh at the sinew" (Gen. 32:33).

Looking back, I can see that the dietary practice I arrived at was the result of my having been on four very different but interconnected journeys. What led me to want to no longer chew on an animal's tongue was the journey of *rachamim,* compassion for others. What led me to want to no longer ingest foods harmful to my health was the journey of *shmirat haguf,* caring for the body. What led me to want to connect with Judaism's shared inner values was the journey of *tzibur haruchaniut,* spiritual community. What led to my consciousness of cutlery and cooking utensils was the journey of *kehillah kedoshah,* holy community. In short: compassion for others, compassion for the self, inner spiritual journeying, outer spiritual connecting.[8]

Spirituality amid the Chaos of Four Children

When I was growing up, my mom explained to me why her parents kept kosher but she did not. My grandparents had told my mother stories about the digestive tract being ruined from cheeseburgers, about food poisoning from pork, and wooden mixing bowls that could not become clean if milk and meat were mixed in them. These were the stories passed down to her by generations of Jewish homemakers, but she, being a modern woman of the 1950s, rejected these stories as untrue. None of these stories made sense to me, either. None of this had found a place in my life (yet).

When I became pregnant for the first time, what I ate became very important to me. Everything I put into my body had to pass a rigorous test. When my first daughter was born, that test seemed frivolous compared to my new standards! I was no longer just eating for two, I now saw myself as responsible for the health and well-being of another life and as a role model for good eating habits. Although nutritional consideration was now being given to my family's food consumption, being "holy" hadn't yet entered the picture.

As my family grew, so did my search for spirituality in my own life and that of my family. I couldn't just go through the motions of parenting; I wanted to create a home that was a place of love, joy, and deep meaning. Four daughters later, and with hectic schedules that only a computer or a mother could keep straight, it became harder to do this without a solid foundation, an infrastructure. I slowly came to realize that the foundation had already been built, one that would support an environment filled with love, joy, and deep meaning. It is called Judaism, and although it seemed distant, it was also surprisingly familiar (and comfortable).

As our family explored ways of reclaiming a Jewish identity and formulating a Jewish context for our spiritual expression, it seemed only natural to incorporate the laws of kashrut into that structure. As busy as we were, we had to eat. For the past thirteen years, I have kept a kosher home. For me, the power of the dietary laws is that the Torah takes a simple, human act that we must do every day and teaches us how to raise it to a level of holiness that we may not reach on our own. Could we remember God's presence in our life—who we are as Jews every day, at every meal—if it weren't for these laws? I find comfort from this structure in a world that is rife with chaos.

My great-grandmothers would not recognize my experience as a wife and mother as "homemaker" (because I work outside the home as much as in, and my husband works as much inside the home as out). Still, for me, having a kosher home is a way of taking my place in that line of generations of Jewish homemakers.

I will tell my daughters a different story. Forget about wooden mixing bowls. Forget about what mixing milk and meat will do to the digestive tract. Forget about the danger of eating pork in the days before refrigeration. We need only to remember that kashrut gives us the opportunity as Jews to "sanctify ourselves and be holy" every time we eat. I hope that my daughters will also find comfort in this structure and will practice it too.

SANDY SLAVET

SOME MYTHS ABOUT KASHRUT: KOSHER QUESADILLAS?

There are many misconceptions about kashrut. Early on, one of the biggest misconceptions I had was that it meant a style of food, like bagels or blintzes. Indeed, nonkosher restaurants and caterers sometimes advertise their food as "kosher style," adding to the confusion.

Food advertised as "kosher style" often means dishes that were popular among Eastern European Jews: bagels, blintzes, *cholent,* and *kasha varnishkas.* For Jews who grew up on this diet, it is by definition "comfort food." A mere morsel of pastrami can affect, in the soul of one so raised, a profoundly Proustian response. The spirits of relatives now thirty years gone will often seem to gather upon the first sip of matzo-ball soup. (So much for those who question whether "kosher style" can be spiritual.)

There are many Jews throughout the world, however, who have never tasted these foods. To the Jews of Morocco, Jewish food is pita and hummus and falafel. To the Jews of India, it would be inconceivable to prepare a holiday dish without curry. "Kosher style," then, admittedly means many things to many people.

Kosher food, on the other hand, means a system, not a culinary style. The meat has been humanely slaughtered in a particular way; there is no lard in the baked goods; the preparation of the food has been rabbinically supervised. Hence, it is increasingly common to find kosher Chinese, Mexican, and Italian restaurants in the major Jewish centers of the world. There is no reason this cannot be. A challah may or may not be kosher. The same may be said of a quesadilla.

Some people talk about the origins of kashrut in terms of health benefits. Hygiene is still sometimes offered as a reason to keep kosher, or as a reason it is no longer necessary to keep kosher. Some of the Rabbis offered this as one of the reasons for the dietary laws. It makes sense to me that this has a place in a matrix of reasons in support of a kosher diet, but I think it's a myth that hygiene was or could be the principal reason behind the system.

Often people think that "eating kosher" is the required practice of Orthodox Jews exclusively. The Conservative movement also affirms the importance of a kosher diet. Reconstructionist Jews place a high value on observing a kosher lifestyle. Those who locate themselves within the Jewish Renewal movement are perhaps more likely still, by reason of their vegetarianism, to embrace a kosher diet. Reform Jews, who in previous generations spurned kashrut, are once again discussing the importance of it and many are "eating kosher" again. That would make the founder of American Reform Judaism, Isaac Mayer Wise, quite happy. He was passionate about the observance of kashrut.

One of the greatest misconceptions that people have about a kosher diet is that all aspects of it are relevant only for Jews. Actually, one of the first dietary laws in the Torah (the prohibition of eating blood) was given not to Jews but to all humanity. Eating the limb of a living animal was also outlawed for all humanity, and it is counted as one of the universal Noahide laws. Likewise, the vegetarian ideal was given to Adam and Eve, the (non-Jewish) parents of all peoples.

HUMANE SLAUGHTER

Because the Torah allows for the conditional consumption of meat, the Rabbis take up the question of what ritual slaughter, or *shechitah*, consists of—that is, what methods will cause an animal the least amount of suffering. The following requirements are established: the slaughterer's knife must be exceedingly sharp, perfectly smooth with no dents or nicks; there can be no pausing, or delaying, as the knife moves across the throat; chopping into the throat, or burrowing in and thrusting upward is forbidden; one may not cut outside the specified area (the cut must be below the larynx); the trachea and esophagus must be cut with the blade—they may not be torn out or lacerated in any way. Before the slaughter takes place, the *shochet*, or ritual slaughterer, is required to say a blessing (. . . *asher kidshanu bemitzvotav vetzivanu al hashechitah*, or "who has sanctified us with your commandments and commanded us about slaughtering"). The smallest infraction of the established rules—such as a momentary pause or delay in the movement of the knife—renders the animal unfit for consumption, unkosher. This is not just about rules. It is about taking the sacredness of life, even animal life, extremely seriously.

Finding God and Honoring God

I found God while eating a lobster in Maine. When I was a kid, my family would go on vacation every year in Maine and enjoy the natural beauty of the Northeast—rocky cliffs, green forests, sandy beaches, and, yes, yummy lobster. A true crustacean lover, I looked forward to pulling apart my dinner and dipping it in hot drawn butter. Well, one summer at age eleven in the middle of eating my meal, I became transfixed by the mechanics of the lobster's shell. I bent and straightened its legs and claws, examining the workings of this lobster's exoskeleton. The construction of its joints just awed me. In that very moment I knew for sure there is a God. Who else could be behind such an elegant, brilliant design? The whole time I rejoiced in God's handiwork, I enjoyed my favorite dinner wholeheartedly.

As of today, I have been keeping kosher for twelve years. I found God while eating *treyf;* I honor God by keeping kosher. Both insights and decisions remain good ones for me. I know that lobster is delicious, but I find kashrut to be a compelling part of my religious life. Not once in twelve years have I missed eating lobster or other *treyf.* While I know that they taste delicious, I do not feel denied. Honestly, the only challenge I have ever felt in my keeping kosher is the issue of logistics. On rare occasions, it just seems as if it would be easier not to keep kosher. I would not have to think twice before I eat—at home, in restaurants, at friends' homes—but that is the point! I decided to keep kosher because it infuses the most basic instinct of putting food into my mouth with thought. Every time I eat, I must think about what is going into my body and, hopefully, that moment of thought reminds me of my connection to God and Judaism.

Now a parent of a young child, I am modeling kashrut for my son. I do not pour milk into his sippy cup when he eats a meatball. Sometimes I picture taking him to Maine to climb on the rocks of the white beaches and I wonder: by raising my son in a fully kosher lifestyle, do I deny him the joy of encountering God while eating a lobster? I know that my son will have to find his own path to God, but I just hope it will be through noodle kugel instead of lobster.

RABBI MARY L. ZAMORE

BROAD STROKES OF OBSERVANCE

My great-aunt Nettie used to tell a joke about a man who had two chickens. The first chicken got sick, so he had the second one killed to make chicken soup for the first.

This is such a Jewish joke; Judaism is noted for its appreciation of (even reverence for) internal paradoxes. It may not always seem so, but there are few absolutes in Judaism. For example, Jewish law requires that in matters affecting a person's health, dietary laws can be suspended. As a result, Jewish law states that a pregnant woman who craves pork should be given pork (at first only a little juice through a straw; but if the craving doesn't subside, a dish of the forbidden meat itself should be provided). After ten years of abstinence I am, for health reasons, eating some fish again. We're always trying to balance one good against another. So we end up with exceptions to the rules and a spectrum of "normative" practice.

A few Jews today, mostly American Reform Jews, keep what may be termed "biblical" kashrut (no mixing of milk and meat and the avoidance of biblically prohibited foods). Many more Jews practice so-called rabbinic kashrut (all that is now generally included in the system of kashrut). Now there is a new term, eco-kashrut, coined by Rabbi Zalman Schachter-Shalomi to refer to an emerging set of practices, rooted in and arising out of Jewish tradition, that seek to respond to the global ecological crises.

Eco-kashrut is simply the application of the biblical and rabbinic imperatives of *bal tashchit* and *tzaar baalei chayim* to the modern world. Teachers of eco-kashrut, such as Reb Zalman, Rabbi Arthur Waskow, Rabbi Rami Shapiro, and Rabbi Sam Weintraub, ask us to grapple spiritually with questions posed by the modern world.

If it is forbidden, even in a time of war, to chop down a fruit-bearing tree, can it be kosher to clear-cut our precious, oxygen-producing forests? If it is forbidden for a king to amass an overabundance of horses (Deut. 17:16), can it be kosher to purchase gas-guzzling, ozone-depleting, super-size SUVs? If it is forbidden to remove eggs until one has chased the mother bird from the nest, can it be kosher to violently force-feed a duck or goose sixty to eighty pounds of corn with a wooden plunger rammed down its gullet, for the sole purpose of creating the "delicacy" known as *foie gras?* If it is forbidden to plow with a weak animal yoked to a stronger animal, can it be kosher to use cosmetics whose creation "necessitated" the torture of animals in testing the safety of the preparations for humans?

Much like the vastness of the dietary laws, the questions posed by eco-kashrut are endless when we consider everyday tasks. Can Styrofoam or unrecycled paper be considered kosher? Can nuclear power or genetically altered food be considered kosher? Can beef filled with potentially dangerous growth hormones and antibiotics be considered kosher? Can veal, the meat of tortured calves—purposely made anemic by the deprivation of nutrients and exercise, chained to stalls where they can neither move nor lie down—be considered kosher? What about any product made from child labor or other oppressed labor—can it be considered kosher? These are the sorts of questions with which eco-kashrut asks us to wrestle.

Rabbi Rami Shapiro defines eco-kashrut as "ethical consumption." He calls it "the Jewish way of making your consuming holy"; an attempt to ensure "that all your consuming is morally right and environmentally sound."[9] Rabbi Arthur Waskow sees eco-kashrut as "a constantly moving standard in which the test is: Are we doing what is more respectful, less damaging to the earth than what we did last year?"[10]

FENCE AROUND THE TORAH

Siyag ha-Torah, "a fence around the Torah." The Torah forbade boiling a kid in its mother's milk. The Mishnah (the "oral law") declared that "every kind of flesh is forbidden to be cooked in milk."[11] In the Gemara, which expounds upon the Mishnah, the prohibition is understood to extend to the mixing of all milk and meat, and even the eating of separate milk and meat dishes at the same meal.[12] To ensure this, the Rabbis set a further prohibition on the technically permissible mixing of milk and fowl, in accordance with the dictum "Be patient in justice, rear many disciples, and make a fence around the Torah."[13]

WHERE TO START AND HOW TO CONTINUE

If you're just starting out, you might want to experiment with biblical kashrut by trying first to remove all blood from your diet (abstain from gravy; avoid meat that is cooked "rare"; check eggs for blood spots). Then refrain from one or more of the traditionally forbidden foods (such as clams or pork). Does the first affect your compassion and concern for all living things? Does the second affect your relationship to God? As the range of your consumption contracts—as you limit your palate—does something else within you expand?

Rabbinic kashrut also provides a number of different entry points. Without making wholesale changes to your diet, you might decide, for instance, to observe the precept of *tzaar baalei chayim* (the prohibition against cruelty to living creatures) by buying only meat which has been slaughtered according to the rules of *shechitah* (i.e., kosher meat); to observe the precept of *bal tashchit* (the prohibition against wastefulness) by limiting your consumption of meat even further; and to follow a *siyag ha-Torah* (an additional stringency) by refraining from eating milk products and meat or fowl at the same meal. Does this discipline affect your compassion and concern for others? To what extent do these practices help to integrate secular and spiritual time for you? How much more aware are you of the web of life and your place within it?

If eco-kashrut speaks to your soul, you might want to experiment with a few additional practices rooted in *bal tashchit* and *tzaar baalei chayim*. Think about your role as a consumer, and consider how you might consume in more planet-friendly ways. Does one practice lead you to want to do more?

WHERE AM I TODAY AND WHERE AM I PLANNING ON BEING TOMORROW?

"Mitzvah goreret mitzvah," goes the famous rabbinic saying, *"v'averah goreret averah."* One mitzvah leads to another, and one transgression leads to another.[14] The Jewish dietary practices are not only ends in themselves. They are part of the establishment of a pattern of living, in which one mitzvah does lead to another; a system whose ultimate goal is *kedushah,* the establishment of a sense of holiness, included within which, in Rabbi Dresner's words, is a "reverence for life." With kashrut, Rabbi Dresner writes:

Judaism takes something which is common and ordinary, which is everyday and prosaic, and ennobles it, raising it to unexpected heights, informing it with profound significance by laws of *what* to eat and *how* to eat, by teaching that every act of life can be hallowed, even the act of eating. Abraham Joshua Heschel gave classic expression to this thought when he wrote that "perhaps the essential message of Judaism is that in doing the finite, we can perceive the infinite."[15]

RECOMMENDED READING

Berman, Louis. *Vegetarianism and Jewish Tradition.* New York: KTAV, 1981.

Dresner, Samuel H. *The Jewish Dietary Laws: Their Meaning for Our Time.* New York: Rabbinical Assembly, 1982.

Klein, Isaac. "The Dietary Laws." In *A Guide to Jewish Religious Practice,* chaps. 21–26. New York: Jewish Theological Seminary, 1992.

Schwartz, Richard. *Judaism and Vegetarianism.* Marblehead, Mass.: Micah Publications, 1988.

Waskow, Arthur. "What Is Eco-Kosher?" In *Down to Earth Judaism,* pp. 117–129. New York: William Morris, 1995.

———. *And the Earth Is Filled with the Breath of Life.* Available online at http://users.erols.com/jsblevins/waskow.htm.

4

שֶׁל שַׁבָּת. כִּי לְעוֹלָם

Entering Shabbat

RABBIS DANIEL JUDSON and KERRY M. OLITZKY

THE BASICS OF SHABBAT: KERRY'S PERSPECTIVE

Maybe it's middle age, but I can actually feel my body begin to shut down as I make my way home each Friday afternoon for Shabbat. It has been routinized for such rest. I can push all week long, early mornings and late nights, but come Saturday afternoon, I need my soul refreshment, that soul-doubling that the Rabbis talk about. The Shabbat nap is more than just a quick snooze; it has followed a morning of prayer and a lunchtime celebration of Shabbat with family and friends. It isn't just the bodily rest that I crave; it is the deep spiritual nourishment that Shabbat provides. By separating myself from the frenzy of the world that surrounds me all week long, Shabbat gives me the opportunity to focus on the needs of the soul. It is an island away from secular intrusions on my spiritual world.

Shabbat is unlike any other day. For starters, it is twenty-five hours long. By extending its holiness, we get a head start on what it has to offer us. My succumbing to the changing time it begins each week, a reflection of the weekly changing time of sunset, forces me to admit that I am not in control of the world around me. So I consciously let go and let God lead the way to holiness for me.

Shabbat begins eighteen minutes before sunset with candlelighting, the short blessing marking the time as sacred and special, when we have readied ourselves for the period ahead. This is followed by kiddush (over wine or grape juice), the blessing of children and spouse, a festive meal with singing, and *Birkat Hamazon,* a prayer of thanksgiving that follows the meal. The basic elements are repeated with certain variation in a modified form at Shabbat lunch on Saturday and for a third meal *(seudah shlishit)* late Saturday afternoon or early evening, depending on the time of year, with worship and study along the way.

The primary goal in observing Shabbat is to limit the intrusion of the workday world so that we might focus on the more important issues of spiritual renewal. The Rabbis established prohibited labors to guide us, deducing them from the various activities that were required to build the ancient Tabernacle. In this way, they were able to transform the idea of building sacred space into building sacred time.

MY JOURNEY TOWARD OBSERVING SHABBAT: DAN'S PERSPECTIVE

Because I am Jewishly observant, I sometimes get the question from people I meet as to whether my parents were observant. I always respond emphatically, "Yes, my father was a golfer. Every Saturday morning, he religiously played golf unless it snowed, or Yom Kippur fell on Saturday (and even then he might get a quick nine in)." This is to say that a sense of traditional Shabbat was simply not part of my home when I was growing up.

My grandmother, however, was rigorously observant, and maybe somehow through her doing, Shabbat seeped into me as a child. Maybe she stuffed Shabbat into the little kosher frankfurters that took the place of ham in the split pea soup she would bring to our home every Thursday morning. I think she must have fed Shabbat to me in my soup, because it does not feel as though at some point in my life I "began" to observe Shabbat, it feels as though I "returned" to observing it.

I got back into Judaism before I returned to Shabbat. I had become intellectually open to learning about Judaism and was excited about Jewish study and the rich existential questions that Jewish study provoked. As I took a few classes in Jewish thought at the local Jewish Community Center, it became clear to me that intellectual exploration in Judaism was meaningless without an exploration of what Jews *do,* and the center of what Jews do is Shabbat.

I began by going to shul on Friday night, but I would go out afterward to a bar or a movie to meet my friends. I was at a bar with some friends when I realized that I needed a deeper commitment to Shabbat. We were all standing around when it sort of struck me that I was really bored, that my life was short, and that I needed to do something different that centered on finding meaning. I turned to my friend and said that this was the last time I was ever going to be in a bar on Friday night, and it was.

From that point on, my Shabbat observance continued to evolve, and in large part it has felt oddly like a return—to the place that I had hoped I would come to when I was young. I was one of those kids who secretly paid close attention to what the Hebrew school teacher was saying. I was interested in questions about God and what Judaism says about how we should live, but pretty much everything in my life around me rejected those questions as important. The observance of Shabbat in my life has returned me to that place. I surround myself with people who are also interested in those questions. Shabbat has given me rest, joy, time for reflection and discussion, and with all of this I have returned to the sense of meaning I always wanted my life to have.

BROAD STROKES OF SHABBAT OBSERVANCE:
DAN'S PERSPECTIVE

My friend Rachel and my cousins all observe Shabbat, but they do so in different fashions. My ultra-Orthodox cousins in Williamsburg, Brooklyn, observe Shabbat by following a vast array of rules as to what they can and cannot do. They spend all Friday cooking and cleaning, readying themselves for Shabbat, when they will not use electricity, watch television, use the computer, or spend any money. Rachel says that she observes Shabbat as well. She wakes up on Saturday morning and goes to the gym to work out. She then comes home, spends time with her husband, and spends the afternoon in her favorite bookstore, which has wide comfortable chairs, serves good coffee, and doesn't mind people spending a few hours reading. She believes that Shabbat is about giving oneself joy in life, and few things bring her as much pleasure as an afternoon browsing through books.

My cousins in Williamsburg would surely not begin to recognize that Rachel is observing Shabbat by working out at the gym and reading at the bookstore. On the other hand, Rachel would surely not resonate with my cousins' extensive Sabbath preparations. Nevertheless, the Jewish observance of Shabbat runs the spectrum from my cousins' all-encompassing Shabbat to Rachel's exercising and café latté.

For my cousins in Williamsburg, the observance of Shabbat is anchored in *halakhah* (Jewish law). The laws concerning Shabbat were laid out in the Mishnah (the "oral law"). The Rabbis of the Mishnah tried to define "work." In various places in the Torah, we are told that we should observe Shabbat as rest, because God rested on the seventh day after creating the world, but the Torah does not detail precisely what constitutes "rest" or "work." The Torah does tell us about a person who was caught gathering wood on Shabbat and summarily stoned to death for working on the holy day. Besides gathering wood and lighting a fire, however, no further information is given on what constitutes work. The Rabbis of the Mishnah thus attempt to spell it out. They take their lead from the work that was required to build the Tabernacle that the Israelites brought with them during their desert journey from Egypt to Canaan, and they deduce thirty-nine categories of work, which they call *melakhah*. These include activities that we might not consider part of our daily work today: planting, tearing, writing, building, and mixing. Most of the activities on the list are agricultural, reflecting the farming society in which the Rabbis lived.

The traditional Shabbat my cousins observe is rather stringent. Following the categories of prohibited work (and the activities derived from this list), one is not permitted to drive or carry anything beyond private space (that means one's home, unless it is encompassed by an *eruv*, an artificial enclosure of space). One is not permitted to use the phone, to go online, to see a movie, or to shop. One cannot cook, write a letter, or garden. Although the list seems overwhelming, the goal is simply to make sure that individuals separate themselves from any activity that potentially could be work or lead them to work. Thus, individuals can't even touch such items (pens, money, garden tools) even if they have no intention of using them.

These prohibitions may appear burdensome, but the restrictions are an attempt to help create holy space by removing individuals from the ordinary and the everyday and raising them to a more sacred and spiritual plane. By limiting what one is permitted to do, individuals are forced to give up the facade of "control" of their lives. Instead, they strip down to life's essentials by just being together with others for eating and talking and celebrating being alive. If you can't rush off to the shopping mall or work just a little bit more, you can create sacred space in your life to linger over conversation or to be intimate with your partner. You are able to enter what Rabbi Abraham Joshua Heschel calls "a sanctuary of time." This is a period in which you remove yourself from trying to change the world to one in which you strive to simply be in harmony with it.

Unlike my cousins, Rachel does not believe that such rules are necessary for experiencing Shabbat. For her, observing Shabbat is much simpler. The Rabbis must have anticipated her attitude when they wrote in a well-known midrash that "Shabbat was given only for pleasure." For her, Shabbat is about trying to do things that bring her pleasure: working out, reading, sipping coffee. She believes that as long as she is mindful that the activities she is doing are connected to Shabbat, then she is indeed observing Shabbat.

My cousins and my friend represent two ends of the Shabbat spectrum. One sees Shabbat as being primarily about bringing joy to one's life without any specific rules and regulations; the other sees Shabbat as an attempt to differentiate one day of the week for complete rest from the world, and that can be accomplished only by following a specific set of guidelines.

Most of us seem to live somewhere in between, and both extremes seem right to me. I try to keep both of these Shabbats at once. I try to do things that bring me joy while also recognizing that removing myself from daily activities frees me in a profound way to experience inner peace.

My own observance is quite simple. I am with my wife and son and friends for Shabbat meals, because my family and friends are the center of my life. I study Torah on Shabbat morning because I love it. I embrace the intellectual opening to ideas wrapped in the holiness of the Torah. Furthermore, although I don't sing too well, I sing on Shabbat whenever it is possible, whether at worship services or after a meal. I sing because it is a way for me to experience joy.

In terms of what I don't do, there are two Shabbat restrictions in particular that shape my observance. I don't turn on my computer, and I never spend money or engage in any commerce. These limit what I am able to do and help to form a spiritual circle for me. If I don't turn on my computer, I have removed the possibility of doing work, because so much of my work is done on the computer. If I won't spend money, I cannot go to restaurants or movies or any other place where an exchange of money is required. It is not that I am particularly driven by money, but I am conscious that the best way to differentiate one day of the week is to remove money from my life.

Franz Rosenzweig, the great Jewish philosopher, said, "The Sabbath is a world revolution." It may seem odd to call Shabbat a "revolutionary" idea when it is three thousand years old, but even if the observance of Shabbat in our day is not revolutionary, it is indeed subversive. There is something subversive about attempting to remove oneself from the various objects and activities that occupy the world on a daily basis. While the rest of our culture is engaged with commerce, Shabbat gives us the opportunity to not take part in that. That may mean just spending Shabbat evening drinking wine with the one you love, reading Harry Potter with your child, or being by yourself and enjoying the solitude.

For some people, it is almost incomprehensible to think about spending Friday night or Saturday not going out or working. There are occasions when I see a listing for a concert or a show or I am invited to a friend's party on a Friday night that I momentarily regret my decision not to participate in these activities. However, the spiritual discipline of not spending money provides me with benefits that transcend the limited joy of a party or a movie. In consistently observing Shabbat, one can feel "an intuition of eternity," as Heschel calls it. For me, this is not about a magical or even mystical experience. Rather, it is something about consistently trying to differentiate Shabbat from the other days. This feeling of Shabbat overwhelms me with a profound appreciation for slowing down, resting, and appreciating the blessing of time itself.

Returning to the Root of All Life

Here's how one man, the spiritual leader of Ger, Poland, in the nineteenth century, once described the Sabbath:

> The Sabbath completes each thing; it is the fulfillment of all, for it is the root of all life . . . that is why Sabbath is called "rest," because it returns each thing to its root. . . . All week long we should look forward to this returning to our root and the place of our rest, for this is where we truly live.

Where is my root? Where is the place that I rest? Where do I truly live? Although the first question may take my whole life to answer, I do know this: I rest best on a green couch in the living room of my home in Montclair, New Jersey. Resting and returning to one's root may not be as easy as it seems. Part of the problem is apparent in the very meaning of Shabbat. The word literally means "to stop," yet from one of its first descriptions in the Torah it is spoken of as a day when we are instructed to *"shabbat vayinafash,"* stop and resoul. But how does one "resoul"?

When I consider the meaning of "resouling" I think of the poet-mystics of the hill town of Safed in sixteenth-century Israel who imagined that resouling is a meditative spiritual practice of coupling with the radiant Divine Bride. Those ancient mountain men saw in Shabbat a soft, sensual, erotic encounter that completed them. Reading their poems, I must admit that I am drawn to their fantasy—"Come, my beloved, my bride, come in peace, my crown, rejoicing and frolicking"—one in which Shabbat is the romance that sustains life's commitments. However, mystical romantic fantasies don't always come to life in American suburbia. The real question is: How do I do Shabbat here? How traditional will I be? How do I structure such a day of rest and keep it each week?

For me, I have to start with a structure of dos and don'ts. I begin with the questions that set boundaries: Do I have the right balance of solitude, family time, and community interaction on Shabbat? Am I disengaged with the things that stress me out? Am I bored and restless? Do I engage in Torah learning? Do I feel closer to my Creator? Does attempting a stress-free day actually induce stress?

For someone who has grown up with a traditional understanding of Shabbat, my pattern of observance contains quite a bit of irony. Of the thirty-nine categories of prohibited work, the very first one is a prohibition of planting. I violate this precept with full knowledge that the Shabbat violator is, according to Torah, liable for stoning with the very rocks I am tossing to the side of the garden in order to plant strawberries. I have to admit that every time I go back to the garden and work on some project or other, I feel somewhat guilty. For the last three thousand years, Shabbat has been about letting the land rest while we rest. As I uproot and pick, I always feel the irony of my actions. Nevertheless, I understand my behavior to be reflective of a powerful paradigm shift that results from a technological age in which the work in this world has been turned upside down in the same way that the agricultural revolution supplanted hunter-gatherers. What once was our work—intensive agriculture—

described as a curse of the ground as Adam and Eve were thrown from Eden ("by the sweat of your brow"), is now a great joy. (Women, I sense, got the worst of the curses with the pain of childbirth.) Tilling the soil, digging in the dirt, and growing things in my backyard now epitomizes Shabbat for me. This is such a form of rest, a removal from the world of work, a return to the root (quite literally), that I must say "Is this not Shabbat, to have my hands covered in mud as I plant tomatoes?"

I understand that for some people, gardening, or its indoor counterparts of cooking and baking, are indeed serious activities that involve commercial consumption, articulate planning, and even professional consultation. If you fall into that category, then such activities are not Shabbat activities. Rabbi Eugene Borowitz, the preeminent liberal Jewish philosopher, reports to have gardened on Saturday afternoons but stopped many years ago when the gardening (and the schlepping of fertilizer and the like) began to feel more like work and less like relaxation. For the amateur gardener, an afternoon of flowers and shrubs is one way of returning to one's root, literally and metaphorically.

RABBI DANIEL BRENNER

SETTING BOUNDARIES FOR SHABBAT OBSERVANCE: DAN'S PERSPECTIVE

To create some space in your life to observe Shabbat, it is necessary to have some sense of boundaries in order to create an island of peace for yourself. It can be hard to do that, especially if you are very busy all week long. A friend told me that the sole rule of Shabbat that she and her family observe is to have Friday night dinner together, the only meal of the week where they are together. At dinner, they go around the table and describe their week, the difficulties they had and the blessings they felt. Sometimes it is a wonderful experience right from the moment they all sit down together. Her teenage daughter opens up in a way that she does not the rest of the week.

At other times her husband will call and say he is going to be late, and her daughter will grumble as she sits down, in that young-teenager-grumbling sort of way, about having to make blessings and then share her week with her parents. Sometimes it is such an effort that everyone will be angry at each other right through the blessings and into the salad. It seems that if the point of Shabbat is relaxation, the stress of getting everyone together has put everyone in such a bad mood that Shabbat is backfiring. However, my friend says, eventually—somewhere between the main course and dessert, when everyone has decompressed long enough to realize that the goal is to be together just this one time a week—they relax and the transcendent experience of Shabbat sets in.

Evolving Boundaries of Observance

Since I started going to Torah study and Shabbat services, I have found that Shabbat just evolved for me. Once I realized what celebrating Shabbat does for me and my soul, I've continued to set my own boundaries as they feel right for me. Some Shabbats are perfect. Others need more work.

Most Shabbats I go to Friday evening services, have dinner with my husband, go to Torah study and Saturday morning services, and then try to spend the rest of my day gardening, writing, reading, or whatever activity I can that I have little time to do during the week. It's not that complicated. I really feel that this twenty-five hours is sacred time. Even if I don't go to services on Friday night, and instead I spend time with my husband (who is not Jewish and does not go to services), sitting down with him to a long dinner with a glass of wine, I don't feel less of an experience of Shabbat because of this. If I can be at most of the services, take a nice drive with my husband, talk about the Torah portion that morning and really understand it, that is Shabbat to me.

I think there are many people who are necessarily involved in the world on Saturday, whose job or family obligations means that they are not going to be able to seclude themselves at home, who can still have a very meaningful Shabbat experience. I know that for me, once I really take on the "beingness" of Shabbat, the actions I do become less important than how I do the actions.

This is not to say that I have stopped thinking about what to do or not do on Shabbat. It's a continuous, growing, natural process that comes as my perception and awareness changes of where I want to set my boundaries.

ANN STRICKLAND

TO "REMEMBER" AND TO "GUARD": THE DOUBLE OBSERVANCE OF SHABBAT

The Ten Commandments appear twice in the Torah. The revelation at Mt. Sinai is recorded in Exodus and then retold in Deuteronomy. In the Book of Exodus, it says that one should "remember" the Sabbath and keep it holy. In Deuteronomy, it tells us to "guard" the Sabbath. To Jewish readers of the Torah, the slight difference becomes rather important. Commentators have seen two ways of observing Shabbat. "Guarding" Shabbat means the myriad restrictions imposed by Jewish law that ensure that a person will not work. It represents the passive aspect of Shabbat, refraining from work. "Remembering" Shabbat means taking positive actions to increase the joy and peacefulness of your life.

Jewish tradition commemorates the two times the Ten Commandments appear by having two candles lit on Shabbat. This is just one of a number of rituals on Shabbat that, like the animals on Noah's ark, come in pairs. "Everything pertaining to Shabbat is double" (*Midrash Tehillim* 92:1). Customarily, two loaves of challah are used to represent the double portion of manna that fell on Friday for the Israelites to gather when they were in the wilderness. We even have two souls on Shabbat; the Talmud says that on Shabbat one receives a second soul, and at the conclusion of Shabbat the second soul goes away (Babylonian Talmud, *Betzah* 16a). The Talmud also says that a pair of angels escorts a person home from the synagogue on Shabbat evening (Babylonian Talmud, *Shabbat* 119b).

Yet for all of the doubling, Shabbat is ultimately about two becoming one. For the mystics it was the male and female aspects of the Divine uniting. The *Zohar* says that as the male and female aspects of the Divine unite above, so also do they unite below in the mystery of the oneness. Some take this to mean that we should engage in the "double mitzvah" of Shabbat—that is, to have sex with our partner, the ultimate symbol of two becoming one. Even the two times that the Ten Commandments appear, the Rabbis say, God actually spoke them, in the mystery that is the oneness of God, at the exact same time. The Shabbat prayer *Lekha Dodi* says this quite simply, "*Shamor vezakhor bedibur echad.*" God uttered "guard" and "remember" as one word.

WHERE TO START AND HOW TO CONTINUE

To help you think about ways to begin or enhance your Shabbat observance, we have divided Shabbat into five separate time periods: preparation, candlelighting, Friday night, Saturday, and *havdalah*. In each section, we have made suggestions to spiritually deepen your Shabbat experience. They are all steps to glimpses of paradise, which the Shabbat experience can offer us in the midst of the real world. We have been there; we invite you to join us on the journey.

Preparation

Anticipation and preparation are crucial elements to experiencing Shabbat. Because Shabbat begins on Friday at sundown, one has to be ready by that time. The sun does not wait to set until you finish that one last project on your desk—and neither will Shabbat wait. Some people say that every week, on Friday just a few hours before the beginning of Shabbat, the heart of the Baal Shem Tov (the founder of Hasidism) would beat so loud that all who were with him could hear it. Others report that as they leave work on Friday afternoon, in anticipation of Shabbat, they can actually feel their bodies begin to shut down.

Refraining from work. Prior to the beginning of Shabbat, place your wallet in a drawer and close it. Leave it there for the duration of Shabbat. A crucial aspect of Shabbat is to remove oneself from business and commerce. Stay away from bills and purchases. You may even want to leave Saturday's mail—or, at least, its bills—until Saturday night or Sunday.

Experiencing pleasure. The Talmud tells us that Shammai, one of the talmudic sages, would spend all week putting aside food that he wanted to eat on Shabbat (Babylonian Talmud, *Betzah* 16a). Throughout the week, be conscious of what you might want to eat on Shabbat, what you might want to read on Shabbat, what you might want to wear on Shabbat, and then prepare these things so they are ready for you.

The sixteenth-century mystics of Safed immersed themselves in a *mikvah* and then put on white linens to prepare themselves for Shabbat. Take a shower and change your clothes just before Shabbat. Make this one of your final acts of preparation. It is a simple way of making the transition into Shabbat.

Creating a spiritual environment. A Hasidic rabbi who lived in a small town in Hungary in the early twentieth century used to prepare for Shabbat by cleaning and shining the shoes of all the members of his household. This was a task undertaken by his wife during the rest of the week, but he wanted to prepare for Shabbat by doing humble work for his family. Follow his lead. Do one thing before Shabbat for the other members of your family. Consider buying flowers for your partner, calling your parents, cleaning your kids' shoes—or even their rooms—for them.

Learn one new song each month to be sung on Shabbat. As you prepare for Shabbat, sing it repeatedly to yourself until you can claim it as your own. If you keep singing it over and over, others will learn the melody as well.

Lighting Shabbat Candles

Candlelighting is traditionally done eighteen minutes before sunset. Adhering to this practice forces you to let go of control over time and the environment. However, for many Jews who observe Shabbat, lighting candles to commence Shabbat before sunset is impossible. Many people get home from work when the sun is setting and can begin preparing only at that point, so they light candles when they sit down for dinner, whatever time that is. In many Reform synagogues it is the custom to light candles at the beginning of Friday night services even if those services are taking place significantly later than sunset. For all of these groups, the essence of lighting candles is to signify the beginning of Shabbat, that the time to rest has arrived.

Refraining from work. Consider what is work for you. That's where to begin to frame a Shabbat experience. If you do a lot of reading for your job, then make sure that the kind of Shabbat reading you do is unrelated to that. If your workweek includes a great deal of physical labor, then make sure to rest your body. The idea is to make Shabbat holy (wholly different) from your weekday experiences.

Experiencing pleasure. Customarily, two candles are lit for Shabbat. There are a number of different explanations given for this custom. Some families go beyond this two-candle minimum and add a candle for each child. Others use a third candle to represent all of their children. Because of the significance of the number 7 in Judaism (e.g., seven days of creation), some have a custom of lighting seven Shabbat candles. Regardless of the number of candles you have chosen to light for Shabbat, fill your home with Shabbat light. (See the sidebar on candlelighting customs, pp. 75–76.)

Creating a spiritual environment. In most homes, women light the candles. Men are required to do so when there are no women available to do it. Even though we strive to build egalitarian families, you might want to preserve those few customs, traditions, and laws that are specifically related to women. Light the candles, then cover your eyes. As you do this, say a silent prayer for your family after making the blessing. You may want to consider saying the prayer aloud so that they may hear your deep-seated wishes for them, as an expression of your love.

After lighting the candles, spend some time meditating, gazing at their soft light. The Book of Proverbs says, "The soul of a person is the light of God." This is a moment to reflect on your soul, your inner being, who you are in the world, and how your inner light is connected to God's divine light.

Friday Night

The Talmud says that a person is accompanied home on Friday night by two angels who guard the way (Babylonian Talmud, *Shabbat* 119b). Shabbat evening begins with kiddush (a blessing that sanctifies the day and is said over wine) and the *motzi* blessing over challah. This is followed by a Shabbat meal.

SHABBAT CANDLELIGHTING CUSTOMS

The classic Jewish image is of a woman lighting two Shabbat candles before the sun sets. She closes her eyes intently and circles her hands in the air, as if to draw the energy of the candles into her, and she recites the blessing over the candles. Why are there two candles? Why is it a woman's job? Why just before sunset? And why the hand circling? All good questions; we're glad you asked them.

Two candles: Customarily, there are two candles to represent the two times the commandment to observe Shabbat is given in the Torah, and specifically the two different words—*shamor,* guard, and *zakhor,* remember—that begin the commandment. More candles may be added. Some add a candle for each member of their family or light seven candles to reflect the importance of the number 7.

A woman's job: The commandment is for men as well as women; however, the custom became for the woman to light the candles. The mystical explanation for this relates to the characterization of Shabbat as feminine (a Bride or Queen); the mundane explanation is that women are the ones at home. In liberal Jewish circles men often light Shabbat candles, although it is remarkable to note that the custom of women lighting candles remains in place even in Jewish communities where women are rabbis and lay Jewish leaders.

Covering the eyes: Candles are lit, and then the blessing over the Shabbat candles is said with the eyes closed. It is said that the gates of heaven are particularly open to women at this time, and so many women use this opportunity to add a silent blessing for their family. The reason the eyes are closed is actually not so simple. My mother used to remark that no custom in Judaism is ever "so simple." Customarily, you say a blessing before you do an act—for example, you say the blessing over bread before eating the bread. However, the blessing over the candles marks the beginning of Shabbat, and on Shabbat it is forbidden to create light. Thus one would be breaking Shabbat by saying the blessing and then lighting the candles, yet one needs to say the blessing before the act is done. The custom became to light the candles but to close the eyes so as not to see the light while reciting the blessing. When the hands are removed, it is as if one has said the blessing before the candles were lit.

Just before sunset: Tradition prescribes that one lights the candles eighteen minutes before sunset. Shabbat commences officially at sunset, but the lighting of candles marks the beginning of Shabbat for those who lit them. Candlelighting is done early, to provide a cushion of time to prevent the possibility that one might accidentally light candles after sunset, and because it was difficult (before clocks and astronomers' tables) to determine exactly when sunset occurs.

Waving the hands around the candles: Shabbat light is the symbol of joy and harmony. One is drawing this joy and harmony into oneself and one's home. Shabbat is also imagined as Bride or Queen, and the waving of the hands welcomes Her to the house.

Refraining from work. Although the Rabbis did not have to deal with questions concerning electronic communication, they would undoubtedly state that you must stay off the Internet on Shabbat. It is another way of keeping your daily world out of Shabbat. If you are a TV watcher, try to spend just this one day without television. (It's good for you *and* for the kids.) Such things also keep us from really interacting with people, something that Shabbat encourages. Be present with the members of your family, your friends, and yourself.

Experiencing pleasure. Be intimate with your partner if you are blessed to have one. Having sex on Shabbat is considered a mitzvah.

Creating a spiritual environment. At the dinner table, invite everyone to share the most significant event that happened to them that week, and encourage them to express appreciation for it to God.

In addition to the traditional blessings that are offered on behalf of spouses and children, offer a blessing for each person. Use the traditional formula for blessing, adapt the one for a spouse or children, or use whatever words emerge from the depths of your soul. (See "Easy Steps for Entering Shabbat," pp. 79–84.)

Shabbat Day (Saturday)

Shabbat morning is traditionally a time when people go to synagogue. The highlight of the service is the reading of the Torah portion of the week, which is designed to help people reexperience the revelation at Sinai. We go to pray, to be with friends, and to celebrate the joys of Jewish community.

Refraining from work. Try to minimize your use of an automobile by driving only to the synagogue or to visit those with whom you are celebrating Shabbat, or perhaps refrain from driving completely. Part of the mystery of Shabbat is helping us to reconnect with the natural world away from the hectic pace that is implied by using machinery. If you do drive, avoid long trips.

Experiencing pleasure. Sleep a little later than normal in the morning. Take a nap in the afternoon. The essence of Shabbat is rest, so take the opportunity to just slow down.

Creating a spiritual environment. Study the weekly Torah portion. Find a partner with whom to discuss it in detail.

Read aloud from Rabbi Abraham Joshua Heschel's classic book *The Sabbath* or another work that focuses on the spiritual meaning of the Sabbath.

Havdalah: Leaving Shabbat Behind Yet Taking It with You

Just as Shabbat is ushered in with a ritual act of candlelighting, so too we leave Shabbat with a similar ritual act that involves light. It is a bittersweet time. It is also a time steeped in mystery as the daylight slips into darkness. We hate to let go of Shabbat. It is one of the reasons that we are permitted technically to hold on to Shabbat until Tuesday night—but then we have to make *havdalah* so that we can prepare for the next Shabbat. This brief ritual marks the end of Shabbat and helps us to make the transition back into the workday world, even though most of us don't work on Saturday night or Sunday. The *havdalah* ritual takes place forty-two minutes after sundown, or twenty-five hours after lighting Shabbat candles. This lovely, simple ceremony includes wine, a special braided candle, and fragrant spices. The ceremony is a sensuous experience of enchanting lights and sweet-smelling aromas.

Refraining from work. After *havdalah*, take Shabbat with you into the week. Don't rush to check e-mail, use the telephone, turn on the computer, or get back to work. Luxuriate in the Sabbath just a little while longer. Take the Sabbath moments that you have acquired along with you.

Experiencing pleasure. Before drinking the *havdalah* wine, follow the custom of the mystics by taking a small drop of wine and gently rub your eyelids or another's eyelids with it. During Shabbat, we gain an extra soul; this is meant to fortify and renew our soul, weary from the week. The wine is meant to comfort our soul, which loses its "partner-soul" at the end of Shabbat.

As a way of adding to the *havdalah* experience, leave the lights off. It is also nice to do it outside under the light of the stars.

Creating a spiritual environment. Pass the *havdalah* candle to each person before extinguishing it. Invite each person to say what they are hoping to be blessed with in the coming week.

The Talmud says that those who leave wine from the *havdalah* cup for the following week's observance of Shabbat are worthy of a share in the world to come, for such people are already anticipating the next Shabbat even as they say good-bye to the current one (Babylonian Talmud, *Pesachim* 113a). Instead of rushing to clean up after *havdalah*, leave some wine in the *havdalah* cup and set it aside for the following Shabbat.

WHERE AM I TODAY AND WHERE AM I GOING?: KERRY'S PERSPECTIVE[1]

It is a transcendent moment. Each Friday evening, as I sit at the head of the Shabbat table, my boys come to me for my blessing. (Even if I am away for Shabbat—the only time they voice any objection to my absence—they still ask me to bless them over the telephone before they sit down for dinner.) It's a brief moment, just enough time to whisper a few carefully selected words chosen by Jewish tradition for Jacob's final blessing to his own children, and augmented by the priestly benediction. Then, finally, a kiss—something particularly precious for the father of adolescent boys, who normally eschew such display of emotion. On other occasions, in other settings (especially in front of their peers), they will shriek, "Dad!" as they wriggle out from my lingering embrace, complaining loudly, "You're embarrassing me." Secretly, I rather enjoy the scene they make for their friends.

Shabbat is different for them. It offers them permission to break free of the conventions of their youth culture. No matter what has happened during the week, even if it's something that took place only moments before we sit down for a Sabbath meal, that everyday world becomes eclipsed. The fights, the arguments, the exchange of ill-considered and often hurtful words—all are set aside for the sake of this one moment that defies time. It is only in these few brief seconds that I am able to even approximate the intense physical bonding that God gives to mothers who are able to bear children. And so on Shabbat evening, after my wife leads us all in lighting the Sabbath candles, I set my principles of equality aside; my boys come to me alone for blessing.

EASY STEPS FOR ENTERING SHABBAT

1. Candlelighting

Close your eyes and bring the light into your heart and soul by encircling the flames with your hands three times. Then say this blessing: *Barukh ata Adonai Elohenu melekh ha-olam asher kidshanu bemitzvotav vetzivanu lehadlik ner shel Shabbat.* (Praised are You, Adonai our God, Sovereign of the universe, who makes us holy with mitzvot and instructs us to kindle the lights of Shabbat.)

2. Sing or Read *Shalom Aleikhem*

Shalom aleikhem, malakhei hashareit, malakhei Elyon,
Mimelekh, malekhei hamelakhim, hakadosh barukh hu.
Boakhem leshalom, malakhei hashalom, malakhei Elyon,
Mimelekh, malekhei hamelachim, hakadosh barukh hu.
Barkhuni leshalom, malekhei hashalom, malekhei Elyon,
Mimelekh, malekhei hamelakhim, hakadosh barukh hu.
Tzeitkhem leshalom, malakhei hashalom, malakhei Elyon,
Mimelekh, malekhei hamelakhim, hakadosh barukh hu.

Peace be to you, ministering angels, messengers of the Most
    High, of the supreme Sovereign, the Holy One, ever to
    be praised.
Enter in peace, ministering angels, messengers of the Most
    High, of the supreme Sovereign, the Holy One, ever to
    be praised.
Bless us with peace, messengers of the Most High, of the
    supreme Sovereign, the Holy One, ever to be praised.
Depart in peace, ministering angels, messengers of the Most
    High, of the supreme Sovereign, the Holy One, ever to
    be praised.

3. Bless Your Spouse and Your Children

Speak words of the heart or these words of the tradition.

The traditional blessing for a wife is from Proverbs 31 and is
often referred to as "A Woman of Valor." Try this egalitarian version
for women and men by Rabbi Susan Grossman:

A good wife, who can find her?
She is worth far more than rubies.
She brings good and not harm
all the days of her life.
She girds herself with strength
and finds her trades profitable.
Wise counsel is on her tongue

and her home never suffers for warmth.
She stretches her hands to the poor,
reaches her arms to the needy.
All her friends praise her.
Her family blesses her.
She is known at the gates
as she sits with the elders.
Dignity, honor are her garb.
She smiles at the future.

A good man, who can find him?
He is worth far more than rubies.
All who trust in him
never lack for gain.
He shares the household duties
and sets a goodly example.
He seeks a satisfying job
and braces his arms for work.
He opens his mouth with wisdom.
He speaks with love and kindness.
His justice brings him praises.
He raises the poor, lowers the haughty.

Sometimes, their children are invited to add:

These two indeed do worthily.
True leaders in Zion.
Give them their due credit.
Let their works praise them at the gates.

Then the children are blessed, usually in chronological order from oldest to youngest.

For boys the blessing is "May God make you like Ephraim and Manasseh." For girls the blessing is "May God make you like Sarah, Rebecca, Rachel, and Leah."

Then comes the text from the Torah known as the priestly blessing, for both boys and girls.

May God bless you and protect you.
May God show you favor and be gracious to you.
May God cause light to shine on you and grant you
    tranquility of spirit.

4. Make Kiddush (Friday)

Vayekhulu hashamayim ve'ha-aretz vekhol tzeva'am vayekhal Elohim bayom hashevi'i melakhto asher asah. Vayishbot bayom hashevi'i mikol melakhto asher asah. Vayevarekh Elohim et yom hashevi'i vayekadesh oto ki bo shavat mikol melakhto asher bara Elohim la'asot.

(Now the whole universe—sky, earth, and all their array—was completed. On the seventh day God rested with all the divine work completed. Then God blessed the seventh day and called it holy, for on this day God had completed the work of Creation.)

Include this traditional formula of invitation to others to join in: "Savrei" (Folks).

(They respond, *"L'chaim."*)

Barukh ata Adonai Elohenu melekh ha-olam borei pri hagafen. (Praised are You, Adonai our God, Sovereign of the universe, who creates the fruit of the vine.)

Barukh ata Adonai Elohenu melekh ha-olam asher kidshanu bemitzvotav veratza banu veshabbat kadsho be-ahavah u'vratzon hinchilanu zikaron le'ma'asei bereshit ki hu yom techilah lemikra'ei kodesh zekher l'tziyat mitzrayim. Ki banu bacharta ve'otanu kidashta mikol ha'amim veshabbat kadshekha be'ahava u'vratzon hinchaltanu. Barukh ata Adonai mikadesh ha-Shabbat.

(Praised are You, Adonai our God, Sovereign of the universe, who makes us holy with mitzvot and takes delight in us. In love and favor You have made the holy Sabbath our heritage, as a reminder of the work of Creation. It is first among our sacred days, and a remembrance of the Exodus from Egypt. O God, You have chosen us and set us apart from all the peoples and in love and favor have given us the Sabbath Day. Praised are You, Adonai, for the Sabbath and its holiness.)

5. Make Kiddush (Saturday Midday)

Veshamru bnei Yisrael et ha-Shabbat la'asot et ha-Shabbat ledorotam brit olam beini u'vein bnei Yisrael ot hi le'olam ki sheshet yamim asah Adonai et hashamayim ve'et ha-aretz u'vayom hashevi'i shavat vayinafash.

Al ken berakh Adonai et yom ha-Shabbat vayekadsheinu.

Include this traditional formula of invitation to others to join in: "Savrei" (Folks).

(They respond, *"L'chaim."*)

Barukh ata Adonai Elohenu melekh ha-olam borei pri hagafen.

6. *Hamotzi* (Blessing for Bread)

Barukh ata Adonai Elohenu melekh ha-olam hamotzi lechem min ha-aretz.

(Praised are you, Adonai our God, Sovereign of the universe, Who brings forth bread from the earth.)

7. *Birkat Hamazon* (Grace after Meals)

Birkat Hamazon contains a series of blessings that express appreciation to God for food, the Land of Israel, Jerusalem, and for doing good things for us. Although there is a lengthy *Birkat Hamazon* in most prayer books, some people begin the process of adding *Birkat Hamazon* to their spiritual discipline by simply offering thanks to God, either using words of their own or through these two blessings:

Barukh ata Adonai Elohenu melekh ha-olam hazan et hakol.

(Praised are You, Adonai our God, Sovereign of the universe, who nourishes everyone.)

Berikh marei d'hai pita. (Praised are You for this bread.) (Babylonian Talmud, *Berakhot* 40b)

8. *Havdalah* Blessings

Behold, God is my deliverer. I trust in You and am not afraid. For Adonai is my strength and my stronghold, the source of my deliverance. With joy we draw water from the wells of salvation. Adonai brings deliverance, blessings to the people. Selah. Adonai is a powerful God: the God of Jacob is our stronghold.

Give us light and joy, gladness and honor, as in the happiest days of Israel's past. I lift up the cup of my salvation and call out the name of Adonai.

Barukh ata Adonai Elohenu melekh ha-olam borei pri hagafen. (Praised are You, Adonai our God, Sovereign of the universe, who creates the fruit of the vine.)

Barukh ata Adonai Elohenu melekh ha-olam borei minei besamim. (Praised are You, Adonai our God, Sovereign of the universe, who creates a variety of fragrances.)

Barukh ata Adonai Elohenu melekh ha-olam borei meorei ha-esh. (Praised are You, Adonai our God, Sovereign of the universe, who creates the light of fire.)

Barukh ata Adonai Elohenu melekh ha-olam borei hamavdil bein kodesh lechol, bein or lechoshekh, bein Yisrael la-amim, bein yom hashevi'i lesheshet yamei ha-ma'asei. Barukh ata Adonai hamavdil bein kodesh lechol.

(Praised are You, Adonai our God, Sovereign of the universe, who distinguishes between the sacred and the everyday, light and darkness, Israel and other peoples, the seventh day and the six days of labor. Praised are You, Adonai, who distinguishes between the sacred and the everyday.)

RECOMMENDED READING

Elkins, Dov Peretz. *A Shabbat Reader: Universe of Cosmic Joy.* New York: UAHC Press, 1997.

Greenberg, Irving. *The Jewish Way: Living the Holidays.* New York: Summit Books, 1988.

Heschel, Abraham Joshua. *The Sabbath.* New York: Farrar, Straus & Giroux, 1996.

Matlins, Stuart M., ed. *The Jewish Lights Spirituality Handbook: A Guide to Understanding, Exploring and Living a Spiritual Life.* Woodstock, Vt.: Jewish Lights Publishing, 2001.

Peli, Pinchas. *Shabbat Shalom: A Renewed Encounter with the Sabbath.* Washington, D.C.: B'nai B'rith Books, 1988. Paperback ed: *The Jewish Sabbath.* New York: Schocken Books, 1991.

Strassfeld, Michael. *A Shabbat Haggadah: For Celebration and Study.* New York: Institute of Human Relations Press/American Jewish Committee, 1981.

Wolfson, Ron. *Shabbat,* 2nd ed.: *The Family Guide to Preparing for and Celebrating the Sabbath.* Woodstock, Vt.: Jewish Lights Publishing, 2002.

5

Daily Prayer

DR. MARK KLIGMAN

One Rosh Hashanah I decided to pray in an ultra-Orthodox *shtibel* (small synagogue). The building looked worn and the decor was vintage 1950s. The room was not very big, and there were more people than could comfortably fit in the space. Of the seventy men present in the men's section, some were seated in pews while others sat around long rectangular tables. An equal number of, or perhaps more, women were in the back of this little shul behind the *mechitzah* (partition separating men and women in traditional prayer). I sat in a pew with a table in front of me. Several men sat on either side; both men and boys sat in front of me. I felt like I was in a football huddle seated around this table. Conversation occasionally ensued; facing each other in this arrangement made discussion easier. I had not experienced prayer this way before.

The cantor's repetition of the *Amidah* (the central prayer of the service) was lengthy during the morning service of Rosh Hashanah; it took well over an hour. As the cantor sang, some men followed along in the prayer book while others studied a Hebrew text. I tried to follow the service in the prayer book. Before the *Musaf* part of the service began (i.e., the lengthy final portion of the morning service), a middle-age man seated across from me stood up and prepared himself. He was wearing a dark suit, white shirt and a large tallit that was draped around him; the tallit covered his head and upper body. He took his *gartl* (a thin black cord that some traditional men wear like a belt) and tightened it into a knot, as if he were "strapping himself in." He said to all of us who were seated around the table, "Okay, I'll meet you on the other side." I felt like he was directing his comment only to me. Where was he going? Where were we going? His message to me was simple: "I'm preparing myself for this spiritual journey. I'll meet you at its conclusion."

This man provided me with an entirely new formulation for the experience of prayer. Previously, I always had my eye on the final page of the service, counting down the pages one by one until the conclusion of the service. Although his mode of prayer was not one that had previously resonated for me, this man's comments challenged my entire notion of prayer. He anticipated the prayer experience as transformative. I had only considered prayer obligatory and rote. By preparing himself, he created a sacred space and journeyed with his soul into prayer. For the first time, the silent portion of the *Musaf Amidah* became truly silent. Instead of being distracted by every chair squeak, I was able to shut out any potentially intrusive noise. Men shuckled (swayed) fervently; the communal responses during the repetition of the *Amidah* were heartfelt. I ventured into my own prayer space. I read each of the words of prayer in the prayer book slowly and deliberately for the first time. Those who surrounded me pleaded to God and made gestures with their arms toward heaven. I felt drawn closer to God as well. At the end of the service, I found myself on the "other side." Through prayer, I was able to experience an intimate encounter with God, perhaps for the first time in my life.

THE BASICS OF PRAYER

The Hebrew word for prayer is *tefillah*. Grammatically, the verb "to pray" *(hitpalel)* is in the reflexive form; it is thus understood as an activity done to the self. The term therefore reflects Rabbi Eliezer's call in the Talmud for prayer as personal assessment: "A person should always assess oneself [before praying]; if one is able to concentrate one should pray, and if not, one should not pray" (Babylonian Talmud, *Berakhot* 30b). Such assessment can take the form of *cheshbon hanefesh* (introspection and self-evaluation; literally, an accounting of the soul). As you reflect on yourself and your personal spiritual journey, you reach out to God for guidance through prayer. Prayer becomes a way to connect yourself to holiness and measure your thoughts and actions according to standards set forth by the Divine. Prayer provides you with an opportunity to enter into a dialogue with God, personally and intimately. Rabbis call the state of mind during prayer *kavanat halev* (literally, "focusing of the heart").

Because prayer is deeply personal, your own motivation and mindset is certainly relevant to it. Prayer is typically described by its content and form; this is known as *keva,* the "fixed" text of prayer in a prayer book, and *kavanah* ("intention"), the spontaneous prayers, or those that are not fixed in the liturgy. These two aspects, *keva* and *kavanah,* form the basis of the interplay of prayer.

The Rabbis of the Talmud tell us that prayer should not be a burden, and saying something new in one's prayers is important (Babylonian Talmud, *Berakhot* 29b). This reminds us that that one should pray when one can concentrate fully and spontaneously. Although this is certainly the ideal, it seems that this is possible only for a limited few and only on limited occasions. Perhaps that is why fixed prayers (normally referred to as the liturgy) have often eclipsed spontaneous prayer in the Jewish tradition and in the synagogue.

MY OWN ENCOUNTER WITH PRAYER

I studied music in college. My goal was to teach music history and theory to college students. I did not want to be a pianist, but piano study helped me to understand and really get to know music. I committed myself to practicing the piano many hours each day, and it became a routine part of my life. Some days I felt like playing, many days I did not, but I learned discipline through the task. Playing music allowed me to express my thoughts, emotions, and experiences in ways that words did not express. Little did I know that my piano practice would serve as a model in my later quest to experience real prayer.

After seriously engaging in the study and performance of music for several years, I realized that music itself was not enough for me. Although I felt satisfaction studying and performing music, I felt that something was missing. I longed for a deeper, more profound mode of expression that connected me to the Divine and to Jewish tradition. Music was not able to answer my questions, such as "Why be a good person?" I searched for answers through prayer. I tried to follow Rabbi Hayim Halevy Donin's advice:

> "It is true that at times I pray only because it is my duty to obey the Jewish law that requires me to pray. But there are also times that I pray because I sincerely want to pray. These are the times when I want to reach out and talk . . . when I want to cry out to the Supreme Being, to communicate" [with God].[1]

I learned that such moments are rare, and they come when one feels distress or lonely and isolated from the world. Praying regularly in a routine, Donin taught, helps to facilitate prayer when it is most needed.

It occurred to me that every day I had my own rituals of getting ready for my day—showering, grooming, and the like—but I did not have similar Jewish rituals as part of my daily life. I found the parallel from my piano practice to Donin's description of prayer to be inviting. I knew that regularly engaging in prayer was not going to be a powerful experience every time I prayed. However, I felt certain that if I prayed regularly, the routine would aid me when I needed it the most. *Kavanah* in prayer goes hand in hand with *keva*. When my *kavanah* is at its peak, I find deeper meaning in the fixed text of prayer.

It didn't happen overnight. I began slowly. I started with the *Shema* and the *Amidah* each morning and then added other blessings. (The literal understanding of every prayer came later.) Gradually I increased the prayers that I recited and later added *Minchah* and *Maariv*, the afternoon and evening prayer services, into my daily routine. I took classes on prayer to understand the structure of the prayer book and to gain insights into the purpose and meaning of prayer. In time I started attending a daily minyan (prayer quorum). Although I have never attended three daily minyans on a regular basis, I do try to attend at least one minyan a day, and I pray on my own otherwise. I find that praying with others deepens my prayer experience and helps me to concentrate on it more.

Praying Daily Can Be a Struggle

I know the prayer service, but I am constantly struggling with how to pray. Some days I wake up groggy and I daven by rote. Before I know it, I have reached the blessings after the *Shema,* not fully aware of how I got there. I console myself by realizing that at least now I am awake. Sometimes I dive into the words. I try to enunciate them clearly. I find myself drawn to certain words and slow down and linger over them as certain images appear before me. As I say the phrase *Or chadash al tzion ta'ir,* "a new light will arise upon Zion," I stare at the floor and realize that every atom in the wood is energized by God's light, which is new every second. Or, as I come to the phrase *V'yerushalayim irkha b'rachamim tashuv,* "And Jerusalem your city may return [to You] in compassion," my mind is drawn to the pain in Jerusalem from last night's terrorist bombing. Other days, I mumble the words in a rhythmic hum and it is almost like a mantra—all sound and no meaning. That can be hypnotic and meditative or simply deadening. Or I may not feel like using the fixed liturgy at all—too much Hebrew for me to think about today. I will slowly put on my tefillin, repeat the

Shema ten to twenty times, and stay silent for ten minutes. If I have something on my mind, I may take a minute or two and actually talk (aloud or inwardly) to God about what I want from the day to come.

All of this I do by myself, in the room next to my bedroom, with tefillin and tallit, after I have showered and dressed, and before I have spoken a word to anyone. I leave for work or the gym each day between 5:15 and 6:15 A.M., and I pray for the half hour before I leave. It may not be precise according to traditional Jewish law (because it is still dark during much of the winter at that time), but it is my morning and so I daven *Shacharit* (the morning service). If I step off the plane after an all-night flight on business, I will find someplace to put on tefillin and pray (the cab from the airport, even a locker room at the office) before I begin my day. I will not miss a day—I always pray at least a little. It orients my day, consoles me if I am in a bad mood or if someone is sick, reminds me of what is important in life, and—on the good days—connects me to God. Prayer lifts me just a tiny bit off the ground.

I wish I had a minyan that I could pray with, but none is close enough to fit my schedule. Even if I could find one, I would be trading the precious flexibility to mold my prayer to where I am at the moment for the joy and power of community prayer. At my workplace, there is a group of Orthodox Jews who daven *Minchah* every late afternoon. I join them when I can. I suspect I am the only liberal Jew in the group. They do speed davening. When I say speed, I mean *speed*—a *Minchah* service with a full repetition of the *Amidah* in seven or eight minutes. Finding a prayerful space in that environment was not easy at first. Over time, I have been able to make the experience meaningful by directing my attention to a limited section of the liturgy (rather than trying to keep up with the prayer leader). What is most remarkable to me about this community that gathers together for high-speed prayer, though, is not that they are praying so quickly but that they have broken away at all. They choose to take a few moments out of the intensity of their business lives to be with each other and with God. There is a palpable warmth in that room that is remarkable.

ROBERT MASS

The experience of prayer helps me to make a personal connection to God. It enables me to find a way to constantly encounter holiness. I have been working at it for twenty years, and I feel that it is part of my spiritual journey. I am reminded of the maxim that ultimately the journey is not about getting there, the joy is in the journey. Getting to know God has been the most challenging part of the journey. I thought that once I took a leap of faith, everything about God would fall into place. However, my faith did not come as a result of a sudden inspiration or specific event. Rather, it emerged from learning, questioning, and encountering others who have been my guides. An experience of the Divine was not part of my vocabulary.

Now I pray to feel closer to God, to pull myself out of my daily struggles and gain perspective. Prayer has allowed me to reach beyond myself, to encounter the Divine. Watching TV and movies may be fun, but they cannot help me to reach heavenward. When I am deeply involved in prayer and experience the Almighty, it allows me to reflect on the beauty in others and myself, allowing me to experience and feel what rational thought cannot capture.

One summer I studied at a music camp in Interlochen, Michigan, a serene setting surrounded by forests and two lakes; music could be heard everywhere. Large ensembles played in open-air concert settings while small groups and individuals practiced on the grass or in a clearing in the woods. One afternoon I walked past an outdoor concert just as the sun was about to set. Through a distant clearing of trees, I saw a reflection of the sun on the lake; the air and water were still. I could hear the beautiful sound of two hundred flute players playing J. S. Bach's *Air on G String*. The ethereal sound of the flutes in this calm and relaxed setting captured me. It took my breath away. I thought to myself, "Only God could make this beauty possible." I carry this experience with me into prayer. I know that heaven must be similar to this.

Learning to Pray from My Bubbe

The first person I ever saw "pray" was my Bubbe Ida Paperny, my grandmother. She was Russian-born and did not go to synagogue very often, but she prayed every week in her living room when she lit her Shabbat candles. Bubbe would put a little scarf on her head, light the candles, and then move her arms in a circle three times over the flames, ending with her hands covering her eyes. Then she would enter a kind of trance, rhythmically moving back and forth as she mumbled the blessing under her breath. She continued this shuckling for what seemed like an eternity, until she uncovered her eyes to reveal tear-stained cheeks. Why was she crying? Wouldn't you, if you had just talked with God? You see, Bubbe had just had her weekly conversation with the Almighty. She asked God for many things: good health for her family, success in Zadie's business, happiness in the neighborhood, peace in the world.

Bubbe's example taught me about the two most important aspects of Jewish prayer. The *keva* routine of regularly offering prayer at specified times gives me a structure and a formula to follow that creates the opportunity for moments of spiritual encounter. The *kavanah* intentionality of prayer is more elusive; it is what I bring to the prayer experience—my emotions, my state of mind, my life journey.

My colleague Rabbi Elliot Dorff has taught that Jewish prayer is like baseball. The more "at bats" we have, the better our chances for hitting a "home run" in prayer. In baseball, a player can be an All-Star by hitting .300—fewer than one out of three times. The important point is to "step up to the plate" as often as possible. In my own experience with Jewish prayer, I seek out the structured opportunities to pray—in my daily life and in the appointed synagogue services, hoping to find the *kavanah* that elevates my soul. I praise God, I sing songs, I study, I move, I engage in ritual, I join in community. I don't always hit it "out of the park," but when I do, prayer can shake me to my core, inspire me to change, and lead me to a life that matters.

RON WOLFSON

PRAYING WITH A COMMUNITY

Although prayer is self-directed, it is also a communal activity. Certain prayers like the *Barkhu* (call to prayer); the public repetition of the *Amidah,* including the *Kedushah* section (a proclamation of God's holiness); and the Kaddish (memorial prayer) are traditionally said only in the presence of a minyan. The language of prayer also focuses on personal and communal needs. In the three paragraphs of the *Shema* (Deut. 6:5–9, 11:13–21, and Num. 15:37–41), the role of the individual and collective responsibility is the focus of the text. The words of the first line of the *Shema* are stated in the plural, not the singular: *Shema Yisrael, Adonai Eloheinu, Adonai echad* (Hear O Israel, the Lord is our God, the Lord is one). That's what leads me to seek out a minyan with which to pray. Praying with a minyan is a reminder that I do not stand alone; I am part of a community, and this requires participation and responsibility.

Attending prayer services regularly in a daily minyan adds to my circle of those close and dear to me. If someone is not present one morning because they are ill or busy caring for a sick loved one, I know that I have a responsibility to reach out to them. Saying a *Mi Sheberakh* (prayer for healing) allows the community to reach out to God for help. Likewise if someone comes to observe a *yahrtzeit* (the anniversary of the death of a loved one), doing so in a familiar environment may help the bereaved. To pray with them and support them adds to my personal spiritual experience.

Although I want to see the immediate results of prayer, I am constantly reminded of Maimonides' teaching that fulfilling the commandments in Judaism should not be done for the sake of a reward but to shape our heart in service to God (*Mishneh Torah, Hilkhot Teshuvah* 10:1). When I am praying for myself or another, I hope that God will grant my requests. I know that ultimately I cannot will or determine the outcome of life; answering my prayers positively is up to God. At times I receive what I asked for, often in ways I do not anticipate. Sometimes I even receive them in abundance, and I am humbled by the extent of my riches. I try to gear my response of gratitude for what the Almighty has given with the same intensity as the request. When there are difficult events in my life, I am reminded that our tradition teaches that we should pray for our own needs and also pray for the needs of others. The Rabbis of the Talmud remind us that praying for others actually adds to our own benefit for our prayers to be accepted (Babylonian Talmud, *Baba Kamma* 92a).

Rather than viewing prayer as an activity that I go to do, I see it as something that I take with me. Committing myself to prayer means making the necessary arrangements to pray every day and anywhere. This is a challenge, with the pressures of family schedules, commuting to work, and everything else that occupies the routine of everyday life.

THE BASIC STRUCTURE OF THE PRAYER SERVICE

The relationship between spontaneous and fixed prayers plays itself out in the various prayer books that have been developed for use by the Jewish people throughout its history. The *siddur* was created to provide people with the text of fixed prayers for the required worship services (three times daily) and with some room for spontaneity. The conventional daily ritual of prayer begins with *Shacharit*, continues with *Minchah*, and concludes with *Maariv*.

The basic service is built around the *Amidah*, named as such because it means "standing prayer." Praying fulfills the commandment "And you shall serve the Lord your God" (Exodus 23:25). Although the service was once accomplished in the form of animal sacrifice, that gave way to prayer after the destruction of the ancient Temple in Jerusalem in 70 C.E. (Prayer and sacrifice coexisted for a period of time prior to its destruction.) The *Amidah* is also known as the *Shemoneh Esreh* (literally eighteen, referring to the original number of blessings, which have grown to nineteen) or *hatefillah*, "the prayer," using the more general term for prayer. The individual blessings of the *Amidah* are grouped into three sections: praising God; petitioning God (for personal things as well as for the needs of the Jewish people); and thanking God. At first, reciting various blessings and saying the *Shema* and the *Amidah* constituted the entire ritual of required prayer. During the first millennium, the prayer leader improvised a great deal beyond the basic prayers. By the ninth century, the order of the prayers became relatively fixed. In the traditional community, things have been added to it, but little has been taken from it.

Since the *Amidah* forms the core of all of the services, individual prayers are usually added at its conclusion, somewhere in the middle of the service. (They are also added elsewhere.) In traditional prayer books, the portion that immediately follows the repetition of the *Amidah* in the morning service is known as *Tachanun* (petitions or pleas). This section consists of requests to God for help and protection. In its prayer books, the Reform movement calls this moment of reflection a "silent meditation." To emphasize the humble nature of these petitions, it is customary to sit down (after the *Amidah,* which is said while standing) and to lay your head on your arm (very similar to the way children in classrooms do when asked to "put their head down"). Beyond the structured worship service, there are other opportunities for prayers and prayerlike texts, such as the reciting of psalms.

Prayers for Each Stage of Life

The regular morning service comprises six sections:

- *Birkot Hashachar,* the preliminary blessings
- *Pesukei d'Zimra,* songs and psalms that praise God
- The *Shema* and its blessings
- The *Amidah,* the standing prayer
- The Torah service
- The concluding service

Each of these sections is independent, but they all work together to form the service as a whole. This is how I see them reflecting the human life cycle.

In *Birkot Hashachar,* we begin silently. The first blessings in the *siddur* we don't even do out loud. Before we have speech, we are infants. In these prayers, we acknowledge the basic trust we have in a God who restores us back to life every morning. As an infant begins to develop, it focuses on the first things it sees in its immediate surroundings; fingers, toes, mom and dad, the crib. So too, in our morning blessings, we focus on those things in our immediate surroundings; our bodies and our souls; our material, intellectual, and spiritual needs. We focus on us. We thank God for providing the things that keep us going.

Then like toddlers, our focus shifts outward toward our relationship with the rest of the world. And so in the *Pesukei d'Zimra* section, we recite psalms and biblical verses that focus on God as the primary force in nature and in history. We are like little children who exclaim in awe at the wonders that surround us. "God, You created the mountains, the streams, the plants, the animals, all the living beings. God, You acted wondrously in history, saving us from Egypt, giving us the Torah, bringing us to Israel." This is the transcendent God, whom we know is in control of everything, whom we need to be in control. This is the big God, before whom we feel very small and insignificant.

Then we continue to mature and we hit adolescence. Every parent of an adolescent child knows that adolescence is about being in relationship. It's about hanging out with your peers, being part of a clique. So rather than praying as individuals, we come together with the *Barkhu,* the call to prayer, to be in our community and in a communal relationship with God. We move from the perception of God as a transcendent God of creation to the immanent and loving God who cares for each of us and for all of us as God's people.

In the prayer *Ahavah Rabbah,* which precedes the *Shema,* we describe God as a parent who demonstrates love for us by giving us the most precious gift of Torah: a system of boundaries and rules within which we are allowed to flourish and grow. Then in the paragraph immediately following the *Shema,* the *ve-ahavta,* we reciprocate by talking about our love for God and how we will demonstrate that love by following God's Torah and by seeking to develop our personal relationships. The life cycle continues.

We come to the *Amidah,* and now we are all grown up. The *Amidah* is about the mature love relationship that we seek to develop with God. It's a much more complex relationship, and the prayer becomes much more complex and nuanced. Symbolically, at the beginning of the *Amidah,* we take three steps back to separate ourselves from the group that we've belonged to, and three steps forward, as it were, to enter under the *chuppah,* entering into a marriage, an intimate relationship with God. Some people at this point even choose to wrap themselves in their tallit, a practice that is also observed by some under the *chuppah* with the bride and groom, and so it recalls that imagery.

In this prayer, we are now in a mutual relationship. Being in a mutual relationship means that we must give but we may also request. So we ask God to take care of our needs, both individual and communal. We finish up with a prayer for *shalom*, or peace and wholeness, for a relationship with God that's like a happy marriage.

Rabbi Louis Finkelstein, former chancellor of the Jewish Theological Seminary of America, once said, "When I pray, I talk to God; when I read Torah, God talks to me." Part of being in a successful, mature, adult relationship is that true sense of give-and-take, of speaking and truly listening to the other. The Torah service, then, is our chance to hear and process God's word and God's will. In addition, we find at this point in the service that we take the opportunity as mature adults to address other communal needs. We say prayers on behalf of those who take care of the community through their labor and their financial support. We pray for the ill, we say special prayers for our country and for the State of Israel. We attend to the political, spiritual, and material needs of those whom we love.

Finally, the concluding service is like our senior years. We have gained wisdom, we possess integrity, and we have a much more global view of the world. We sum up where we have been and we look forward to what lies beyond. The *Alenu* prayer reflects our hope for a perfected world and for the redemption that is yet to come. The Mourner's Kaddish, which also speaks about ultimate redemption, serves to bring us face-to-face in confronting our own mortality. We don't know how much longer we will live, so we ought to make the most of every day.

RABBI TRACEE ROSEN[2]

PRAYER AND MEDITATION

Praying three times a day on a daily basis is done primarily by people who are engaged with the traditional form of prayer. However, one of the alternative modes of daily prayer that has undergone much renewed interest is Jewish meditation. Many people are surprised to learn that there are meditative techniques in Judaism at all, because they associate meditation with Eastern religions. In fact, Judaism has

a long tradition of meditative techniques, most of which are associated with Kabbalah, or Jewish mysticism.

Some suggest that meditation has even been a part of mainstream
Jewish practice. Avram Davis, a leading practitioner and teacher of
Jewish meditation, suggests that the word *tefillah,* prayer, was in fact
used by the Rabbis of the Talmud to mean both prayer and simple
meditation. "When they [the Rabbis] use the term *tefillah,* they can
easily be referring to either meditation or prayer or possibly to both.
It is both a strength and a weakness of modernity that we feel so
sharply the need to differentiate between these transformative tools."[3]

Jewish meditation has many different techniques, and there is
much new and rich material on the subject to spark one's interest (see
"Recommended Reading," pp. 103–104). Basically, Jewish meditation
seeks to clear the mind through focused intention on certain phrases
from the prayer service or images from Jewish tradition. The goal of
this meditation is not just relaxation, but *devekut,* a "cleaving" to
God through quieting the mind and making the ego smaller. A Jewish
meditator might practice on a daily basis or follow the traditional
pattern of *Shacharit, Minchah,* and *Maariv* and meditate for three
periods during the day.

One particular form of meditation is chanting, which attempts
to create a meditative state through the repetition of a particular
phrase with a melody.

Chanting and Meditation

Like many Jews, I am a lover of words. I loved Hebrew even when I didn't
understand a word of it. The sounds seemed to open up a place inside me
that wanted to pour itself out to God. They turned me inside out in ways
that made me feel visible to God so I could be seen and known and loved.
As my love for the sounds grew along with my knowledge of Hebrew
words, I found myself seriously out of step with formal communal prayer.
My thirst to drink deeply from certain phrases in the liturgy that called to
me was constantly being frustrated by the pace and volume of traditional
prayers. I began to look for what was essential in prayer and to search for
the deep structure of the prayer service that would help me to under-

stand the function and not merely the content of each prayer. My background in music and many forms of meditation prepared me to develop a chanting practice that treated the sacred phrase as a doorway. Repetition became a way to still the mind and open the heart so wide that it felt as if the sacred phrases were planting seeds there.

My own chanting evolved from searching for a form of prayer that would let me experience the Divine and would deepen and develop with practice. Indeed, the experience of chanting has enhanced my silent meditative practice. My "base" practice remains the same and is the foundation for other practices that evolve and change according to whatever I feel is needed. That core practice is a silent, twenty-minute daily meditation that I call *devekut*. It is a practice of intention. My intention is to be in God's presence and to gently let go of all thoughts that arise that may take me from God's presence. One of the purposes of meditation is to develop an ongoing, vital relationship with the Divine, which then becomes the foundation for prayer. I believe that different forms of Jewish meditation can strengthen one's prayer life. When I work with a sacred phrase from the liturgy, exploring its meaning with the intuitive senses of the heart and letting that meaning expand and affect my inner life, then that phrase has a new power for me. The cumulative experience of using many phrases from the *siddur* in meditation gradually injects new life and new depth into my prayer.

RABBI SHEFA GOLD[4]

WHERE TO START DAILY PRAYER
AND HOW TO CONTINUE

Start slowly and gradually. Don't rush. Find the right time—and a comfortable place, if you can—in your day for prayer. It will probably be easier to find a time at the beginning of your day or at the end of it. Afternoon prayers are the most difficult—and probably the most important as a result—because you have to steal yourself away from your work or leisure activities in the middle of the day in order to make room for prayer.

Begin with the simple words of prayer that emerge from your heart. Once these more spontaneous prayers become part of your spiritual discipline, you can ready yourself for the fixed prayers of the traditional liturgy.

Then you are ready to continue with the daily blessings and then the opening verses of *Pesukei d'Zimra*.

Next continue with the *Shema* and the blessings that follow.

Then focus on one unit (out of nineteen) of the *Amidah* at a time. They are divided by themes, which are stated in the opening blessing and repeated in the closing blessing of each section. Before focusing on the specific words of the prayers, meditate on the themes that are addressed in each section.

Next add the blessing before and after the *Shema* to create a cohesive unit that connects the *Shema* with the *Amidah*.

Then add the final sections of the service.

WHERE AM I TODAY AND WHERE AM I PLANNING ON BEING TOMORROW?

Today I pray three times a day. I am not always successful in finding a minyan. I find that my morning prayers are enhanced when I pray in the same synagogue with the same friends and neighbors each day. As personal and world events constantly remind me of my fragility, prayer anchors me and lifts me heavenward at the same time. My *kavanah* is not always ideal. If possible I try to study a little before I pray. I usually read a portion of a book by Abraham Joshua Heschel or another spiritual teacher. It helps to put me in the direction of leaving my day-to-day world behind and focuses on my relationship with God.

Finding my inner voice for prayer leads me to more active engagement. When praying a passage silently, I often think of a melody I like and sing the prayer to this melody. This may be a traditional melody (in liturgical music this is known as *nusach*), a melody I heard from a recording, or one I have adapted for myself. The power of music and prayer is often experienced in the communal realm, but music helps me to express my inner voice. The author of the *Sefer Hasidim* from the thirteenth century says it this way:

> Say your prayers in a melody that is most pleasant and sweet to you. Then you shall pray with proper *kavanah,* because the melody will draw your heart after the words that come from your mouth. Supplicate in a melody that makes the heart weep, praise in a melody that makes the heart glad.

Seeing prayer as a journey to experience the "other side" takes effort and a commitment that comes from within. Personalizing prayer is an ongoing challenge, but it is worth the effort.

RECOMMENDED READING

Davis, Avram, ed. *Meditation from the Heart of Judaism: Today's Teachers Share Their Practices, Techniques, and Faith.* Woodstock, Vt.: Jewish Lights Publishing, 1997.

Donin, Hayim Halevy. *To Pray as a Jew: A Guide to the Prayer Book and Synagogue Service.* New York: Basic Books, 1980.

Green, Arthur, and Barry W. Holtz. *Your Word Is Fire: The Hasidic Masters on Contemplative Prayer.* Woodstock, Vt.: Jewish Lights Publishing, 1993.

Hammer, Reuven. *Entering Jewish Prayer: A Guide to Personal Devotion and the Worship Service.* New York: Schocken Books, 1994.

Heschel, Abraham J. *Man's Quest for God.* New York: Charles Scribner's Sons, 1954.

Hoffman, Lawrence A., ed. *My People's Prayer Book: Traditional Prayers, Modern Commentaries.* 8 vols. Woodstock, Vt.: Jewish Lights Publishing, 1997–.

———. *The Way Into Jewish Prayer.* Woodstock, Vt.: Jewish Lights Publishing, 2001.

Matlins, Stuart M., ed. *The Jewish Lights Spirituality Handbook: A Guide to Understanding, Exploring, and Living a Spiritual Life.* Woodstock, Vt.: Jewish Lights Publishing, 2001.

PRAYER BOOKS

Reform

Gates of Prayer: The New Union Prayer Book. New York: Central Conference of American Rabbis, 1975.

Gates of Prayer for Shabbat and Weekdays. New York: Central Conference of American Rabbis, 1994.

Conservative

Siddur Sim Shalom. Edited by Rabbi Jules Harlow. New York: Rabbinical Assembly and United Synagogue of America, 1985.

Sim Shalom for Shabbat and Festivals. New York: Rabbinical Assembly and United Synagogue of America, 1998.

Orthodox

Daily Prayer Book: Ha-Siddur Ha-Shalem. Translated by Philip Birnbaum. New York: Hebrew Publishing Company, 1969.

The Complete Artscroll Siddur. Translated by Rabbi Nosson Scherman. Brooklyn: Mesorah Publications, 1984.

Reconstructionist

Kol HaNeshamah: Shabbat Vehagim. Philadelphia: Reconstructionist Press, 1995.

6

קצת דברים א

Torah Study

RABBI RUTH M. GAIS

THE BASICS OF TORAH STUDY

Barukh atah Adonai Eloheinu, melekh ha-olam, asher kidshanu bemitzvotav vetzivanu la-asok bedivrei Torah. (Praised are You, Adonai our God, Ruler of the universe, who has made us holy through Your mitzvot and instructed us to busy ourselves with words of Torah.)

This is the blessing for studying Torah, recited as part of the morning service. Its placement in the service reflects the value that Torah study has in the Jewish tradition. In the set of standard morning blessings, it comes right after the blessing that expresses thanks to God for keeping all of our vital organs functioning. First we thank God for keeping us alive and then we thank God for being able to study Torah. Why do we exist? Our tradition teaches us that we exist to study Torah, the "tree of life to all who hold fast to it" (Prov. 3:18).

What is Torah study? In its narrowest sense it's the study of the Torah itself, the first five books of the Bible: Genesis, Exodus, Leviticus, Numbers, and Deuteronomy, sometimes called the Five Books of Moses. There is also a broader meaning of Torah study that includes the entire Bible, such as the Books of Prophets and the collection known as Writings (Psalms, Proverbs, Job, Song of Songs, Ruth, Lamentations, Ecclesiastes, Esther, Daniel, Ezra, Nehemiah, I Chronicles, II Chronicles). The classic term for the Hebrew Bible is *Tanakh;* the word is formed from an acronym of the three sections: *Torah* (the Five Books of Moses); *Neviim* (Prophets); and *Ketuvim* (Writings). Some people employ the term *Pentateuch* (from the Greek word for "five") when referring to the Five Books of Moses. Some use the term to describe the entire corpus of Jewish law and commentary, including midrash, Talmud, and *halakhah*. This chapter uses the term primarily to refer to studying the first five books of the Bible.

In contemporary Jewish life, Torah study is often associated with a class on Shabbat morning led by a rabbi or some other person knowledgeable in traditional Jewish texts. However, Torah study can also be a daily practice, in the same way that prayer can be a daily practice. Jewish tradition encourages us to spend some time studying Torah each day. This can happen at a synagogue, a community center, or at home; on a bus, in a subway, on the phone, or in an online study group.

How to go about studying Torah is not so complicated. The simple part is that the basic equipment list is pretty short: a copy of the Torah. The more challenging part comes in learning how to study Torah in a Jewish way, a way that lets us know that we are part of a long chain of students all seeking to find the holiness in the text and use it to inform our lives.

MY OWN JOURNEY

I was the only child of older parents. We lived in an apartment in Manhattan. It was a solitary childhood. I spent a lot of time reading, and the characters I read about became very dear and important to me. However, they lived in their world and I lived in mine. I could imagine what they might do if they were in my life, but mostly I wanted to live their lives. I wanted to be them; the whole point of reading so intensely was to lose the real me and become someone else. I never realized that this was a traditional Jewish posture for study: to become the Torah text.

I have always been an intense reader. In high school and college I studied poetry eagerly—first the poems of John Donne, George Herbert, and Sylvia Plath, then the classical poetry of Virgil and Horace and the sonnets of Shakespeare. I loved to analyze the text, to tease apart each sentence, each word even, to appreciate the nuance and multiplicity of meanings embodied in a great poem. After college, I entered graduate school and a career in academia, and throughout my life, that basic desire to connect with the world I was reading about remained with me.

I stumbled into Torah study, not literally, but it sort of just happened that I ended up in a Torah study group. Like many of my peers, my religious education ended shortly after my bat mitzvah. I didn't walk back into the local synagogue until it was time to educate my own children. At that point, I decided that if my children were going to learn, I should take the opportunity to educate myself as well. It seemed that with my love of stories and reading, the obvious place for me to begin was by studying Torah, only it turned out that there was no formal Torah study in that small suburban synagogue. So a group of us set about trying to study it ourselves, without the help of a rabbi or anyone who had a great deal of Jewish knowledge.

Reading through Genesis and Exodus was enjoyable, but by the time we got to Leviticus, with its focus on sacrifices, many who started in our group lost their initial enthusiasm and interest waned. Nevertheless, I persevered. There was something about the experience of studying Torah that brought me home, back to my room when I was young, when I wanted so desperately to connect with the characters about whom I was reading. Little did I know at the time that such study would lead me to the rabbinate. In Abraham, Isaac, Rachel, and Leah, I saw pieces of myself. Brutus, Lady Macbeth, and Othello were all characters I read with great fascination. They taught me about the world, but it was altogether different to study the characters of the Torah. It was deeper, more spiritually satisfying. The stories of the Torah are the stories of the Jewish people, and I instantly recognized them as my stories.

It had never dawned on me that the passion I felt for words and poetry in English or Greek or Latin could be transferred to a Jewish text like the Torah. In analyzing the Torah text with the same rigor with which I approached poetry, I intuitively grasped a core experience of being Jewish—that is, to grapple with the Torah.

There was also something else that distinguished studying Torah from the other types of studying I had done in the past. As I became more actively engaged in studying Torah, I started reading everything I could find about the Torah, trying to expand my understanding of it. Yet there were moments when I would sit alone with the sacred text, reading it to myself, searching for its meaning. I used to sit in our synagogue library, studying a section of Torah, and I was just beginning to understand what I was reading. I knew it was a holy moment. Torah study is a sacred act. The space in which it takes place becomes sacred; its students become sanctified.

CONVERSATIONS WITH RASHI, IBN EZRA, AND MY *CHEVRUTAH* PARTNER

The Jewish way to study Torah begins with the understanding that Torah study is really an ongoing conversation, as intimate as the dialogue of prayer. This is a conversation that extends through both time and space.

My friend and I studied Torah together. Jewish tradition calls one's study partner a *chevrutah* (a companion, a study buddy). We used to spend some time each morning going over the week's Torah portion, analyzing and arguing about meanings. In fact, it wasn't just the two of us arguing with each other; it was the two of us arguing with people who were no longer alive but who were nevertheless seated around the table with us. Whenever we studied, we always had a few classic commentaries of Jewish sages to help guide our thinking about the text. Commentators like Rashi, Ibn Ezra, and the Ramban (Nachmanides) inspired or annoyed or prodded us enough to keep us searching deeper and deeper through the layers of meaning. We talked about them in the present tense: "Rashi says . . ." "No, I don't think he means that. He's really saying . . . and Sforno disagrees." In studying the Torah text with commentators, one is not just studying the text but is also studying how the great Jewish sages searched for meaning in the text.

I loved these sessions. They were fun and exhilarating. I always had the sense that we were burrowing away toward sacred truth. These conversations were sacred. We talked to each other and to the earlier commentators, but we also felt that someone else was there, too. Somehow we knew that God was listening in, maybe even helping out in the give-and-take of holy talk. We knew that Rabbi Chananya ben Teradyon was right when he said, centuries ago, that "when two sit together and exchange words of Torah, then the Divine Presence dwells with them" (*Pirkei Avot* 3:2).

"SHOW ME YOUR PRESENCE": AN ENCOUNTER WITH THE TORAH

There is another aspect to studying Torah in a Jewish way. For me, the goal of studying Torah is not simply to understand the Torah better, but to figure out its meaning in order to inform my life. Torah exists only when we engage it. This is a way of saying that the Torah invites us into its text, and only when we enter its depths are we able to fully absorb its profound spiritual message for our lives. Our interaction with the text is what makes the Torah so sacred and alive, but how do we do it? We enter the characters of the text and become them. In our study, we become one with the text. We struggle with Abraham and Sarah and the others as they navigate their own spiritual journeys through a developing relationship with the Divine. At the end of the process, when it is time to suspend our study—if only temporarily—we leave the character. As a result of the process, however, we have left a little bit of ourselves in the ongoing story of our people, and the text has become embedded in our soul.

There is one text in particular that exemplifies this power of Torah study for me. The scene is described in Exodus 34:17–23. It is a conversation between Moses and God that occurs after the making of the golden calf. God is angry with the people and threatens to remove the Divine Presence from among the people. Moses ascends Mt. Sinai and pleads with God to remain with the people. The text continues:

> And the Lord said to Moses, "I will do this thing that you have asked; for you have truly gained My favor and I have singled you out by name." He [Moses] said, "Oh, let me behold Your Presence!" And God answered, "I will make all My goodness pass before you, and I will proclaim before you the name Adonai and the grace that I grant and the compassion that I show. But," He said, "you cannot see My face, for humans cannot see My face and live." And God said, "See, there is a place near Me. Station yourself on the rock and as My Presence passes by, I will put you in a cleft of the rock and shield you with My hand until I have passed by. Then I will take My hand away and you will see My back; but My face must not be seen."

The Jewish way of studying often begins by raising questions about the text, and there are certainly a lot of questions that emerge from this story: Why would you die from seeing God's face? Why can Moses see only God's back? What does it mean for "God's goodness" to pass before Moses? Why does Moses wish to see God's presence?

It is the last question that for me is so crucial. Moses has already seen the power of God on Mt. Sinai. He has already spent forty days and nights on the top of Sinai scribing the Torah, but he still wants more. He desperately wants to see God, to be intimate with God, to know God in a way that no one else did. I hear the plaintive longing in his voice. Moses is pleading with God for this favor. Every time I study this story, I feel the power of it because I feel that same desire: to see God. It is one of the deepest yearnings I have. When I study this text I recognize a kinship with Moses and everyone else who wishes to see God, to know God intimately.

There is one commentator on this passage whose words also speak powerfully to me. He is a Hungarian rabbi who lived at the turn of the nineteenth century. Moses Sofer, also known as the Chatam Sofer, was the leader of Hungarian Jewry at the time. The Chatam Sofer responds to the question of what it means to see God's back:

> We are only able to comprehend God's ways and recognize how God works in the world in retrospect. Only then is it possible to fathom even a little of what God does. But at the time the event itself is happening, our understanding is unable to grasp God's doing. . . . And this is the real meaning of "You will see My back."[1]

It is not referring to God's body, but to our perspective on time itself. According to the Chatam Sofer, God is telling Moses that God can be seen only after the fact; God's "fingerprints" can be seen, but never God's "fingers." When I first heard this commentary from one of my teachers, I let out an audible, "Yes! That's it exactly." It was a piece of eternal wisdom that I had some sense of but had never been able to articulate so simply. I have the feeling all the time that I see the aftereffects of God, and although I may yearn for it, I will never be able to see God in the moment.

I often think about this scene in the Torah and mull it over, looking for other questions to ask or other commentaries to give me wisdom about its meaning. Sometimes I just meditate on what it means to desire to see God. I often think about God's response to Moses' impossible request. God does not balk but grants Moses something unique in seeing God's back. It is a loving and compassionate response from God, which reminds me of the need for loving and compassionate responses to people in my life.

When all of these ideas about seeking God and loving others are running through my mind, I know that I am studying well. This is the power of daily Torah study for me. I am constantly engaged with asking questions about the nature of God, truth, sacred obligations, love, and the meaning of life. When I began to study regularly, I began to live in a different way because of all those ideas swirling in my mind. Even if I studied for just twenty minutes in the morning, the ideas would seep into me for the rest of the day. I found that all the parts of my life were acting out of a deeper sense of God than I had ever known before. Torah study provided an impetus for living a life more open to God's presence and to the mystery that fills the world.

Study, She Said

Fifteen years ago, I was a very alienated Jew. I was so angry at God that I made sure that if I ate a ham and cheese sandwich only once a year, it was on Yom Kippur! Judaism seemed to have no place for me. It was all prayers babbled so quickly that I couldn't keep up and rules that were to be followed without question or explanation. What I learned (or perhaps, remembered) from six years of Hebrew school, and my parents' and grandparents' admonitions, were the sins and the penalties for those sins. There was nothing to entice me, no community, and certainly no spirituality.

My son had joined a scout group that met at a local Conservative synagogue, and they were leading a Friday night service followed by a presentation by a Conservative and a Reform rabbi about the differences between the two synagogues. My wife and I were there for my son and decided to stay for the presentation. The Reform rabbi was a dynamic, firebrand woman who so captivated us that we joined the Reform temple.

Six months later, having attended Saturday services regularly, I went to her with the complaint that I still felt very much like an outsider as a Jew and wanted to know if she could suggest a remedy. I told her about my family's religious background, how my mother would rush home from work before sundown on Friday nights to light Shabbat candles and then return to work. I also told her about my own religious education, most of which left very little impression on me. I waited to see what she might have to say about a situation I viewed as hopeless.

"Study," she said. "Attend Torah study every week, go to lectures and discussions about Jewish biblical and secular issues, and do it for two years. Then come back and tell me what you think." That was it? I gave that some thought. I wanted a quick fix. Two years wasn't quick, but no previous advice had worked. My son would be in Hebrew school for at least two more years, so I decided to give it a try.

What happened was that my life began to change in unimaginable ways. I developed a sense of community that I could not have imagined. A spiritual cosmos developed around me that influenced my thinking and behavior. I developed a personal relationship with God that I never knew existed. It almost feels like too trite a testimonial, but I went from ham and cheese on Yom Kippur to feeling the nurture and care of a loving God. "Study," she said, and I did.

STUART FRANKEL

THE TRUTH OF THE TEXT

One of the stumbling blocks for many people in beginning to study Torah is the basic question of who wrote the Torah. Jewish tradition teaches that God revealed the Torah to Moses, who acted as God's scribe and wrote it down. Thus, every letter of the Torah is God's revealed word. However, I think that it is easy to recognize a human hand in its writing. There are sections of the Torah that seem to disagree with each other, there are sections that are repetitive, there are sections that are just plain obscure, and there are sections that I wholeheartedly reject as God's plan for us (such as the Torah's commandment to stone a rebellious son). To dismiss the text out of hand makes it too easy. Why had those who came before me left these "contradictions" in the text? They must have seen it, too.

Modern academic scholarship of the Bible suggests that the Torah is an edited or "redacted" compilation of the writings of different authors. While I recognized the truth of this scholarship, at some point in the course of studying I realized that I had to take the question of the holiness of the Torah text seriously. If I didn't, there was no difference between studying it and studying anything else. This is not about "who wrote the Torah." This is about something much more profoundly spiritual. So I had to study Torah in a way that highlights its sanctity even while recognizing the participation of humans in its writing. I had to commit to what Samuel Taylor Coleridge called "the willing suspension of disbelief." The willing suspension of disbelief is the conscious act of putting aside my modern sense of skepticism and cynicism and understanding that the Torah is holy. It is to say to myself, "Yes, the Torah was written by human beings, but I also know that every word I read is holy." Whether or not I believe in the idea of the Torah as God's word revealed or whether I think of it as the writing of "religious geniuses," as Rabbi Eugene Borowitz says, doesn't really matter.

This is, in essence, an act of spiritual humility. If I want to be able to have conversations with my ancestors, I have to believe as they believed—that the Torah is sacred, and that it was revealed to us at Mt. Sinai. Not only do I have to believe this, I also have to believe that the words that make up the sentences of the text are sacred, the letters that form these words are sacred, and even the spaces between the letters are sacred. I have to agree to study Torah in the way that it has always been studied, and that means accepting it as revealed truth, even temporarily.

This awareness of the sanctity of the text does not mean that I'm not enraged or disturbed by certain ideas or stories I read. On the contrary, the more thoroughly I scrutinize the text, the more questions and problems arise that I have to face. However, I've come to understand that I can't just brush these difficulties aside or use them as a way to devalue everything in the Torah. I'm caught up in an ongoing conversation with the text and with anyone else who cares about it; I hope this conversation will eventually let me understand the text, "forgive" the text, and see its eternal truth.

TORAH SPONGES

The way that I prepare myself for Torah study allows me to focus on my sacred task. For me, putting on a *kipah* is a way of making a tran-

LEARNING TORAH AS A LOVE AFFAIR

There is a famous text in the *Zohar,* the central text of Jewish mysticism, that depicts the Torah as a beautiful maiden isolated in a palace. In rare moments she chooses to reveal herself to her smitten suitor:

> Torah may be compared to a beautiful and stately maiden who is secluded in an isolated chamber of a palace and has a lover of whose existence she alone knows. For love of her he passes by her gate unceasingly and turns his eyes in all directions to discover her. She is aware that he is forever hovering about the palace, and what does she do? She thrusts open a small door in her secret chamber, for a moment reveals her face to her lover, then quickly withdraws it. He alone, none else, notices it; but he is aware it is from love of him that she has revealed herself to him for that moment. And his heart and soul and everything within him are drawn to her. So it is with Torah, which discloses her innermost secrets only to them who love her. . . . Hence, people should pursue the Torah with all their might, so that they might come to be her lovers. (*Zohar* II, 99a)[2]

This passage reflects a Jewish worldview that sees the study of Torah as a sensual experience. We are lovestruck and seek the object of our love. She returns our love, but only reveals herself momentarily. Studying Torah may be frustrating at times, just as it is to be lovestruck by one who is unattainable, but when she is glimpsed there is an intense pleasure.

A love affair may seem an overly done metaphor for studying, but for anyone who has experienced that desire to fully understand the meaning of the Torah, "love affair" feels just about right.

sition from ordinary time to sacred time. Just that simple act, putting a little circle of cloth or leather on my head and attaching it with a bobby pin, starts the process. I place the *kipah* on my head and I remember that God is above, involved in this moment and that I need to think and act differently. The next step in this transformation is to recite the blessing for Torah study.

The first ten Hebrew words of this blessing are the standard command-blessing formula used whenever we are about to perform a mitzvah (a sacred obligation). The last three words describe what that mitzvah is to be. Here the mitzvah is "to busy ourselves with words of Torah." This could also be translated as "to be involved in matters of Torah," or even as "to soak up words of Torah"—a wordplay, not an accurate translation, but one that explains this transformation best of all: we are commanded to become Torah sponges.

That's it, really. We are no longer our usual selves, talking our ordinary talk. The blessing transforms us. The blessing does not command us to learn Torah but to be involved in it. We voluntarily enter a covenantal relationship with God. In it, we've been commanded to do something different that will make us holy. Torah is to become part of us; our very pores should ooze Torah; what we learn should go beyond our study and become part of our lives. When I am studying with a group of people, after saying the blessing we all become a bunch of sponges, sitting around a table, all of us waiting to absorb holy words from each other. We open our copies of the Torah. We read the holy words and begin to talk.

Studying Jewish Values

At the time, it wasn't an epiphany. It was just another conversation with an equally Jewishly uneducated office mate, on a long afternoon, in a dreary government agency, off the mall in Washington, D.C. We were fresh out of college doing grunt work for the experts who were writing a federal welfare reform bill. The heated public debate on this issue revolved around the government's role in teaching values and responsibility and in helping people to raise their children. In our windowless space, my office mate and I talked of our own fears about creating lives that would involve meaningful work and time for family. How would we teach our children values, we wondered.

I reflected on my parents, who had raised four solid citizens, and their parents, my grandparents, who must have given them the tools to accomplish that task. Although most of my grandparents and my parents lacked extensive, formal, Jewish education, I assumed that most of their values were probably "Jewish," even if they didn't know it. So even if I had absorbed decent values from my ancestors, could those values be transmitted to yet another generation if I did not have the ability to articulate or even understand the purpose, source, reasoning, and foundation of the teachings? Suddenly, it was clear to my twenty-one-year-old unmarried self that I was not equipped to be a Jewish parent in any meaningful way.

Within months, I was living in Israel and learning from 8:00 A.M. to 8:00 P.M., five days a week, at Pardes, a coed, nondenominational yeshiva. Every class inspired. *Chumash* (Torah) and Mishnah, the core classes, challenged my Hebrew and analytical skills. The classes about Jewish law, and specifically the laws of *ben adam l'chavero* (interpersonal behavior) shocked me. I so clearly remember sitting and learning the Jewish laws about speech—about not speaking, or even letting oneself hear, gossip. The teacher was such a kind, gentle person. Of course he can refrain from gossip, I thought, it's completely easy and natural for him. How is someone like me, far from righteous, supposed to live by these laws, which prohibit not only flimsy gossip but also speaking the known facts, if they are harmful, and even speaking too nicely about someone? I tried to practice the laws I learned, and in the process, to my complete amazement, I was transformed. My only explanation is that there is truth and goodness in Jewish teachings that overcame years of conditioned behavior. Now, many years later, only when surrounded by a very few people in my life, does the temptation to "hear the dirt" arise.

Not all Jewish learning is equally powerful or obviously relevant to the challenges of living a moral life or being a good parent, but regular learning is a constant reminder of the sweetness and genius within our tradition. The sheer breadth of our texts offers constant reminders that one never stops learning or growing. The depth of the arguments, regardless of the seeming relevance of the topic, teaches the invaluable lesson that there is not just one answer to most questions, and to respect different people and their points of view.

Now married with children, I still don't know with certainty if I will have the skill and luck my parents have had in their marriage and in raising children with values. However, in many ways, my job will be easier than theirs. Where they had to navigate hard questions, learn to nurture and to draw lines based solely on their own judgment, ongoing Jewish learning provides me with so many sane and sound tools on which I can draw.

ABBIE GREENBERG

BROAD STROKES OF OBSERVANCE

In the Talmud there are three different answers given to the question "What is the blessing said before Torah study?" One Rabbi suggested the blessing we've just mentioned. Another disagreed and proposed this one:

"May the words of Torah, Adonai our God, be sweet in our mouths and in the mouths of all Your people so that we, our children, and all the children of the House of Israel may come to love You and to study Your Torah for its own sake. Praised are You, Adonai our God, who teaches Torah to your people Israel."

The third rabbi, Rabbi Hamnuna, said that we should say, "Praised are You, Adonai, our God, who has chosen us from among all peoples and given to us Your Torah. Praised are You, Adonai, our God, giver of Torah." He also resolved the dilemma by saying, "These are the finest of the blessings. Therefore let us say all of them" (Babylonian Talmud, *Berakhot* 11b).

These blessings before Torah study are the finest because our tradition finds the commandment to study Torah central to the existence of each Jew. Torah study has been the sweetness that has bestowed meaning upon the bitter lives of our people for centuries. So important is this commandment that after these blessings are said, most prayer books contain the minimum amount of passages from Scripture, the Mishnah, and the Talmud that are required for a person to study each day to fulfill this sacred obligation.

Maimonides, the twelfth-century philosopher and jurist, devotes several chapters in the *Mishneh Torah* to the laws of Torah study. First and foremost is the law that "every Jew is obligated to study Torah, whether poor or rich, of a healthy and complete body or afflicted by difficulties, whether young or old whose strength has diminished" (*Hilkhot Talmud Torah,* 1:8). A person is also required to establish a fixed time for Torah study during the day and the night and continue in this pattern until death. Torah study is not just for scholars. Torah study is everyone's obligation.

Women are traditionally not obligated to study. A woman who studies Torah, Maimonides tells us, will be rewarded, but because a woman is not commanded to study, her reward will not be as great as a man's (*Hilkhot Talmud Torah,* 1:13). We forgive him for that comment, given the era in which he was writing. Women are, in fact, required to study the laws dealing with those commandments that they are obligated to perform, so some learning is always necessary. Even the traditional point of view does not prevent women from studying. It may not always encourage their study of the Torah or Talmud, but we certainly do.

The laws of Torah study show us how vital it is to Jewish life. Each Jewish community is obligated to build a *beit midrash,* a house of study, which is more important than a synagogue. If necessary, we are permitted to destroy a synagogue in order to build a house of study (Babylonian Talmud, *Megillah* 27a). Torah study overrides building the Holy Temple (Babylonian Talmud, *Megillah* 16b), and a child's desire to study Torah is a permissible reason for him to ignore his parent's wishes (*Shulchan Arukh, Yoreh Deah* 240:5).

After the Romans destroyed the Temple in 70 C.E., the future of Judaism was fragile at best. Rabbi Yochanan asked the Roman emperor Vespasian for permission to set up a yeshiva, an academy for Torah study, in Yavneh. The request seemed ludicrous to the Roman. But Rabbi Yochanan understood that it was constant study of our sacred texts that would preserve Judaism, more than any buildings or riches (Babylonian Talmud, *Gittin* 56b).

Jews have stubbornly continued to study Torah no matter what the circumstances. Torah is the crown, waiting for each of us; it is our inheritance (*Hilkhot Talmud Torah* 1:6). Why is Torah study supreme? We study Torah *lishmah,* for its own sake. We are not supposed to exploit our learning or use it for anything other than trying to understand how we should lead our lives. The beauty of studying Torah *lishmah* is that being truly "involved in the words of Torah," as the blessing directs us, leads us to positive action that compels us to try to improve our world. Maimonides says that "the study of Torah is equal to all the other mitzvot because study leads to deed. Therefore study takes precedence over deed" (*Hilkhot Talmud Torah* 3:3).

Although traditional Torah study is part of the daily morning prayer routine, non-traditional Jews can reframe the idea of Torah study in terms of time commitment, place of study, and what we study. What remains the same, though, is our attitude toward Torah study: however, wherever, and whenever we study, the time we set aside becomes sacred. During the time we study, it is as if we are in a bubble, outside ordinary time and space. Ways to help us enter this bubble might be a period of meditation before we begin, or a song or a chant or our own personal blessings as we enter and as we emerge.

According to Jewish tradition, there are four layers or levels to the classic approach to studying Torah: *peshat* (the literal meaning of the text); *derash* (the midrashic meaning of the text); *remez* (the hints that are contained in the text); and *sod* (the secret meaning of the text).

THE VARIETY OF APPROACHES

Jewish tradition has an endless supply of interpretations of the Torah. One can find commentaries from a variety of perspectives: mystical, rational, scientific, feminist, literary, post-modern, or ethical. For any perspective you might like to explore, there is probably a learned Jew who has written a commentary about it. If you want to study Torah with a twelfth-century Yemenite, a sixteenth-century German, a fifth-century Babylonian, or a nineteenth-century Russian, you can find it; there are commentaries from almost every place and time where Jews have lived. There have also been attempts in the past decades to study Torah in alternative models. In place of the text of the Torah and books and books of commentaries, you might have dancing shoes, a therapist's couch, or pieces of colored paper in front of you. Here are some of the alternative approaches you can try.

Bibliodrama is a recently coined term used to describe studying Torah by inhabiting a character the way an actor does. The technique recognizes that there are so many parts of the Torah where it remains silent about what the characters said to each other. Perhaps the most famous example is found in the story of Abraham's almost-sacrifice of Isaac. The Torah says that they walked three days together to get to the place where Abraham was going to sacrifice his son. The Torah does not tell us what they said to each other, and the reader cannot help but wonder what Abraham might have said to his son, whom he has been commanded to sacrifice. The rabbis of all generations have seen these silences as an opportunity to interject their own dialogue in the form of stories, which are known as *midrash*. There are well-known collections of midrash from Jewish tradition, and new books of midrashim are being created all the time.... (see Bialik and Ravnitzky in "Recommended Reading," pp. 127).

Bibliodrama seeks to inject dialogue in a different way. If you were studying with a group of people, two people might volunteer to be Abraham and Isaac, and they would act out the scene of the three days of walking, ad-libbing the dialogue. In determining what the characters would say to each other, one is, in effect, doing a type of Torah study. Advocates of this kind of study also see its potential for therapeutic application. For the actors who are playing Abraham and Isaac, they may be revealing something about their own sense of what it means to be a parent, and their relationship with their parents and their children. Acting out these parts may be a kind of therapy, in which the participants can articulate some of their struggles through the biblical dramas. Just as a trained therapist can facilitate deeper explorations of the self, a trained bibliodrama leader can facilitate deeper understandings by the participants. Peter Pietzele, author of *My Father's Wells: A Personal Encounter with the Myths of Genesis* and an adjunct faculty member at the Jewish Theological Seminary, is the most well-known practitioner of this work.

Jo Milgrom, in her book *Handmade Midrash*, seeks to do something very similar through the medium of art. Instead of acting out the scene of Abraham and Isaac, she suggests taking different colored paper and creating a collage that depicts the scene. This is but one of a multitude of art projects she suggests in the book. The art that you produce will be a type of Torah study. Based on how you represent the characters and the colors you choose, you will be interpreting the scene in some way.

Similarly, scenes from the Torah can also be danced. There are many dance companies, such as the Avodah Dance Company and the Liz Lerman Dance Company, that specialize in helping people to study Torah (and do Jewish ritual) through dance.

DAF YOMI: A PAGE A DAY

In some traditional circles, the practice of *Daf Yomi* is a popular form of daily study. The concept of *Daf Yomi* is quite simple. Every day one studies one page of Talmud. This may sound simple, but given the tremendous length of the Talmud, to go through it a page a day takes seven years. There are different types of audiotapes, online sites, and even some phone-in lines to help one through the process of studying each day.

Studying Talmud is said to sharpen the mind in a way that almost no other type of Jewish study does. Judith Abrams' book *The Talmud for Beginners* can provide a way into Talmud study. Some groups have taken an alternative road, studying a page a day of *Encyclopedia Judaica*, the master work of Jewish scholarship on everything related to Judaism.

WHERE TO START AND HOW TO CONTINUE

Shammai said, "Make your Torah study a habit" (*Pirkei Avot* 1:15).

Daily Torah study, as our morning liturgy reminds us, is one of the commandments for which there is no time limit. It would be nice to be able to study Torah all day, but this is clearly unrealistic for most of us. I try to study something Jewish at least once a day. I commute to work by train, so I often study alone as I go to and from work. I decided to do this when I realized that I couldn't get up, get dressed, make lunches for my children, walk the dog, get the children off to school, get myself off to work, and still have time to study at home. I sit in my train seat (or stand, if I am unlucky) and read the text I have chosen to study. I have discovered a variety of shortcuts to this approach, which I recommend adapting, depending on your plans for study—like pocket-size editions of the Bible or the Mishnah and other Jewish texts. Sometimes I print pages from the World Wide Web. I usually say the blessing to myself, and then I start studying. Every now and then I meet someone on the train who knows what I am doing and wants to study along with me.

With some creative thinking, most of us can find opportunities to study, either alone or with a friend, at a study breakfast or a study coffee break during the week. Other possibilities are audio materials to play in your car, instant messaging on the computer, or a study conversation over the telephone. The crucial point is to specifically set aside some time and make that time a *zeman kavua,* a fixed time, just like a regular time for exercise or having lunch with a special friend. Studying on Shabbat morning, before or after prayer or anytime on Shabbat, is especially precious.

We should study anywhere we can. A kitchen table is fine; so is Starbuck's, in a comfortable chair, on top of a mountain, or at the beach. Many of us belong to a synagogue and can study in a space there, but Torah study can be done anywhere, anytime.

My Shabbat Torah study group meets in the library of our synagogue. We sit around a large table that has plenty of room for books, coffee, and bagels. Some of us are Hebrew readers, but most of us read in English translation. If we all can read and understand biblical Hebrew, we use as our main text a good edition of the *Mikraot Gedolot,* literally "The Big Writings." This is basically a study Bible in Hebrew. It packs a lot between two covers. There are many editions, but in general all have the biblical text in large Hebrew print, in the center, surrounded by the *Targum Onkelos,* an Aramaic translation of the Hebrew, and a good selection of the major commentators on the text. Rashi will always be there; others include

Ibn Ezra, Sforno, the Ramban, the Rashbam, and the Kli Yakar. These commentators, who lived from the eleventh to the sixteenth centuries, are more than eager to help the Hebrew reader to begin to study.

If Hebrew is out of the question, as it is for so many of us who study regularly, good translations are indispensable. Any standard Jewish edition of the Bible (such as those published by the Jewish Publication Society) will have the first five books as part of the larger Bible, but you may do better with an edition of just the Torah. An edition that provides a fair amount of commentary as well as the biblical verses is better still. It doesn't matter if people have different translations. In fact, it's often better to have as many different translations of the Torah as possible, to capture the real essence of the Hebrew. This is the best way for the non-Hebrew reader to approximate a close reading of the text—especially since all translation is interpretation.

I generally follow the ancient tradition of reading the Torah according to an annual cycle. The five books are divided into fifty-four portions *(parshiot),* and one portion *(parshah)* is read per week, with some doubling (two in one week to make it fit into the solar calendar). Many Torah study groups assign one member to lead the discussion. That person might give an overview of the weekly portion and then focus on a few verses or a particular aspect of the portion. If nothing leaps out at you, try reading a particular commentary; it will usually point you in a direction you might not have noticed.

It's easy to find out about the particular portion of the week, the *parshat hashavua,* by checking most Jewish calendars, Jewish newspapers, or Jewish websites. Studying this way, I feel part of the rhythm of Jewish life. I like to think of Jews everywhere on Shabbat morning reading and thinking about the same *parshah.* My Torah study group has gone through the entire Torah about nine times now, and we are always finding new things to discuss. This is what the first-century rabbi Ben Bag Bag meant when he stated, "Turn it and turn it again, for everything is in it. Reflect on it and grow old and gray with it. Don't turn from it, for nothing is better than it" *(Pirkei Avot* 5:22).

If entering the world of study by beginning with the Torah doesn't appeal to you, try starting with another classic Jewish text. This could be *Pirkei Avot,* often called *Ethics of the Fathers* (we like to say "Ancestors"), a collection of pithy sayings written two thousand years ago. You could also begin with a more contemporary work. There is more to study than any one of us could hope to accomplish in several lifetimes. Centuries ago, Rabbi Tarfon (first to second century) offered these soothing words to those who felt just as overwhelmed. "It is not up to you to finish the work, but you are not free to avoid it" (*Pirkei Avot* 2:16).

GO AND STUDY!

Find a fixed time for study, either by yourself or with a friend. What you study is up to you. You might want to follow the weekly Torah portion. You may want to make index cards of the Psalms or Proverbs and study one a day. The most important thing you bring to this ritual is your attitude. Set realistic goals for yourself. Start slow. If you only have ten minutes, then focus on a verse or two or a paragraph or two. Say the blessing for Torah study to help you move from ordinary time to sacred time. You might want to add an additional prayer of your own. Cover your head, if you are so inclined, sing a *niggun* (wordless chant) or Jewish song; do whatever it takes to help you achieve this transition.

Prayer on entering a place of study to learn: "May it be Your will, God of my God, and the God of my ancestors, that You guide my eyes with the light of Your Torah and save me from stumbling and making mistakes . . . for God gives wisdom and from God's mouth comes knowledge and understanding." (Abridged and translated by Raphael Zarum from the *Taz Commentary on Tur, Shulchan Arukh* 110:8.)

Prayer on leaving a place of study after learning: "I thank you, God of my God, and the God of my ancestors, that you have established my portion with those who dwell in the *beit midrash* and have not established my portion with idlers. I get up early and they get up early; I get up early for words of Torah, while they get up early for idle words. I work hard and they work hard; I work hard and receive reward while they work hard and do not receive reward. I run and they run; I run to the life of the world to come, while they run to the well of destruction, and I will trust in You." (Abridged and translated by Raphael Zarum from the Hadran prayer on completing the study of a tractate of Talmud.)

RECOMMENDED READING

The Torah

Most of these editions provide both the Hebrew and the English texts as well as commentaries.

Fields, Harvey. *A Torah Commentary for Our Times*. 3 vol. New York: UAHC Press, 1998.

Fox, Everett. *The Five Books of Moses*. New York: Schocken Books, 1995. The translation seeks to render the English as close to the original Hebrew as possible in terms of style and rhythm.

Hertz, J. H., ed. *The Pentateuch and Haftorahs*. London: Soncino Press, 1936. Commentary from an Orthodox perspective by the late Chief Rabbi of Britain.

Lieber, David L. ed. *Etz Chaim*. Philadelphia: Jewish Publication Society, 2001. Commentary from the Conservative movement reflecting both academic and spiritual concerns.

The Metsudah Chumash with Rashi, 5 vol. Hoboken, N.J.: KTAV, 1996. Rashi's commentary translated and explicated.

Plaut, Gunther *The Torah: A Modern Commentary*. New York: UAHC Press, 1981. Extensive commentary and essays on ancient Near Eastern literature as well as a liberal perspective on the theological and religious issues raised in the Torah.

Sarna, Nachum, ed. *The JPS Torah Commentary*. 5 vols. Philadelphia: Jewish Publication Society, 1989–1996. Erudite commentaries by modern biblical scholars.

Modern Commentaries

Frankel, Ellen. *The Five Books of Miriam*. New York: HarperCollins, 1996.

Greenberg, Aharon Yaakov, ed. *Torah Gems*. Translated by Shmuel Himelstein. 3 vols. Tel Aviv: Yavneh Publishing, 1992.

Goldstein, Elyse. *The Women's Torah Commentary: New Insights from Women Rabbis on the 54 Weekly Torah Portions*. Woodstock, Vt.: Jewish Lights Publishing, 1999.

Holtz, Barry, ed. *Back to the Sources: Reading the Classic Jewish Texts*. New York: Summit Books, 1984.

Kushner, Lawrence. *God Was in This Place And I, i Did Not Know*. Woodstock, Vt.: Jewish Lights Publishing, 1991.

Leibowitz, Nechama *Studies in Bereshit*. 6 vols. Jerusalem: World Zionist Organization, 1972–1980.

Zornberg, Aviva. *Genesis: The Beginning of Desire*. Philadelphia: Jewish Publication Society, 1995.

———. *The Pursuit of Rapture: Reflections on Exodus*. New York: Random House, 2001.

Other Resources

Abrams, Judith. *The Talmud for Beginners*. 3 vols. Northvale, N.J.: Jason Aronson, 1991–1997.

Adler, Rachel. *Engendering Judaism: An Inclusive Theology and Ethics*. Philadelphia: Jewish Publication Society, 1997.

Bialik, H. N. and Y. H. Ravnitzky. *The Book of Legends [Sefer ha-Aggadah]*. Translated by William G. Braude. New York: Schocken Books, 1992.

Cohen, Norman J. *Self, Struggle and Change: Family Conflict Stories in Genesis and Their Healing Insights for Our Lives*. Woodstock, Vt.: Jewish Lights Publishing, 1994.

———. *Voices from Genesis: Guiding Us through the Stages of Life*. Woodstock, Vt.: Jewish Lights Publishing, 2001.

———. *The Way Into Torah*. Woodstock, Vt.: Jewish Lights Publishing, 1999.

Goldstein, Elyse. *Revisions: Seeing Torah through a Feminist Lens.* Woodstock, Vt.: Jewish Lights Publishing, 2000.

Hebrew-English Tanakh. Translated by Harry Orlinsky. Philadelphia: Jewish Publication Society, 1999.

Kravitz, Leonard, and Kerry M. Olitzky, eds. *Pirkei Avot.* New York: UAHC Press, 1993.

Milgrom, Jo. *Handmade Midrash: Workshop in Visual Technology.* Philadelphia: Jewish Publication Society, 1992.

Pietzele, Peter. *Scripture Windows.* Los Angeles: Alef Design Group, 1997.

Steinsaltz, Adin. *The Talmud: A Reference Guide.* New York: Schocken Books, 1989.

Tanakh: The Holy Scriptures. Translated by Harry Orlinsky. Philadelphia: Jewish Publication Society, 1985.

7

Blessings throughout the Day

RABBI NINA BETH CARDIN

THE BASICS OF BLESSINGS

In the crucible that was the week of flurried preparations and mixed anticipation as my husband and I prepared to take our second son to college, everything we did seemed to be lit from above. The spotlight settled on all the little events that we otherwise regularly ignore in our everyday lives. A cozy, casual pizza dinner became a celebration of all the years we all called the same place home. Our goodnight routine announced that for at least one more night, all my children would sleep safely under my roof. Every echo of my children's voices conjured up

all the years when the family was young, when we had seemingly endless days to fill. In that last week, we sensed every moment as precious. No one complained of boredom. All were aware of the big
separation that was looming. That week was profoundly bittersweet.
I was so thankful for having a son, for having a family, but there was
also the pain of separation. So I made a blessing; in it, I thanked God
for it all. The words were not poetic, nor did they arise particularly
from Jewish tradition, but they were my own, and they came from the
depths of my soul.

Rabbi Norman Cohen tells a similar story of a woman who tear-
fully put her young daughter on the school bus for the first time, on
her way to kindergarten. He asked why she was crying so profusely,
and he told her not to worry, that her daughter would be home that
evening. Her response, "You don't understand. My daughter will
never be home again." I understand her tears, as I imagine most parents do. It is at times like these that I use blessings as a way of
responding to my feelings.

Although the distinction between a blessing and a prayer is often
very subtle, blessings are generally short, begin with the familiar formula *Barukh ata Adonai Elohenu melekh ha-olam* (Praised are You,
Adonai our God, Sovereign of the universe), and are connected to
specific acts or activities (especially when the acts are required by
Jewish tradition). Prayers are often longer, may contain blessings in
them (sometime to begin and end a theme that is elucidated in the
prayer), and do not require any connection to an act. They are often
requests made by individuals to God.

There are two types of blessings in Judaism. The first type is a
blessing said in response to a moment of awe. These moments may be
bittersweet, such as the moment described above of my son going off
to school; they may be moments of intense sadness, such as hearing
the news of a death or an illness; or they may be an experience of the
awe of the natural world, such as seeing a rainbow or upon the birth
of a child. When we experience these moments of awe, Jewish tradition has a blessing to be recited.

Besides these blessings that respond to awe, there is a second type of blessing, which seeks to conjure up awe. As humans, we seek and settle into a routine that often numbs us to the wonders of the world around us. We may even become inured to the everyday miracles that surround us. Thus, the recitation of blessings can become an emotional prod, a reminder of all that we take for granted. Rabbi Abraham Joshua Heschel tells us that blessings help us to "take notice of the wonder, to regain a sense of the mystery that animates all being."[1] It is not just awe that stimulates blessings; blessings can stimulate awe. Blessings can be like a four-year-old perpetually tugging us along the path of life, inviting us to turn over rocks to peer at the vibrancy underneath, to sail across the ocean in a driveway puddle, or to reach for a beloved's hand or hug whenever we desire it.

The Rabbis tell us that we should attempt to say one hundred blessings a day. By encouraging us to do so, they are teaching us a profound lesson. One hundred times a day we should be alert to the wonders of life around us. If we are awake about sixteen hours a day, that means we should open ourselves up to the opportunity of blessing about six times per waking hour. That's once every ten minutes. How rich would our lives be if we were awed by a sight, a sound, a meeting, a word, an act, a face, a taste, or a bit of news that took our breath away even for a moment, once every ten minutes?

What would happen if each of us took a day, just one day, in our personal calendar, and designated that as our day of awe, to see if we could find one hundred things that caused our hearts to soar heavenward? If we cultivated both the art of awareness, and a receptive attitude that is eager to witness all that the mind and the senses can absorb, how different would our experience of the world around us be?

MY OWN JOURNEY

Unlike the time I decided to keep kosher or to keep Shabbat, there is no one moment or event that was pivotal in my coming to the tradition of reciting blessings. It has been a slow evolving process in my life, something that has become as second nature to me as walking or breathing. Some of the blessings I say use the traditional formula, whereas others are just the words I formulate at the moment. Maimonides says in his code of Jewish law that blessings can be recited in any language; their purpose is simply to have God in mind constantly.[2]

Part of my embrace of the discipline of blessing has to do with my family. When I got married and had children, there were so many moments that called for some recognition. When my children were very young, I began the practice of giving them a blessing for each significant book that they finished. At first it was Dr. Seuss; as they reached high school it was *The Catcher in the Rye;* now that they are in college it is works of philosophy and political science. When they are at home and they have finished a book, they still come to me looking for a blessing.

Family provides such experiences of joy and pain, and in both of these extremes I am left with such feelings of awe. I say a blessing after the joyous moments out of gratitude, and I say blessings after the painful moments to steady myself, and remind myself of the larger picture. I am not sure when the blessings I said in response to certain occasions were joined by saying regular blessings over meals and when I awoke, but slowly my life has become replete with blessings. I do not quite match the Rabbis' recommendation of saying one hundred blessings a day, but the discipline of saying blessings provides me with the constant awareness of the One who sustains and nurtures me.

THE ORIGINS OF BLESSINGS IN JEWISH TRADITION

The Rabbis of the Talmud ordained the structure of blessings. As you will see throughout this chapter, Judaism has fixed blessings for a multitude of occasions, and almost all are found in the first tractate of the Talmud, appropriately called *Berakhot,* "Blessings." In this tractate of the Talmud we read about both types of blessings: those that respond to awe and those that seek to conjure up awe. The latter type is seen in the following discussion about blessings to be said before eating. The Talmud says: Rabbi Hanina bar Papa says, "Anyone who enjoys this world without saying a blessing, it is as if he robbed God" (*Berakhot* 35a). This may seem to be an odd thing to say; how can you "rob God"? The idea, according to Rabbi Lawrence A. Hoffman, is that everything belongs to God—all food, all objects, all of us belong in some sense to God. There is a famous psalm that makes this clear: "The earth is the Lord's and the fullness thereof" (Ps. 115:16). You say a blessing before eating to transfer the food from God's realm to the human realm. The blessing therefore reminds you to be conscious of the fact that you are partaking in something that was in God's realm. The blessing evokes God's awesomeness, that the whole earth is full of God's glory.

The other type of blessing, which responds to awe, is also found in this tractate of the Talmud. A miracle, shooting stars, seeing unusual-looking people, or any moment that brings up awe is cause for a blessing—surprisingly, even upon hearing tragic news. "One says a blessing for evil, similar to that said over good" (*Berakhot* 54a). This is a deep theological statement compacted into one sentence. It reflects the basic idea of monotheism: God is ultimately responsible for our lives, and whenever we discern God's presence, whenever we are filled with awe, either for good or bad, we are obligated to bless God.

BLESSINGS THAT STIMULATE AWE AND AWARENESS

Morning Blessings

Jewish tradition obligates one to begin each day by saying blessings. The very first in the list of morning blessings is a blessing of awareness: "Praised are You, Adonai our God, Sovereign of the universe . . . who gave our minds the wisdom to discern between day and night." This blessing is not just a way of thanking God for giving us the ability to determine the difference between obvious opposites—dark and light, sleep and awake, labor and rest. This blessing is about the consciousness of discernment, the mindfulness of our existence; what the philosopher Emanual Levinas called the awareness of awareness.

Rabbi Akiva teaches (in *Pirkei Avot*) that we are a doubly beloved people—once because we are the recipients of divine gifts (being made in the image of God, being called God's people, receiving the Torah) and again because we know that we possess these gifts. This self-awareness, and the ability to check our behavior in light of this self-awareness, may be the most profound difference between humans and animals. It is probably the fundamental characteristic that explains how we can be seen as being made in the image of God. Active awareness is not just a divine gift. It is a quality of the divine, and it is a necessary prelude to living a life of satisfaction and holiness.

Even more, life requires awareness and discernment, for life requires change. Growth, advancement, development, building, and everything else in life depends on change. However, it is change within the framework of routine that is welcome, healthy, and exciting. Change that disturbs the routine is usually unwelcome. It upsets the body and the mind. Routineness gives us security: to be able to set your alarm clock knowing that you can sleep soundly in your house, to stop off at the same coffee shop, to know the layout of your local grocery store by heart, to have a kitchen that is well stocked, to be secure in your job, to know the best shortcut to work, to know that you can expect to do today exactly what you planned. These are signs of blessing and they indicate mental, physical, financial, and social health. Moreover, they also point to no illness, anxiety, worry, poverty, war, famine, terrorism, or natural disasters.

However, life is not always so predictable. When change upsets our routine—a move, divorce, new job, new spouse, even new neighbors or the closing of a favorite store—we need an anchor of stability to hold on to as we establish a new routine. Prayers that remind us of the stable core to which we belong help, through both their content and their performance. That is, the message of the blessings—telling us that God is with us, that we continue to benefit from our daily gifts, that even disruptive change is part of life's mystery—supports us. So does the recitation of the blessing. The act of reciting the blessing itself is comforting, a sign of stability, a reassertion of routine in a time of upheaval. More than any other liturgical prayer, the morning litany of blessings, a repetitive run of fourteen blessings said in a singsong tone, helps to reestablish our comfort of routine every morning.

Most of the time we take for granted that our loved ones will return home from work, that our bodies will do for us today what they did yesterday, that the water will come on when we turn the faucet, that the stoplights on our way to work will be functioning, that our voicemail will keep track of our calls, that those who love us today will be there tomorrow. This blasé attitude toward the infra-structure of everyday life is itself one of life's precious gifts. However, as with many things in life, it is a gift noticed most when it is absent.

Other blessings that Judaism bids us to say in the morning remind us of these everyday gifts: "Praised are You . . . who made me free; who opens the eyes of the blind; who clothes the naked; who causes those who stoop to stand straight; who releases the bonds of those who are constrained." These blessings make us aware of the gifts we enjoy often without even noticing them. Our daily blessings draw our attention to the gifts we are likely to take for granted.

The first blessings of the morning liturgy explicitly focus our attention on the need for, and gift of, this awareness. Even more, every blessing implicitly serves this purpose.

Blessings before Eating

The blessings recited before eating food reflect our awareness of participation in the divine. We could have only one version of the blessing to be recited before eating. It could go something like: "God, thanks for the food." Such an approach would reduce all food to one common category, something to be consumed by us. It would ignore the variety, diversity, and grandeur of nature. That's why Judaism is not satisfied with only one blessing for food. Instead, we offer several specific blessings to be recited before eating: one for bread (which can encompass the others); one for other baked goods; one for vegetables and all foods that grow out of the ground; one for fruits and all foods that grow on trees; and one for meat, milk, fish, eggs, liquids, candies, and other categories not included in the previous ones.

These blessings remind us, the consumers, about the diverse and sensitive environment in which we live. They subtly encourage us, through self-interest, to attend to the diverse needs of the world. If we like the variety of foods we are eating, we need to tend to the world to enable it to sustain this abundant produce. In Judaism, blessings before eating are about our appreciation of having food, the majesty of nature and technology, and the ideal blending of the two. We are even more acutely aware of this when fruit that was once only seasonally available is now available to us year-round. Transportation and refrigeration enable us to eat any kind of food any time of the year. Selecting the appropriate blessing before we eat helps us to be mindful of the labor, the ingenuity, the efforts, the luxury, and the costs of such diversity and availability.

Blessings and Corn Chex

As I sit and stare into my bowl of Corn Chex, preparing to satisfy my natural feelings of hunger after a night of sleep, I stop and take a moment to ponder the deeper meaning of breakfast. As someone who lives in the wealthiest country in the world and in an urban setting, I am wholly disconnected from the process of food production. I do not even know what ingredients are needed to create Corn Chex. I have never risen before dawn to milk a cow in order to have milk on the table. Feeling somewhat inadequate and ignorant about my place in the food chain, what can I do to reconnect myself to the earth, to this food that sits before me? All of these thoughts go through my head as I close my eyes, meditate on my hunger and how it will be satisfied, and recite the blessing: "Praised are You, God, Source of the world, for everything is created by your word." With this, I can now begin my meal.

Blessings before I eat are an integral part of my life. By stopping to recognize God, I have elevated my meal—whether it is as mundane as Corn Chex or as elaborate as a seven-course feast prepared by the finest chef—to a holy act. Judaism gives us the road map to illumine every moment of our lives with God's presence, and eating is the most obvious one. By taking a moment in silence, closing my eyes, and thanking the Source of Life for my food, I regain a sense of connection to the earth, to all those other human beings who helped to make this food, and to my own soul. With the incredible pace of our hi-tech world, we are in greater need of blessings. By saying a blessing before and after I eat, I also allow myself to slow down, appreciate and actually taste the food that I am eating. I acknowledge that I am being sustained and nourished by a source greater than myself, and that offers me a sense of humility and gratitude. Spirituality is available right here, right now. Eat a Snickers, say a prayer.

The greatest lesson that we can take from blessing our food is the one that our ancestor Jacob realized when he awoke from his famous dream: "God was in this place and I, I did not know it." I might travel the mountains, the seas, and the great plains of the earth in search of holiness, yet the moment before I take the first bite of Corn Chex is for me greater than them all. Praised is God, the Source of Life and Sustenance.

JOSHUA LEVINE-GRATER

The blessings before eating all begin with "Praised are you, Adonai or God, Sovereign of the universe . . ." and continue as follows:

(for bread) ". . . who brings forth bread from the earth."
(for grain products other than bread) ". . . who creates all sorts of grains."
(for wine) ". . . who creates the fruit of the vine."
(for meat, milk, fish, eggs, drinks, candies, etc.) ". . . whose word brings all life into existence."
(for fruits and produce from trees) ". . . who creates the fruit of the tree."
(for vegetables and produce that grows from the ground) ". . . who creates the fruit of the land."

Blessings after Eating

Judaism is one of the few traditions that asks us to recite blessings after the meal, too—as if to say it is not sufficient to give thanks for the food when you are hungry or needy; you also have to be thankful once you're sated. If the blessings before the meal speak of our place in nature and our connection to the land and to God, the blessings after the meal speak of our place in history and our connection to our homeland and God.

On holidays and Shabbat, we begin with a psalm: "A Song of Ascent: When God restored our exiles to Zion, it was like a dream." After the first paragraph, which gives thanks to God for graciously sustaining us with ample food, the second paragraph continues: "We thank you, God, for the rich, spacious, and good land that you gave to our ancestors. . . . We thank you, God, for the land and the food." It is in this second paragraph that we insert seasonal blessings, thanking God for delivering us from our enemies time and again throughout the ages.

The series of blessings continues: "Have mercy on your people Israel, on Jerusalem Your city. . . . Praised are You, God, who rebuilds Your city Jerusalem." This six-paragraph postmeal blessing (not including holiday inserts and a closing vision of an idealized world) casts our gaze back and forth from satiety to history; from food to divine fortune.

Why this emphasis on *ha-aretz,* the Land, in the blessing after the meal? Before the meal, our hunger focuses us on our common human instincts—that we are creatures dependent on the earth; humans in covenant with God eager to satisfy our earthly, creaturely needs. Before the meal, we focus on sustaining life itself.

With the gift of a satisfying meal, however, our attention turns to the purpose of life. We eat to survive, but for what purpose? What meaning do our lives have?

Every time we eat a meal, we remind ourselves to whom we belong: our people, our land, our God. In the company of friends and family or by ourselves, we declare that nourishment is not just a gift, it is a calling. We may eat alone or in small groups, but we live in community, bound to our history and our future. Every act of eating is an act of communion and rededication to the mission of Israel.

The Shortest Proper Blessing

At one Shabbat dinner, both children were ill. We spent more time trying to pacify them than we did on making a holy meal. Thus, as so often happens at such times, the end of the meal with its sharing and singing and blessing simply disintegrated. I was left alone at the table without even enough dedication to sing the final blessing. It was then that I remembered that a friend had pointed out to me the shortest ritually sufficient concluding prayer.

As it happens, God gave me a good hand and I am something of a calligrapher. I decided to write the blessing in as beautiful a script as I could. I convinced myself that the prohibition of writing on the Sabbath had not been intended to thwart so personal a mode of thanks. Not only would I fix the words in my mind, but I might, on this confused evening, offer the work of my hands in gratitude.

It was one of those beautiful sunset evenings with the long shadows of the trees gently blowing in the evening breeze. Just as I made the last dot, I became aware that someone was in the room. I looked up and expected to find Karen (my wife) or one of the kids (who are very good at sneaking up on us), but no one was there. It was just a presence and the fading shadows.

Blessed be the Compassionate One, Master of this bread.

RABBI LAWRENCE KUSHNER[3]

Kavanot: Personal Meditations as Blessings

Waking up in the morning and eating meals are part of the daily routine of life. There are myriad other moments of routine, though, which are worthy of blessings: acts that we do repeatedly throughout our week but that are defining acts for us, such as the moment of walking into our office or picking up a novel.

Judaism encourages the creation of meditations, *kavanot,* at such times. These heighten our awareness about the significance of what is happening and enable us to articulate our hopes and fears and dreams and gratitude. It is a humbling and hallowing exercise to sit down and identify those common acts that define our days and our lives. Upon identifying those moments, we can then write or say a short personal meditation that can guide us as we make our way in the world. Sometimes these *kavanot* are carved out of simple words and phrases from the sacred texts of our tradition. At other times, they are just wordless chants that incline the heart.

Gregory J. Davis, a forensic pathologist who is often called upon to render expert testimony in criminal and civil courts, created his personal *kavanah*:

> Adonai, let me be an instrument of Your will in utilizing all the resources I am able to call forth in fulfilling Your command to pursue justice. Grant that I may use the strength of my learning, scholarship, and experience to formulate and articulate opinions not for special interest, but only for the truth.[4]

One particular moment of the day that seems appropriate for a personal *kavanah* is the moment we leave home. As we cross the threshold to step into the car, catch a bus, go to work, or take the kids to school, we might say a quick prayer. It needn't be in lofty language. These are the everyday words that I use to express the most precious of my everyday thoughts: "Dear God, fill my hands, my heart, and my mind with the tools I need to manage this day well, in holiness; let me be there for others as I hope others will be there for me."

BLESSINGS THAT RESPOND TO MOMENTS OF AWE

Shehecheyanu: The Essential Blessing of Awareness

One of the most popular fixed blessings is the *shehecheyanu*—a blessing all about being aware of and delighting in the moment. The blessing says: "Praised are You, Adonai our God, Sovereign of the universe, who has given us life, sustained us, and brought us to this very moment [of joy]." This blessing is said at bar and bat mitzvah ceremonies, commencements, retirements, dedications, and other important milestones, but it can also be said for quiet extraordinary moments at home: when a child takes a first step; when we cut the tags off our new clothes; when our child gets a driver's license; when parents celebrate their fiftieth wedding anniversary. This is a blessing that awakens us to the moment's splendor.

Birth and Death

Throughout our lives, we hear news of births and deaths, graduations and retirements, weddings and divorces. The Rabbis help us to process this news, to place it in the context of the broad stream of life. They crafted two different responses in the form of fixed blessings.

When we hear the news of a death, we are told to say: "Praised are You, God, the Judge of truth." When we are angry or confused or lost, this blessing shows us the way. It reminds us what we can and cannot control. It affirms our faith at a time when faith seems so hard to attain. It reminds us that we cannot fully understand the mysteries of life. When we place our faith, our trust and our hope in a power bigger than us, we can relax our fists, release the urge to control, and let go of what we never had anyway.

Likewise, when we hear good news, we are to say, "Praised are You, God, the One who is good and who brings goodness." These words place our feelings of gratitude in a greater context. We do not mourn alone and we do not rejoice alone. These blessings crafted by our tradition remind us that others care about our feelings and how we respond to them. But they also remind us that there are others who celebrate, others who hurt; that our experiences, while unique to us, are not unique to humanity. We are not alone in the particularity of our feelings. To recite these blessings helps us to remember who we are and *whose* we are.

Friendship

There is a remarkable blessing found in Jewish tradition that reminds us of the preciousness of constant contact with our friends.

If we do not see or communicate with a friend for more than thirty days, our tradition asks us to greet that friend, the next time we see him or her, with this blessing: "Praised are You, God, who brings the dead back to life." It seems that when we lose touch with a friend, a little bit of us dies. To renew contact is to renew more than the relationship. It is to reawaken that part of us that our friend uniquely animates. For each friend enlivens a unique constellation of our spirit, our desires, our strengths, our hopes, and our memories. Inactive relationships are not necessarily endangered, but they cannot grow, and neither can that part of us. Reciting this blessing reminds both friends how long it has been between visits, how valued our time is together, and what a loss it is to be out of touch.

Miracles of Time and Place

Just as we may reconnect with a person, Jewish tradition recognizes that we can reconnect with a place. Places stimulate memories, which arouse feelings. That is why, for example, we often celebrate anniversaries at the place we first met our loved one or where we became engaged. Some of us may have experienced a miracle of rescue. Perhaps it was that someone inexplicably appeared to help us in a moment of danger. Or perhaps it was not quite as mysterious, yet it was just as miraculous: when a physician removed a diseased organ or replaced a weakened valve or saved us from infection. Jewish tradition encourages us to mark the place where an act of rescue happened, when we come upon it again, by reciting: "Praised are You, God, who caused a miracle to happen here to me."

A Blessing for Everything

Judaism has a surprising variety of blessings for all types of experiences. Some of them are quite beautiful. Consider incorporating some into your life.

Upon seeing something of extraordinary beauty we say, "Praised are You Adonai, Our God, Sovereign of the universe, who has placed such beauty in Your world."

Upon seeing lightning we say, "Praised are You Adonai, Our God, Sovereign of the universe, who does the work of creation."

Upon hearing thunder we say, "Praised are You Adonai, Our God, Sovereign of the universe, whose power and might fill the whole world."

Upon seeing the ocean we say, "Praised are You Adonai, Our God, Sovereign of the universe, who made the great sea."

In conversation, when we independently awaken to an insight that reflects one from our sages or colleagues, we say, "Praised are You, God, for enabling me to share in the wisdom of sages."

When we see someone distinguished in worldly knowledge, discovery, and invention, we say, "Praised are You Adonai, Our God, Sovereign of the universe, who has given of Your wisdom to those who are flesh and blood."

Health and Recovery

Between life and death are moments of illness or accident. The *Mi Sheberakh,* the classic prayer for health, is recited in the synagogue in front of the Torah scroll on behalf of a loved one in the presence of a minyan. That is not the only opportunity we have to recite personal petitions for health, however. The *Amidah,* the central prayer of every fixed Jewish prayer service, said three times a day with or without a congregation, includes a general prayer for healing: "Heal us, God, and we will be healed; save us, and we will be saved." Jewish tradition also encourages us to add a personal petition for the recovery of a loved one in the midst of this prayer: "May it be your will, God, that you quickly send a full recovery from your domain in the heavens to ———— here. May it be a healing of body and a healing of spirit, for them and all Israel who suffer." One can recite this petition any time of day or night.

The precariousness of life is brought front and center every time an ambulance siren pierces our sphere of comfort. Once, when an ambulance passed my car, I could not help but look at my daughter and be thankful that we were in this vehicle and not that one. My first impulse was to offer a prayer of thanks, but then our thoughts turned to the person in the ambulance. Since then, my daughter and I recite a prayer for the person(s) in the ambulance whenever one passes us: "Heal them, God, and they shall be healed, for You are the true and merciful source of healing."

Learning the Lesson of Blessing

I struggled with the requirement to praise God for the bad my whole life. It was easy to praise God for all the blessings that have been bestowed upon my family and me. I never fully understood the Rabbis for making a requirement to say thanks for the evil as well, nor could I ever bring myself to actually fulfill it. Then my wife became ill and I spent many hours waiting for her and with her at Memorial Sloan-Kettering Hospital in New York. The unending procedures became routine and familiar. One day, as I was sitting in the surgical waiting room as she underwent yet another diagnostic biopsy, I was rather self-absorbed in my own pain and I looked around the room. I saw parents clinging to young children. I saw misshapen bodies that had been ravaged by cancer. I saw pain and fear in the eyes of those whose names I didn't even know. That night, after thinking about what we were facing and realizing that it was minor—though indeed similarly life-threatening—I realized what others were facing and I was able to thank God for what had been wrought upon us.

RABBI KERRY M. OLITZKY

Responding to Awe with Personal Blessings

The above blessings were formulated centuries ago for our recitation, but Judaism also recognizes that there are moments when we will be moved to recite a personal blessing in our own words and in our own way. It could be upon leaving home every morning, nursing a baby, visiting the home of someone who is sick, or even making dinner for a special occasion. The Talmud records the personal prayer of a teacher who asked that he make no mistakes that day and that no student be misled by what he said. "Before going in to teach,

Rabbi Nehunia ben Kana would say: 'May it be Your will, my God, that no misunderstanding or confusion arise through my teachings. May my colleagues and students value my learning, and may I value theirs.'"⁵

An entire literature of personal prayers and blessings records what Eastern European women used to say on a variety of personal and domestic occasions. When lighting the Shabbat candles, some women recited the following Yiddish *techinah*, a personal petitionary prayer: "Lord of the world, may my mitzvah of kindling the lights be accepted like the mitzvah of the high priest who lit the lights in the dear Temple. . . . May the mitzvah of my candlelighting be acceptable so that my children's eyes may be enlightened in the dear Torah."⁶ Hundreds of books of these prayers and blessings were passed from mother to daughter, published in German, Yiddish, and English over the past two centuries. We can learn from them and extend this tradition of our mothers through our own prayers of desire and thanks. As you prepare to light your own Sabbath candles this week, you may want to share with those you love what is in your heart.

Our mothers had blessings for occasions that we may not think of as a time for blessings. For example, many said a blessing when a child's first tooth emerged: "Your wonders and care over all creatures are so great and numerous they cannot be recounted. When a child begins to wean, You give him teeth with which to chew. For the precious gift, for the little pearl I have found in my child's mouth, I thank You, God, and praise Your Name."⁷ Rather than playing the part of a mythical tooth fairy, when your child or grandchild or even the child of a friend loses a tooth, try to form words of blessing that express how you feel at the moment—about the child and about the mystery of creation, growth, and development.

These women offered blessings for a child about to be married, for a spouse who was away from home, and for a sick child—and we can do the same. Some of their prayers were codified in Yiddish prayer books, but most of them were simply recited, as they lifted their hands and their hearts to heaven. Among their words, we can find a prayer for those who collect *tzedakah* (charitable giving) on behalf of the community, asking that they be sensitive and honorable to both donor and recipient. There are prayers and blessings for those who provide medical care, asking that they carry out their work with expertise and humility, caring and kindness, gentleness and understanding. There is also a prayer for an elderly mother who moves in with her daughter. Their words can be used as guides, and their message to us is straightforward: Use any occasion for blessing.

Sometime in the late Middle Ages, Jewish women in Italy began reciting prayers and blessings surrounding all aspects of their pregnancies: from the desire to conceive to celebrating the birth of a healthy child. The blessings helped them to mark each moment of this dangerous and miraculous event. The blessings they recited speak to every pregnant woman's experience even today, as well as to those who face the ongoing challenge of infertility.

Here is a prayer to be said during the ninth month of pregnancy:

> I thank the Lord with all my heart that I have carried the full nine months and that up to now God has spared me from all afflictions that could harm a pregnant woman and her child. Surely God's tenderness is unending. Again, I seek God's kindness so that God will be with me and support me when my child is pressing to be born. . . . Fill my breasts with milk enough to nurse. . . . Send with my child blessings, abundance, and success.[8]

These prayers offer us both guidance and inspiration to form our own prayers and blessings at times that are special to us. We can either use texts and phrases from our past or write some of our own. We can also blend the two. Those that we take the time to write and plan to recite—by ourselves or in the company of our family and friends—and that are built upon phrases and images from our tradition are among the most powerful.

When you give your children the keys to the car for the first time, place the keys on a special key chain that includes a laminated card with a prayer that you have written or the traditional traveler's prayer.

The following prayer is one I wrote for just such an occasion:

May it be Your will, my God and God of my ancestors, that I go on my way in peace and return in peace. Protect me from all accidents and harm. May I always use my power to drive for good. Remind me of the awesome might of motion every time I sit behind the wheel. And through my acts may my life be a blessing. So may it be Your will.

A PRAYER FOR TRAVELING

Knowing how unsettled we and our loved ones can be at the prospect of a long-distance journey, our tradition provides us with the words to say when we leave home. Though crafted for the traveler, these words can provide comfort for the traveler and the homebound alike. Here is the traditional *Tefilat Haderekh* (Traveler's Prayer):

May it be Your will, our God and God of our ancestors, that You lead us toward peace, place our footsteps toward peace, and guide us toward peace. Bring us to our desired destination in life, joy, and peace. Save us from the hand of all our enemies, from ambush, robbers, and evil animals along the way, and from all types of harm that come to the world. Send blessings to all the work of our hands, and grant us grace, kindness, and mercy in Your eyes and in the eyes of all who see us; hearken to the sound of our supplications, because You are God, who hears prayers and supplications. Praised are You, who hearkens to prayer.

Here is an alternative text:

May it be Your will, our God and God of our ancestors, that You lead me away in peace, guiding and directing my journey in peace. Bring me to my desired destination in health, joy, and peace. Keep me from all the harm and misfortunes that roam this world. Bless my work. Let me find kindness and openness in those I encounter wherever I go, and before You as well. Hear my prayer, God, for You are the one who listens to prayers. Praised are You, the one who hears prayers.

WHERE TO START AND HOW TO CONTINUE

Offering prayers and making blessings do not always come naturally, so we need to train ourselves to be aware of the special nature of the moment and comfortable in marking it through sacred words. At the dinner table, take a moment to share with family and friends the events of the past week: what was learned, what was enjoyed, what wasn't. According to tradition, the Shabbat table is a place where parents offer blessings to their children and guests.

Try and do the same for life's more difficult moments. It is often at these times that we most wish to give some blessing but do not know quite the right thing to say. If it is the night before your child goes to college, recall fond memories of his or her childhood, offer gifts of wisdom and love and fun and comfort that you want your child to take on the journey.

If you are forced to make a difficult decision, such as removing a loved one from life support after consulting with a rabbi or hospital chaplain, prepare your own blessing of understanding and release that such a decision entails.

Every moment of blessing is enhanced both by the moment of celebration and the preparation that brings us to that moment.

Judaism is a religion of many beginnings. The Mishnah speaks of four new years (in the Hebrew month of Tishrei for the calendar, Nisan for kings, Shevat for trees, and Elul for cattle). However, there are more beginnings that are unique to each of us. Every week we enjoy the refreshment of Shabbat, and every month we ask for renewal of spirit. So when we feel stuck, bored, or lethargic, our liturgy offers us encouragement. Imagine a new year for the different parts of our lives today: the school year; an organization's fiscal year; the year marked by the day we began a significant event in our lives, such as our first job. Each new year can be celebrated, or at least marked, in its own way, to allow us to take a moment to assess, regroup, count our successes, note our failures, and prepare for tomorrow.

On the first of each month, surrounded by family and friends, at dinner, or before bed, we can recite the age-old prayer of renewal sung in the synagogue on the Shabbat before the new month:

> May it be Your will, Adonai our God and God of our ancestors, that You refresh us with the coming month, with goodness and with blessing. Grant us a long life filled with peace, goodness, blessing, prosperity and strength. May we be God-fearing, free of shame and disgrace. . . . May all our desires be fulfilled.

Perhaps we can write a *kavanah* for our personal new years, to help guide our vision, our spirit, and our destiny.

Daily, weekly, monthly, or yearly, Judaism offers us ways of renewing, connecting, dreaming, and hoping. Blessings enable us to feel gratitude, seek new beginnings, know that we belong and where we belong, and find the path toward promise and hope.

RECOMMENDED READING

Broner, E. M. *Bringing Home the Light: A Jewish Woman's Handbook of Rituals.* San Francisco: Council Oaks Books, 1992.

Cardin, Nina Beth, ed. *Out of the Depths I Call to You: A Book of Prayers for the Married Jewish Woman.* Northvale, N.J.: Jason Aronson, 1992.

———. *The Tapestry of Jewish Time.* Springfield, N.J.: Behrman House, 2000.

Falk, Marcia. *The Book of Blessings.* San Francisco: HarperSanFrancisco, 1996.

Flam, Nancy, ed. *LifeLights: Help for Wholeness and Healing* [pastoral care booklet series]. Woodstock, Vt.: Jewish Lights Publishing, 2000.

Kula, Irwin, and Vanessa L. Ochs. *The Book of Sacred Jewish Practices: CLAL's Guide to Holiday & Everyday Rituals & Blessings*. Woodstock, Vt.: Jewish Lights Publishing, 2001.

Orenstein, Debra. *Lifecycles, Vol. 1: Jewish Women on Life Passages and Personal Milestones*. Woodstock, Vt.: Jewish Lights Publishing, 1994.

Prager, Marcia. *The Path of Blessing: Experiencing the Energy and Abundance of the Divine*. New York: Bell Tower, 1998.

Tarnor, Norman. *A Book of Jewish Women's Prayers: Translations from the Yiddish*. Northvale, N.J.: Jason Aronson, 1995.

8

Covering the Head

RABBI DANIEL JUDSON

THE BASICS OF HEAD COVERING

My date asked me if I was really going to go outside wearing that thing on my head. "My *kipah?*" I responded. She nodded. I was a little surprised. My date was a Jewish day school teacher; she was deeply immersed in Jewish learning, but she was still uncomfortable being seen on a Saturday night with someone wearing a *kipah*. In her eyes I was a bit of a religious fanatic. It was only our second date, and it proved to be our last. I ushered her out the door propping my *kipah* up a little higher on my head.

Wearing a *kipah* can provoke strong reactions from Jews and from non-Jews. There is perhaps no more identifiable outward sign of one's Jewish identity than wearing a *kipah*. Interestingly, although it is such a recognizable symbol of Judaism, nowhere is it proscribed in Jewish law that one must wear a *kipah*. It is a custom that has developed through the ages, with Jews wearing different types of head coverings at different times and places. *Kipot* are typically round; sometimes they come with prayers inscribed, sometimes with sports team logos or a fuzzy bear stenciled for kids. Most often they come plain and simple, reflecting the simple humility that lies at the core of wearing one: to remind the wearer that there is One greater above.

MY OWN JOURNEY

I grew up associating a *kipah* with a rather ugly satin hat with a name and a date imprinted on the underside of it. *Kipot* were to be worn when one went to synagogue and when one made kiddush on Friday night; when Passover came around, a whole stack of them was brought out—yellow satin ones marked "Andy Judson, Bar Mitzvah, November 14, 1977." Nobody I knew wore a *kipah* all the time. Even as my interest in Judaism grew to the point that I decided to enter rabbinical school, I did not consider wearing one outside the synagogue.

It was not until I had to spend a summer as a hospital chaplain that I began wearing one every day, all the time. It started for very practical reasons; it would help patients to identify me as the rabbi-chaplain. When I walked into the room of a patient whom I did not know and announced myself as the chaplain, I would unconsciously lower my head a little to let him or her see the *kipah*. I guess I did it to prove to both of us that I was a legitimate religious figure. When I would finish work each day, as I walked toward the subway I was faced with a simple decision: Do I take it off or not? At that point, it felt strange to take it off, as if I were performing something unholy by removing it. It seemed to me that if I took off my *kipah* after work, then it really was just part of a costume I wore for my job.

That summer of working as a chaplain was also an experience of drawing closer to God for me. Seeing patients in pain and suffering reach out to God enabled me to have a deeper sensitivity to the experience of God in the world, and my *kipah* had been a witness to it. When I walked out of the hospital each day, the experience of God, which was so real in the hospital, did not dissipate as I went into the subway. I saw God in the faces of the other subway passengers and at the bedside of every sick person. This is what it means to have *yirat shemayim* (to be in awe of God), to feel God's presence and power in all places. I wanted to honor the feeling of *yirat shemayim* that had taken root in me, and I thought that wearing a *kipah* would help me to do this. So I began to wear a *kipah* in all these places: at the bedside of people who are sick, while sitting in a subway car, and when shopping at the local grocery store.

Transformation

For me, when I cover my head, I somehow elevate the act in which I am engaged. Something that previously might have been rather routine is transformed into something that is sacred. Eating moves from the rudimentary process of satisfying my body to something that satisfies my soul as I become conscious of the Source of all food and my ability to process it. Reading becomes sacred study. Prayer is enhanced as I am reminded of to whom I am praying. Thus, once I started keeping my head covered for these occasions, it seemed logical to begin to wear a *kipah* all the time. It helps me to take my life and all life seriously.

When I dress in the morning, there are certain things that are indispensable. Without them, I don't feel like I can navigate my way. It used to be rather simple: wallet, watch, and keys. Now, these items have been extended to include a cell phone and a Palm Pilot. I feel the same about my *kipah*. Without it on my head, I may forget about the work that I am charged to do in this world, about the obligations that I have, and about making sure that all I do is reflective of the covenant I have with God.

RABBI KERRY M. OLITZKY

"SHALOM, MY BROTHER": SCENES FROM STOP & SHOP

Once I began wearing a *kipah* regularly, I realized that it not only reflected a connection with God, it also became a public display of my commitment to Judaism. The *kipah* became a tangible expression of my Jewish identity. This became clear to me in my integrated neighborhood of Jamaica Plains (Boston). In the mix of Dominicans, gays, lesbians, Irish, and others, I seem to be the only person who walks around town wearing a *kipah* regularly. So I get reactions.

"Shalom, my brother." I was in the local Stop & Shop supermarket, and behind me somebody repeated the phrase two or three times: "Shalom, my brother." I finally turned around to see an African-American man in his mid-fifties with a huge smile on his face. "I'm Jewish too," he proudly said. We stood quietly for a long moment until I said, "Ok, well that's great." He continued, "You probably didn't think that somebody who looks like me would be Jewish, but I am. And I am so glad that you are wearing a *kipah,* to let us know that you are Jewish and proud. Shalom, shalom, shalom." Then he was gone, leaving me with only an affirmation of pride in Judaism.

This has become a simple truth for me, something that I grew into: I wear a *kipah* because I am Jewish. Leaving aside all religious reasons, I wear a *kipah* all the time as a proud sign that I am Jewish and that I am willing to display my Jewishness, even at the local supermarket. In a place and a time where it is easy to blend in, I have chosen to outwardly display my Jewishness.

One of my friends suggests that all Jews should wear a *kipah* all the time as a symbol of Jewish identity. Many people felt the same way in 1967 after the Six Day War. My friend says:

> It doesn't matter whether they believe or don't believe, whether they keep kosher or eat pork at the movies on Saturday morning—all Jews should wear *kipot*. There are plenty of nonreligious Jews who wear a *chai* necklace [jewelry with the Hebrew word for "life" inscribed on it]

tucked under their shirts. Why are people afraid of taking it out from under their shirts? Why would they not want to wear a *kipah* to tell everyone that they are Jewish?

Her suggestion will probably go unheeded by most Jews. It is a provocative challenge. For most of my life, I too would have been far too uncomfortable to wear a *kipah* anywhere outside a synagogue. Like most young adults, I spent the better part of high school and college wearing only the standard-issue clothes of my generation: T-shirts, jeans, nothing too flashy that might draw unwanted attention. Now, years later, I walk around with the equivalent of a billboard on top of my head that says, "Different, very different" on it. It is not just any billboard, but one that says, "Way into Judaism, Therefore Different" on it.

When I put on my *kipah* some mornings, I get a flash of that high school discomfort. Soon afterwards, the feeling diminishes. I like the reminder, however. I know that I have different responsibilities. Putting a *kipah* on every day means that I am seriously committed to a way of life that places Jewish values at its center.

When I was in the sandwich section of the Stop & Shop a few months later, I felt a woman looking over my shoulder. "You should be all set with that sandwich; there is no meat in it." For a moment, I was confused. How could a stranger know that I was looking for a sandwich without meat? When she continued, "The fake meat sandwiches here are very good, I don't know if they are certified kosher however," I realized that she was making "Jewish talk" with me. It was a Jewish "pickup line." This was not about romance; this was about Jewish identity. She saw my *kipah* and wanted to connect with me. Then we had a long conversation about local Jewish events. I was aware that even in the sandwich aisle of Stop & Shop, in an area of Boston best known for its Cuban food, Jewish souls could connect with one another.

A Tale of a High School *Kipah* Rebellion

At the beginning of my senior year of high school, I began wearing a *kipah* to school. I go to a big public school in central New Jersey. When I made this decision, I really didn't think about how people would react. I didn't consider it a statement; it was a personal thing for me. The possibility that I would cause a large negative reaction at school for wearing a *kipah* had not even crossed my mind.

I was stopped by many teachers in the hall the first day I wore it. They told me to take off my hat. I told them it was a *kipah* and I was wearing it for religious reasons. A few of the more persistent teachers asked if I wore it on a regular basis. They were a little confused and did not know how to react when I told them that I started the practice recently. At lunchtime I passed by a table of teachers. One teacher toed the company line: "No hats," he said. I gave my standard reply, "It's not a hat, it's religious." "Do you wear it all the time?" he asked. We went back and forth. As I walked away, he told me that he "better see me wearing it tomorrow." This would prove to him that it wasn't just a hat. Apparently, hats have a one-week limit in New Jersey.

Then another teacher approached me about it. He was a tad more harsh in his remarks. He said things like "I am going to keep an eye out for you. If I ever catch you not wearing it, I will give you detention so fast your head will spin." During the following period, physical education, he informed me that he "knows what my plan is," that he "knows what I'm trying to do." I told him I had no "plan." He responded with a rather muted "yeah" and walked away. He came back a few minutes later and told me that I would have to bring in a note the next day from my rabbi.

This confused me. A note from my rabbi? Surely this circle of cloth that was clipped to my hair was not a controlled substance. Surely he was not saying that I needed my rabbi's permission to practice my own religion. If that were the case, I already had a note. It was signed by the Continental Congress and said *Constitution* in big letters.

My next encounter was with the hall monitor. She stopped me. I was ready with my well-practiced explanation even before she said anything. I was even prepared to have business cards printed with my response so that I could hand them out to the entire faculty. She said, "Young man, you can't wear hats in school!" "OK," I replied, "but it's not a hat, it's a *kipah*" and continued on my merry way to class. That's when I overheard her say, "That doesn't look like a *kipah* to me." I decided to respond to her, which soon landed me in the principal's office. He wanted to know whether I was wearing my *kipah* for religious reasons. "Obviously you know our school's policy about hats," he said. Before I could fully answer "religious reasons," he told me that he would keep an eye on me just to make sure that I was wearing it "consistently."

I was really tired by the time I got home—and rather angry. Trying to be helpful, my father told me that we could easily get a letter from our rabbi, but I firmly refused. I told him that I was not going to let anyone tell me that I had to get a note that said I was Jewish. Although my father does not always see the logic of my arguments, he readily agreed.

I had wanted to wear my *kipah* previously, in my junior year, but I just couldn't do it. I was afraid of what people might say and how they would react. That fear was one of the worst feelings I have ever had in my life. I felt ashamed: I wasn't strong enough to be the person I wanted to be. I felt bullied. I was not about to make the same mistake again.

I decided to start wearing my *kipah* in my senior year of high school for a specific reason. Too many people say that when young Jews leave high school—even when they were leaders, as I was—they run away from their Judaism or, at least, forget about it during college. Judaism had become a big part of my life. I was not about to forget it.

ADAM POBER

BROAD STROKES OF OBSERVANCE

Unlike many of the other rituals discussed in this book, there is no blessing for wearing a *kipah*. Most rituals have a traditional blessing that praises God for the opportunity to get closer to God through that particular ritual. However, one just puts on a *kipah* and that's about it. This simplicity reflects the origins of the practice. Wearing a *kipah* is not part of Jewish law; it is a custom. This is a major distinction in Judaism. Laws are obligatory, but customs are optional and vary from community to community. In different communities in different times, there has been disagreement over whether to wear a *kipah* in the synagogue, let alone on the street or in a restaurant.

Presently, the custom of wearing a *kipah* has become so accepted in the Orthodox community that it is considered obligatory for men. For many Jews in non-Orthodox synagogues, there is a strong custom of wearing a *kipah* when interacting with the Torah. Many put on a *kipah* when they have an *aliyah*, when they read the Torah, or when they study Torah. Some Jews don a *kipah* when walking into a synagogue for any reason.

The Rabbis of the Talmud tell us that two types of people routinely covered their heads. Mourners were obligated to cover their heads, and married men were supposed to cover their heads in the presence of scholars as a sign of respect. The Talmud also relates a few stories about people who covered their heads and bodies when studying mystical texts or engaged in mystical prayer. One Rabbi even suggested that God covered the Divine's own "head and body" when sweeping past Moses as he hid in the cleft of the rock on Mt. Sinai.

However, the practice of covering the head did not become a custom for all men during prayer until thirteenth-century Germany (a very late date, in Jewish history). The rabbis of that period offered the same reason for covering the head as do most rabbis today: *yirat shemayim*, "awe of God." The word *yirat*, "awe," is central to Jewish life. The ten days of the High Holidays are called the *yomim noraim*, "days of awe," because on these days we stand in judgment before God. *Yirat shemayim* means to be filled with a mixture of fear and wonder of God. We recognize that there is a power greater than our own, and this power is reflected in joy, in sorrow, in mountaintop vistas, even in the food we eat for breakfast. When we cover our heads, we remind ourselves of this fear and wonder of God.

Historically, Jewish women covered their heads for different reasons. The Talmud considered married women who did not cover their hair as "loose" women, and they were subject to divorce by their husbands. The Rabbis equated hair with sexuality. Traditional Judaism is concerned about modesty, and uncovered hair was considered too promiscuous and provocative. As a result, the Rabbis required women to cover their hair during prayer. They required married women to cover their hair at all times, because they should not excite anyone sexually except their husbands.

Until the sixteenth century, married women covered their hair with shawls or scarves. At about that time, women started covering their hair with wigs. This caused a great deal of Jewish legal debate. If married woman covered their hair so that they would not be desirable to anyone but their husbands, the wearing of beautiful wigs was thought to defeat the spirit of the law. As a result, many rabbis opposed wigs. However, the majority of rabbis argued in favor of wigs—perhaps representing the desires of their wives—and wigs became accepted in most traditional communities and remain that way today. Many Hasidic women follow the Hungarian custom and take the prohibition against uncovered hair a step further. They shave their heads for their weddings and often wear a long scarf over their heads.

THE CHANGING HEAD COVERING

Historically, head coverings changed according to local customs and fashions. Jews in nineteenth-century Morocco wore turbans similar to their Muslim neighbors. Eastern European Jews in the nineteenth century wore *shtreimls* (fur hats) that resembled the hat of well-to-do Eastern European men, while rabbis in early twentieth-century England and other European countries wore clerical hats that looked similar to the head coverings of Christian ministers.

Today, it is common for men to wear round hand-knit or suede *kipot*. In synagogues it is not uncommon to see colorful Bukharan *kipot*—that is, a special type of colorfully styled *kipah* from Bukhara, a town in present-day Uzbekistan. In some Orthodox synagogues, it is customary to wear a hat over the *kipah*. In many synagogues of all denominations, married women cover their hair with lace doilies or wear a hat while in synagogue out of respect for the traditional view that they should cover their hair.

There is, however, a growing number of women who have chosen to wear a *kipah* in synagogue, and a small number who have chosen to wear a *kipah* full-time. For those women who have chosen to wear a *kipah* every day, the wearing of it in public is a particularly bold decision. They risk strange looks, and even open disapproval and condemnation from some members of the Jewish community.

Connections to the Divine

The decision to wear a *kipah* was compounded for me by gender. In some Jewish circles women also cover their heads. Ultra-Orthodox married women cover their heads, specifically their hair, by wearing a *sheitl* (wig). Non-Orthodox married women often cover their heads when in synagogue with various lace doilies. Traditionally, the daily wearing of *kipot* was reserved for men. I had to examine what it meant for me, as a woman, to own and embrace this typically male ritual garment as my own. I have had the verses from Deuteronomy that forbid women to wear men's clothing and men to wear women's clothing quoted to me as a challenge more times than I care to count. However, there is no law prohibiting me, as a woman, from wearing a *kipah,* just as there is no halakhic ruling that requires a man to wear one. The fact is that for me, wearing a *kipah* is about taking on its religious symbolism, not its gender identification. *Kipot* are already widely recognized as Jewish. I didn't have to create something new. Wearing a *kipah* for me was a statement of me "owning" my Judaism. It is an expression of pride, a distinct symbol of my connection to God.

In this day and age, when it seems that so many people are looking for a deeper spirituality, I find that wearing an outwardly visible sign helps me to focus internally in the moment. I am more keenly aware of my actions and how I present myself. Most important, I am more aware of God's presence on a moment-by-moment basis. It isn't the *kipah,* per se, that brings me into God's presence; it is dressing in the morning and taking the time to look in the mirror, take a breath, and put it on my head. It is the constant reminder throughout the day that what I do and how I do it are seen not only by others, but by God. My *kipah* can feel like a deep breath being taken in through the top of my head. It is a very grounding experience. Because I am reminded of the spark of God's divine flame that burns in me, I am also reminded of that spark that burns in others. My compassion for others has been greatly enhanced as a result.

HALI DIECIDUE

An Advocate for Tradition

Once, as a fourteen-year-old, I slipped into the empty sanctuary of my Reform synagogue and put on a tallit for a few minutes. It felt daring and also very intimate, as if I had claimed a new kind of spiritual power. The first time I put on a *kipah,* at a Friday night service in college, it gave me the same jolt of spiritual excitement. For me, as a woman, covering the head with a *kipah* was more than a sign that God was always hovering, although it carried that meaning as well. The *kipah* was a way of saying, "I, a woman, help to hold up God in the world. I am a full partner in the covenant with God. No one can subordinate me to their own idea of how a woman should live in God's presence." Now, fifteen years later, I am a rabbi. Many parts of my life are affirmations of the spiritual truth that I am a full and public partner in the relationship between God and Israel, but the *kipah* still carries with it a special sense of sacred rebellion. It is a physical symbol of the courage of Jewish women of my generation who said to the Torah, "I will take you for myself, for my own benefit and for yours."

When I entered college and was able to choose my own religious affiliation, I chose to move into the world of Conservative Judaism. As I began to observe Shabbat, kashrut, and other practices in a more traditional way, I also chose to wear a *kipah* and a tallit. For me, those choices went together. I knew other traditionally observant feminists who prayed in a *kipah* and a tallit, and who sometimes put on tefillin. Sometimes I saw those ritual choices as counterbalances. By wearing a *kipah,* I said "yes" to my tradition; it was a "yes, but . . ." Yes, I will care for the commandments of the Torah, but not when they disempower women. Yes, I will live in a community guided by Jewish law, but I will fight to change that law if it hurts people. Wearing a *kipah* is a crucial part of my religious life because it helps me to proclaim what I accept and what I reject. I make it clear to my religious community that this is the meaning of the *kipah* on my head.

RABBI JILL HAMMER

WEARING A *KIPAH* IN DOMINO'S PIZZA AND OTHER DILEMMAS

If one decides to wear a *kipah* all the time, this decision creates numerous dilemmas for people who try to balance their Jewish and secular lives. Questions that I have asked myself include: Should I wear a *kipah* in a restaurant that serves *treyf* even if I don't eat it? Should I wear a *kipah* if I am driving on Shabbat, even if I am on my way to the synagogue or to visit a friend to share a Shabbat afternoon? Traditional Jews would argue that I should take off my *kipah* when doing anything that reflects badly on Jews or may lead a fellow Jew into a misunderstanding. For example, if I walk into a nonkosher restaurant with a *kipah* on, another Jew might see my *kipah* and presume that I would eat only at a kosher restaurant. That Jew might then mistakenly eat there. This idea is called *marit ayin* (literally, "appearance to the eye").

I used to think that taking my *kipah* off when I entered a nonkosher restaurant was nonsense. Why would my sense of *yirat shemayim,* the awe of God, be diminished in a restaurant because they serve cheeseburgers? Would I really confuse a person who kept strictly kosher if they saw me enter a nonkosher restaurant? Then it happened: I was standing in line at a nonkosher coffee bar when a woman whom I did not know got in line behind me. She leaned over and whispered in my ear just as she was about to place an order, "I am so glad that I saw you in here. I am really excited that this place became kosher." Nonetheless, I still wear my *kipah* all the time, kosher restaurant or not. My sense of Judaism and *yirat shemayim* is not compromised by being in a restaurant that serves nonkosher food. I don't even eat meat, but I have been with friends at restaurants that purport to serve the best barbecue ribs in New York and Boston.

Sometimes I am in situations in which I take my *kipah* off for periods of time, usually if I am doing something that violates my own sense of Shabbat. I admit that it remains a struggle for me. Although I generally do not spend money on Shabbat, as a way of expressing its sanctity, I do drive on Shabbat. On some roads I am forced to pay tolls. When I am not driving, sometimes I have to pay for a taxi. This is a gray zone for me, so I take off my *kipah.* Perhaps I am embarrassed about breaking the Sabbath, or maybe I do it out of respect for traditional Sabbath observers. Every so often a new situation will arise that forces me to consider whether to take off my *kipah.* This is part of living in the gray zone, of trying to be active in the secular world as well as committed to serious Jewish observance. It requires me to act out of my own sensibilities, using Jewish tradition as a guidepost but not a definitive guide.

THE POLITICS OF *KIPOT*

My grandfather served as the vice president of one of New York City's Orthodox synagogues for thirty-seven years, from the mid-1930s until the 1960s. (He said that he never wanted to be president because his father was never president of the congregation.) He was strictly observant in nearly every way, attended shul regularly, and observed Shabbat. Nevertheless, he never once wore a *kipah* outside the synagogue. Now, nearly three quarters of the men who attend the same shul wear *kipot* all the time: to work, on dates, at social gatherings.

In the past thirty years, members of the traditional Jewish community have boldly asserted their identity, taking a stand against acculturation and assimilation. Wearing a *kipah* became part of this rightward shift in observance and practice.

As the Orthodox world has reassessed the wearing of *kipot,* the Reform movement too has engaged in a long struggle over head coverings. In the nineteenth century, many Reform synagogues had a strict policy prohibiting the wearing of *kipot,* even by rabbis. Some synagogues even put up signs that articulated such a policy. Although the Reform movement officially went on record in 1885 in its official platform to disavow head coverings, there has been a strong resurgence among Reform Jews to wear *kipot,* along with other ritual items, during prayer.

THE POLITICS OF *KIPOT* IN ISRAEL

Wearing a *kipah* in Israel may not be as simple as it is in America. The style of *kipah* you wear is often an indicator about where you live and who has the loyalty of your vote. If you are Orthodox and politically to the right, you might wear a colorful knitted *kipah,* called a *kipah serugah.* If you are a bit more moderate, you might choose an all-white knitted *kipah.* Students who study in yeshiva often wear black felt *kipot.* A suede *kipah* generally indicates that you consider yourself modern and Orthodox from North America. The wearing of a *shtreiml* generally means that you are a Hasid, reflecting a tradition that hearkens back to Eastern European shtetl life.

FREEDOM CAPS AND YANKEE YARMULKES

The late Rabbi William Braude of Congregation Beth El in Providence, Rhode Island, delivered an astonishing sermon in 1965 in which the changing attitude of the Reform movement toward wearing *kipot* is dramatically seen. He begins the sermon by attacking those early leaders of the congregation who years before had asked newly arrived Jewish refugees from Europe to takes off their *kipot*.

> [One week after Kristallnacht, the night when Nazis burned and stoned synagogues in Germany, leaders of] Beth-El decided to have a service of grief and sorrow for the synagogues that were destroyed. To the special service we invited all Jewish refugees who were living in Providence. On that Friday night, about ten minutes before the service was to begin, the president of the congregation rushed into the little room at the rear of the temple where I sat: "Did you give permission to these people to wear hats?" The fact was until that instant I had given no thought to the headgear of our guests—the refugees. I did not know whether or not our guests chose to wear yarmulkes; . . . I began to say, "But these people are our guests. They have suffered so much. Whether or not they choose to wear their hats, surely we do not wish to add insult to the injuries they had already suffered." But my interrogator was implacable. "Answer my question. Did you or did you not give permission to those people to wear their hats?" To this day, I don't know the outcome of the battle of the hats. I was too choked up with pain. Involuntarily I thought of comparable demands—of Cossack officers saying to Jews, *Shapka doloi,* "Off with your hat"; of SS men saying, *Hut ab, Jude,* "Hat off, Jew." So when I walked into temple I did not look. My head was reeling . . . to this day I do not know whether ushers took it upon themselves to tell our guests to remove their hats and whether some of the refugees left in protest.

In that same sermon, Rabbi Braude also reflected on his personal experience of wearing a *kipah* while marching with Martin Luther King, Jr. in the famous civil rights march from Selma to

Montgomery. Rabbi Braude never wore a *kipah* in his synagogue. He reflected the posture of the Reform movement of his day. However, as he told his congregation one Rosh Hashanah, marching with Dr. King changed his attitude entirely:

> But it was on the highway—on U.S. Route 80—between Selma and Montgomery, Alabama, that the deep significance of the Jew wearing his yarmulke came to me. Some of you may remember that on Wednesday, March 24, 1965, Rabbi Saul Leeman of Cranston and I were among the marchers from Selma to Montgomery. On that day, the two of us—he quite readily and I somewhat reluctantly—wore our yarmulkes. The reason: to protect our heads from sunburn and to identify ourselves as rabbis. We succeeded on both counts. From all sides, white and black alike, men and women, greeted us with, "Shalom, Shalom." Young Jews, their eyes aglow, came up: "We are glad to see rabbis with us."
>
> And so in the midst of this atmosphere of camaraderie, Saul Leeman and I marched on. Then Sandy Rosen, a fellow rabbi from San Mateo, California, came up from behind me and greeted me with the words *shalom haver* (hello, friend). He, too, was wearing a yarmulke. Knowing that he was a Reform rabbi, I asked him, "Do your people wear yarmulkes?" He replied, "No. But all our colleagues who came to Selma throughout their stay there wore yarmulkes. And the Negroes [the term used then] took to the yarmulkes, [they] began wearing them and calling them freedom caps. Then the rabbis proceeded to bring in large supplies of yarmulkes, which they distributed to many of those on the freedom march. . . . [Rabbi Maurice Davis told me later] 'I tried to get one but I could not.'" I learned later they sent back for a thousand yarmulkes, but all the civil rights workers wanted to wear them. Negro children and white marchers were all sporting yarmulkes. . . . Thus the one-legged man, a white man, who walked the entire distance from Selma to Montgomery, got himself a yarmulke, which he wore from time to time. At the service in Selma on Saturday, March 27, 1965, which followed the killing of Viola Gregg Luizzo, the mother of five children, the Associated Press report stated

that many of those present, white and black alike, wore yarmulkes. On the other hand, the segregationists began calling these head coverings "Yankee yarmulkes."

At the end of the sermon that Rosh Hashanah morning, Rabbi Braude repudiated the Reform movement's position against wearing a yarmulke, recited the *shehecheyanu* blessing (thanking God for having reached that moment), and placed a *kipah* on his head. He wore it in synagogue for the rest of his life. In reflecting on this sermon years later, he noted that a number of the people in the congregation took *kipot* out of their pockets and put them on their heads. This surprised him, because everyone knew that the custom of the congregation was not to wear *kipot*. He thought that some of the men in the congregation must have stuffed yarmulkes in their pockets every service before they left home out of habit, and he wondered how long those yarmulkes had been sitting in those pockets waiting to be worn.

WHERE AM I NOW AND WHERE AM I GOING?

Once in a while, maybe a few times a year, I will forget that I am wearing a *kipah* and walk into the shower with it on. It usually does not immediately hit me that I have done this. It begins with a strange sensation of something waterlogged on my head. I then realize that the shampoo probably is not going to work with a soaking *kipah* on my head. These moments remind me of how accustomed I have become to wearing a *kipah*. It is strange for me to think that I have become so comfortable with something that ten years ago was inconceivable; that I would walk through life proclaiming my commitment to Judaism by having a *kipah* constantly on my head was even beyond inconceivable for me, if beyond inconceivable is possible.

Jewish rituals are about the power of transformation. For me the transformation was from a secular life to one focused on Jewish values. The same ideas that caused me to wear a *kipah* outside the synagogue years ago are still guiding principles in my life: it is important to be bold and proud of one's Jewish identity, and it is important to have *yirat shemayim,* awe of God's presence in all places.

WHERE TO START AND HOW TO CONTINUE

As noted, wearing a *kipah* is probably the simplest practice you will find in this book. There are no relevant traditional blessings. The only question is what style of *kipah* you choose to wear. Nevertheless, you may want to develop your own blessing as you put on your *kipah*. I like to use this blessing, included in a series of morning blessings: "Praised is God for making me a Jew." As an alternative, you may want to consider this blessing, or words that emerge from your own heart: "Praised are You, God, for filling me with awe for Your works."

If you are not yet ready to start wearing a *kipah,* start by wearing a baseball cap or some other head covering that makes you feel comfortable.

Then try wearing a *kipah* for limited periods of time, or for these specific times and places: whenever you walk into a synagogue, even if it is not for praying; when you are doing anything of a Jewish nature; when you are performing a Jewish ritual; and for Shabbat or Shabbat meals.

It may be awkward for you. Wearing a *kipah* is a public display of Jewish identity. It may be more of an adjustment for other people who are not used to seeing you with your head covered than it will be for you. As with most things, however, what may initially be strange will soon become "old hat" in no time.

RECOMMENDED READING

Kula, Irwin, and Vanessa L. Ochs. *The Book of Sacred Jewish Practices: CLAL's Guide to Holiday and Everyday Rituals and Blessings*. Woodstock, Vt.: Jewish Lights Publishing, 2001.
Telushkin, Joseph. *Jewish Literacy*. New York: William Morrow, 1991.

9

Upon Rising and Going to Bed: Traditional Morning and Evening Blessings

RABBI ANDREW VOGEL

THE BLESSING FOR BACK PAIN

I am "blessed" with lower back pain. It is nothing that requires surgery, nothing of major concern. It is just that over the past few years I have become accustomed to the small, sharp pain near the bottom of my spine. Each morning when I awaken I stretch the sleep out of me and get ready for the day. I shower, dress, and as I go down the stairs to begin my day, I remember my discomfort as a "blessing." I consciously recite the traditional Jewish one-line blessings of the morning and pause as I come to the words: "Praised are You, Adonai our God, whose presence fills the universe, *zokef kefufim,* who straightens those who are bent over." As I say this ancient blessing aloud, I straighten my backbone just for a moment, and I am reminded that my back is a gift from God—pain and all. I am thankful for the ability to stand up erect and tall. God has created me the way I am, and I am grateful.

THE BASICS: FOR JEWS, EVERY DAY IS THANKSGIVING

In the Talmud, the voluminous Jewish compendium of law and tales, Rabbi Meir instructs us to recite one hundred blessings throughout the day. His teaching is seen as a foundation for Jews to develop an "attitude of gratitude." Jewish tradition encourages a daily practice of reciting blessings of thanksgiving to God for the goodness in our lives each day.

Although the distinction between a blessing and a prayer is often very subtle, blessings are generally short, begin with the familiar formula *Barukh ata Adonai Elohenu melekh ha-olam* (Praised are You, Adonai our God, Sovereign of the universe), and are connected to specific acts or activities. Prayers are often longer, may contain blessings in them (sometime to begin and end a theme that is elucidated in the prayer), and do not require any connection to an act. They often are requests made by individuals of God.

The Jewish practice of reciting blessings specifically in the morning and the evening originates in the Torah. The passage directly after the *Shema* states, "You shall speak of them . . . when you lie down and when you rise up" (Deut. 6:5). The Rabbis interpreted this verse, in part, as a requirement for Jews to recite certain passages of Torah when going to bed at night, and also as a directive for Jews to praise God when waking up in the morning.

The Rabbis of the Talmud expanded upon the instruction to recite passages from the Torah to include additional blessings that they created. Some of these blessings are lengthy statements of thanks and petition; others are more concise and focused, short one-line blessings. Some of these blessings are for acts as mundane as placing our feet on firm ground, taking our first steps of the morning, and rubbing the sleep from our eyes. Other blessings express thanks to God for creating us in God's image, for making us Jews, and for allowing us to enjoy our precious freedom.

The form of the morning blessings, in Hebrew *Birkot Hashachar* (literally, "Blessings of the Dawn"), evolved over a number of centuries. The morning blessings include the following: a blessing for returning life after sleep; a blessing for the ability to use the bathroom; a blessing for the soul; a series of blessings extolling God's power; and the *Shema.*

MORNING BLESSINGS

As you read through the morning blessings, you may want to note the balance between blessings for the soul and blessings for the body. The first and third blessings thank God for the soul and its purity; the other blessings focus on the physical nature of our beings. The blessings evoke gratitude for both soul and body, calling us to be aware of both aspects of ourselves, implicitly reminding us to care for both parts of ourselves.

"I give thanks to You, living and present Sovereign, for returning my soul to me with love; great is Your reliability."

"Praised are You, Adonai our God, whose presence fills the universe, who has made each human being with wisdom, creating in us openings and cavities. You know full well that if one of them were to be incorrectly closed or opened, it would be impossible for us to exist in Your presence. We thank You, God, who heals all creatures and performs wonders."

"My God, the soul with which You endowed me is pure. You created it, You formed it, You breathed it into me, You preserve it within me. In the future, You will take it from me and return it to me in the world to come. As long as my soul is within me, I thank You, Adonai my God, God of my ancestors, Ruler of all creatures, Master of all souls. We praise You, Adonai, in whose hands are the souls of all the living and the spirit of all human beings."

"Praised are You, Adonai our God, whose presence fills the universe, who gives the rooster the ability to distinguish between day and night."

"Praised are You, Adonai our God, whose presence fills the universe, who made me a Jew."

"Praised are You, Adonai our God, whose presence fills the universe, who created me in God's image."

"Praised are You, Adonai our God, whose presence fills the universe, who opens the eyes of the blind."

"Praised are You, Adonai our God, whose presence fills the universe, who clothes the naked."

"Praised are You, Adonai our God, whose presence fills the universe, who releases the oppressed."

"Praised are You, Adonai our God, whose presence fills the universe, who straightens those who are bent over."

"Praised are You, Adonai our God, whose presence fills the universe, who makes the earth firm upon the waters."

"Praised are You, Adonai our God, whose presence fills the universe, who takes care of all my daily needs."

"Praised are You, Adonai our God, whose presence fills the universe, who guides our steps."

"Praised are You, Adonai our God, whose presence fills the universe, who girds Israel with strength."

"Praised are You, Adonai our God, whose presence fills the universe, who crowns Israel with glory."

"Praised are You, Adonai our God, whose presence fills the universe, who gives strength to those who are weary."

"Praised are You, Adonai our God, whose presence fills the universe, who removes the sleep from my eyes, and who clears away the slumber from my eyelids."

Hear O Israel, Adonai is our God, Adonai is One.

The evening blessings are called *Shema She-al Hamitah* (literally, "*Shema* on the bed"). The blessings consist of the one line of the *Shema* followed by a blessing asking God to protect us while sleeping. The four archangels—Gabriel, Michael, Uriel, and Raphael—are also invoked for protection during the night. There is really no standard version for these evening blessings. Some prayer books include pages of psalms and praises for God, whereas others offer a more basic liturgy.

EVENING BLESSINGS

Following is a basic version of the evening blessings (similar to the one found in many prayer books). As you read through the blessings, do you notice any significant difference between the evening blessings and the morning blessings? We do not praise God in the evening as much as we do in the morning; in the evening, we petition God for protection. We call upon God and the angels to guard us on all sides. The evening blessings respond to a primal fear in humans of the night, of the darkness, of our own inability to protect ourselves as we sleep. It is out of the anxiety that the darkness brings that we call upon God for a shelter of peace.

"Hear O Israel, Adonai is our God, Adonai is One.

"Lay us down, Adonai our God, with peace, and raise us up to life, You who are Sovereign. Spread over us the shelter of Your peace. Set us straight with Your good counsel before You, and save us for the sake of Your name [to protect Your reputation]. Hide us in the cover of Your shadow, for You are our Divine Guardian and Deliverer, and You are a merciful and gracious King. Guard our going and our coming, for life and peace, for all eternity. Spread over us the shelter of Your peace. Praised are You, who spreads a peaceful shelter upon us, and upon all of Your people Israel, and upon Jerusalem.

"For the sake of Adonai, the God of Israel: May the angel Michael be at my right side, may the angel Gabriel be at my left side. May the angel Uriel be before me, the angel Raphael be behind me, and may the Presence of God be upon my head."

MY OWN JOURNEY

In a musty cabin at a midwestern Jewish summer camp, a counselor first asked my fellow preadolescent campers and me to recite the bedtime *Shema.* A dozen eleven-year-olds, we huddled in our sleeping bags, sweating in the humidity after a long day of camp activity. The camp counselor, in his late teens or early twenties, asked that we all climb into our metal bunk beds and, with the cabin's lights off, invited us all to sing with him the one short line of the *Shema.* For me, away from my home, my parents, and my regular routine for four weeks in rural Indiana, the familiar words of the *Shema* were comforting and grounding. I had never before known them to be a nighttime prayer, but I knew them well from Hebrew school. In a cabin of young boys, reciting the *Shema* provided us with a moment of shared intimacy, a few seconds for reflection on the day just ended. When I returned home from camp after that summer, I often softly whispered the *Shema* at night to myself to relive my joyful camp experiences and to feel the beauty this simple practice had brought to my life.

It had been the practice of my synagogue in Cleveland to present all bar and bat mitzvah students with a faux leatherbound prayer book, which most boys and girls promptly placed on a shelf to collect dust. By my high school years I found my copy, and, curious to explore its contents, I thumbed through to the evening prayers. Eventually, I began to expand my frequent practice of the bedtime *Shema,* often testing my Hebrew skills with the words of the Psalms. I remember some nights reciting one psalm, not yet realizing that it was meant for inclusion in the morning ritual: "The heavens declare the glory of God. . . . Day to day makes utterance, night to night speaks out. . . . Their voice carries throughout the earth, their words to the end of the world." The author of the verse portrays nature's praise of God and of the infinite turning of the earth as testimony to God's glory; I considered these to be powerful thoughts. As a teenager who was just beginning to explore my own identity as a Jewish adult, I was amazed to be part of a tradition that acknowledges the cycles of the universe and connects me to them and to their oneness. These words grounded me at a time when I needed them most. Since then, reciting the *Shema* as I close my eyes in bed has been my own personal ritual of comfort and calm after a long day.

Today, years later, my wife and I shut off the light in our infant daughter's room each night after we place her in her crib, then we sing the *Shema* and other evening blessings to her. As new parents, we are laden with anxiety as we leave her alone in her room (although we are only steps away), and perhaps our ritual of singing calms us more than her. I believe that, in time, our evening ritual of blessings and prayers will provide her with a sense of safety as she faces the long darkness of night as a growing little girl. The ancient Jewish prayers will help to connect her to God as the uncertainty of night descends and will make her preparation for sleep an experience that is profoundly Jewish.

My ritual of reciting morning blessings had its own separate evolution, first during a year I spent on a kibbutz in Israel where many young kibbutzniks had come back from their own spiritual journeys to Nepal and India. Their practice of Buddhist meditation seemed foreign to me, but I longed for a Jewish connection with God as I went out to the fields at sunrise to work in the date plantation. Somewhat embarrassed and self-conscious on this "secular" kibbutz, I would sneak away during our early breakfast, wrap myself in my tallit in my room, and recite blessings unfamiliar to me. At first, the ritual did not "work"; I felt no closer to God, too focused on proper pronunciation of the ancient words I was just learning. After a while, however, I began to experience "Aha!" moments, when images in my subconscious would appear as I spoke certain prayers.

I voluntarily accepted the obligation to recite morning and evening blessings some years ago on Cape Cod after a friend inspired me by his own morning prayer ritual, wrapping himself in his tallit and tefillin. It was part of my response to the covenant between God and me that I had accepted. What appealed to me was making a commitment to envelop myself in ancient words whose power and influence on me would certainly continue to grow.

BROAD STROKES OF OBSERVANCE:
PRAYING OUTSIDE THE MEN'S ROOM

The Hasidic rabbi Zusya of Hanipol used to say that his illiterate mother could not pray from the prayer book, but she was able to say her own morning blessings. He noticed that wherever she said a blessing in the morning, "in that place the radiance of the Divine Presence rested the livelong day."[1] Indeed, adopting the practice of reciting morning blessings can brighten one's day and set its tone by heightening one's awareness of the pervasive presence of God in our world and our own lives.

"Praised are You, Adonai, our God, Sovereign of the universe, who has made each human being with wisdom, creating in us openings and cavities. You know full well that if one of them were to be incorrectly closed or opened, it would be impossible for us to exist in Your Presence. We thank You, God, who heals all creatures, and performs wonders."

At the exit of the men's room in a crowded deli in Monsey, New York, I was reminded of the notion that there is a prayer in Judaism for everything, even for relieving one's bladder. A colorful poster over a sink shouted out the words of the second prayer of the morning blessings at me as I wiped my hands on a paper towel: *Barukh atah Adonai . . . asher yatzar et ha-adam bechokhma* (Praised are You . . . the One who has created each human being with wisdom). Suddenly, this mundane and rather routine bathroom activity became elevated, and I became aware of God's presence even here, in the men's room, before I returned to my matzo ball soup served in a Styrofoam bowl.

This bathroom prayer, called *Asher Yatzar* (literally, "the One who has created") serves two purposes. As a morning blessing it acknowledges the complexity of our bodies; as a prayer of thanksgiving, it affirms our appreciation for a successful trip to the bathroom at any other time of the day. Its words are somewhat euphemistic, referring to the various "holes" and "cavities" in our bodies. Some prayer books refer to these orifices as the "veins, arteries, structures, and organs" that allow our bodies to function. The

Talmud, where the original Hebrew text is found, clearly offers it as a post-toilet prayer, and as such it has become incorporated into the traditional morning ritual. As I recited it in the restaurant, I became aware again of the ingenuity with which my human body was engineered, and I was thankful to God for its proper functioning.

Most of us only appreciate our good health when we experience a health crisis. After a friend had surgery for prostate cancer, he experienced incontinence for months. He found this to be both discomforting and humiliating. During his crisis of confidence, he asked me, "What self-respecting adult has to wear a diaper?" He was angry—at feeling powerless, at his body's nonfunctioning, at God for the circumstances that he thought God had created for him. He told me that he had always taken the workings of his body for granted, but now he had gained an appreciation for the dignity that using the bathroom afforded him before the operation. He found the words of the *Asher Yatzar* prayer to be powerful, and he decided to recite them daily, even at a time when his body was not functioning as it should. I think that reciting the blessing helped to change his attitude, as he began to see the holiness in giving thanks for going to the bathroom.

BLESSING A LIFE IN THE BALANCE

Since I began reciting morning and evening blessings, the most profound change in my life is that I have become increasingly appreciative of my breath and beating heart, and aware that one day that breath will stop and so will my heart. However, although my life will end, my soul will not. I have found that morning and evening prayers communicate a sense of life's fragility in different ways. The traditional nighttime blessings address the fear and uncertainty that darkness evokes; morning prayers express the relief, thanks, and wonder at having reached another day.

On my baby's second day home from the hospital, everyone in the house left for a breath of fresh air, and for the first time I was left alone in the house with the baby. Not knowing what else to do, now presented with a little peace and quiet in my home for the first time in over a week, I began my personal morning prayer ritual. I wrapped myself in my tallit, pulled up the rocking chair in my dining room, faced east toward the morning sun, and began singing the prayers to my little sleeping child tucked away in my arms. Then I concentrated on the blessing that spoke most to me at that moment: *Elohai neshamah she-natata bi tehorah hi.* "My God, the soul that You have given me is a pure one. You created it, You formed it. . . . Praised are You, in whose hands are the souls of all the living, and the spirits of all flesh."

As with most newborns, my daughter's first week was filled with the miraculous. The most ordinary activities—her eating, sleeping, breathing, and being—were reminders of the wonder of life. At that moment, however, those miracles became ritualized in the ancient words of the morning blessings. Here I was, thanking God for renewing a soul within *me* that morning, calling *my* soul pure, and my own newborn daughter had just recently taken her first breaths of air, as I had witnessed during her birth.

GOD AND THE ANCIENT ALARM CLOCK

The short, one-line blessings that follow the *Asher Yatzar* prayer (see "Morning Blessings" sidebar, pp. 171–172) likewise bridge the everyday with the transcendent. The first blessing seems odd to our modern ears: "Praised are You, Adonai our God . . . who gives the rooster the ability to distinguish between day and night." Roosters? How is this relevant? Here, the Rabbis of the Talmud call upon us to thank God for hearing the crowing sound, the alarm clock of the rural ancient world, alerting sleepers to the rising of the sun and the start of the day. Today's equivalent for those of us who live in urban or suburban settings, far from the rooster's cock-a-doodle-doo, is the sound of chirping birds filtering through our minds, as our sleep begins to fade. In other words, we should give thanks to God for our very first moment of waking consciousness, as that first daily thought formulates itself in our brains: "Day has arrived."

One by one, the blessings continue, thanking God first for the states in which we live, as Jews, as free men or women, created in God's image.

If the morning blessings describe our thankfulness that our souls have been "returned" to us as we wake, the nighttime blessings address the fear that they will be taken from us at night.

A NIGHTTIME SUKKAH OF PEACE

In the ancient world, nighttime was a fearful time of great vulnerability. The Rabbis taught that sleep is "one-sixtieth of death." In the midrash, they imagined that on the first day of Adam's life, after he had experienced only the beauty of sunshine and light all day, Adam grew profoundly afraid seeing the sun set and disappear for the first time. As darkness approached, Adam feared that he would be enveloped by it; he had trusted all day in the God who had created him, but when the shadows began to fall, he began to lose his faith, afraid that he would be abandoned or killed. However, the midrash tells us, God heard Adam's worried cries, and protected him, teaching him to cope with darkness by lighting fire.[2]

It is no mere coincidence that the Rabbis who imagined this scene chose Adam as the story's main character, as if to say that fear of nighttime is a universal human experience shared by all. When nearly all of us were children, we dreaded the monsters of the night, dark closets and basements. Perhaps we felt anxious at being abandoned, or afraid of the unknown. This fear is not limited to children; on some psychological level all adults are afraid of being deserted, or are uneasy with uncertainty. It is human nature to feel safe and secure in what is known and seen and unchanging, and to fear in times of darkness.

The ancient Jewish authors of the evening blessings (see "Evening Blessings" sidebar, p. 173) sought out God in these moments, asking for God's protection and reaffirming their faith in their fear.

In addition to the *Shema*'s unwavering statement of faith, the *Hashkiveinu* prayer (literally, "Cause us to lie down") is recited as part of the bedtime *Shema* ritual. This prayer asks God to "lay us down in peace, and raise us up, O Sovereign, to life." It can be understood first as a prayer for an assurance of safety during the night until morning, but the prayer also addresses the Rabbis' fear of dying during sleep. The mysterious nature of sleep was connected in the Rabbis' minds to the mystery of death. Thus, the Rabbis asked God to simply let us wake up. The words of the prayer may also be read as though asking God to revive us in the world to come if we do die in the night. Through their ambiguous word choice in this prayer, the Rabbis connected nighttime with death and addressed their fears of both through a prayer for peace.

The prayer concludes by asking God to "spread over us a sukkah of peace." The sukkah is the wooden outdoor booth constructed for the week of the fall holiday of Sukkot; it is a temporary shelter in which Jews are directed to dwell for seven days. However, the Rabbis of the midrash imagined that the sukkah in which God sheltered the Israelites as they wandered through the desert was made not of wood but of six clouds of glory, which represent the Divine Presence. When we recite this prayer at bedtime, we ask God to shelter us with the same sukkah as we sleep—to surround us and protect us with the Divine Presence on all sides.

God's Safekeeping

I had always said personal prayers before I went to sleep, but I decided to add something from the liturgy to this practice. It was part of a growing attachment to my Jewish soul. So I looked at the nighttime blessings and read a traditional version that contains the line, "Into your hand I commend my spirit; You redeem me, Adonai, God of truth." When I first read that, I immediately turned the page. I did not really even notice how quickly I recoiled from reading it; I just rejected the prayer in an unconscious way. When I noticed how intensely I did not want to read it, I realized I needed to go back and reread it. I could see what the problem was. I really like to be in control—and I am not sure I want to commend any part of my being to anyone. That is precisely why I now say this regularly. I like being in touch with the tradition of giving over our souls for safekeeping at night and being thankful for their reappearance when we awake. "Being in charge" is ultimately an illusion, and it is really good discipline to remind myself of that every night before I go to sleep. I commend my spirit to God, not because God will absolutely protect me from all harm, but because there is mystery in the world beyond my control.

BETSY CLOSS

PATTON AND MACARTHUR AT OUR BEDSIDE

"For the sake of Adonai, the God of Israel: May the angel Michael be at my right side, may the angel Gabriel be at my left side. May the angel Uriel be before me, the angel Raphael be behind me, and may the Presence of God be upon my head."

The final section of the nighttime blessings also asks God to surround us with divine protection. It invokes four specific angels by name. (Judaism clearly affirms the presence of angels and their work in the world.) This prayer, which begins with *Beshem Adonai* (literally, "For the sake of God"), asks the angels to stand guard in positions around us, with Michael in place to our right, Gabriel to the left, Uriel in front of us, and Raphael behind us. Why are these angels invoked? The archangel Michael, according to the midrash and some later Jewish mystical traditions, is the angel of God who serves as the prime defender of the Jewish people. Whenever Jews needed to be saved or rescued, the Rabbis imagined Michael playing a key role. (For example, Michael stopped Abraham from sacrificing Isaac, witnessed the sale of Esau's birthright to Jacob, and defended the Jews from Haman.) Gabriel, the second most powerful angel, according to the imaginations of the Rabbis of the midrash, accompanies him in the bedtime prayer to our left side. Asking Michael to be at our right side and Gabriel at our left is like asking the armies of General George S. Patton and General Douglas MacArthur to escort us personally through the night.

Two other angels are also invoked, Uriel and Raphael. These are more minor angels in Judaism's angelology, yet they are chosen for specific reasons. The name of Uriel means "Light of God"; we ask this angel to shine divine rays before us in the dark of night for safety. Raphael, the angel of healing, is understood by the *Zohar,* the major Jewish mystical work, as one who dominates the morning hours, which bring hope and relief to the sick and suffering. The healing that Raphael brings is spiritual as well as physical. If we are to take this prayer literally, God's angels will protect us on all four sides during the night.

I see each angel as a metaphor that describes what I need emotionally and spiritually: strength, courage, insight, and health. Invoking the angels in the prayer helps me to articulate my own limitations as I consider the day just ended and the night ahead. Although I don't believe in angelic figures as they have been represented in Western art, as chubby cherubs with wings, I do believe in a God whose multiple attributes can strengthen me in times of weakness, give me courage in moments of doubt, heal me when I am hurting, and provide light for me in the darkest hours. I express these attributes and how I experience them as angels.

A VARIETY OF APPROACHES

Morning Blessings

Jewish tradition says that the morning ritual begins with our first waking thoughts. The very first words of the *Shulchan Arukh,* the sixteenth-century code of Jewish law, says that one should rise in the morning like a lion ready to serve God. One commentator on the *Shulchan Arukh* says that we should not succumb to the evil inclination that might convince us to stay in bed longer and delay serving God. In recognizing the inherent danger in lingering in bed, this commentator puts it this way:

> In the winter the evil inclination may say to you, "How can you arise now, so early in the morning when the cold is so intense?" In the summer your evil inclination may say to you, "How can you get up now, you have not had enough sleep?" If you would have to go and perform

service to the king, then you would surely rise quickly and not be negligent. So much more must one rise hastily to perform the service of God, the Sovereign of Sovereigns, the Holy One.[3]

Even before we get out of bed, Judaism perceives us to be in a battle between serving God and succumbing to indifference to God's presence. Thus our first coherent action of the day is a blessing that recognizes and thanks God: "I give thanks to You, living and present Sovereign, for returning my soul to me with love; great is Your reliability."

Some follow this blessing with the traditional practice of ritually washing their hands while reciting a verse from Psalms: "The beginning of wisdom is the awe of God; all who practice this gain insight. Praise of God is everlasting."[4] Some have a special cup for the purpose of washing hands called a *kvark* (in Yiddish) or a *natlah* (in Hebrew). Many people who engage in this practice place the *natlah* by the bedside with a bowl, so that the hand washing can actually be done as the first activity of the day. A *natlah* has two handles on it. Although there is some variation in this practice between communities, to ritually wash your hands, hold the *natlah* in your left hand and pour water over your right hand. Then transfer the *natlah* to the right hand and pour water over your left hand. Repeat this procedure two more times, so that you have poured water over each hand three times. Hand washing in the morning symbolizes the notion that you are a new person each time you wake up. Each day contains the potential for being a new world as you approach it. Some continue the morning ritual by donning tallit and tefillin. Some study or meditate or do a little of both.

The traditional custom of using the "blessings for daily miracles" as a time to attune yourself to your body and its functioning is also rather inspiring and uplifting. The first blessing, "Praised are You, Adonai our God, whose presence fills the universe, who gives the rooster the ability to distinguish between day and night," can be said when one hears the rooster. (In our day it is more likely to be the alarm clock.) The blessing that says, "Praised are You, Adonai our God, whose presence fills the universe, who clothes the naked," is recited while dressing. The blessing that thanks God for opening the eyes of the blind is said when you rub your eyes to awaken them, and the blessing that thanks God for freeing the captive is said when sitting up in bed. When standing up for the first time of the day, this blessing is said: "Praised are You, Adonai our God, whose presence fills the universe, who straightens the bent." When walking for the first time of the day, the blessing that thanks God for making steps firm is recited.

Collectively, the morning blessings call upon us to be grateful that all aspects of our body work well, because we all know what it feels like to have something not working well. To wake up with back pain or headaches can be debilitating and painful. The knowledge of how precarious health is calls us to be thankful for the workings of the body. Connecting the body with blessings also reinforces a basic sense of Judaism: the body is a vehicle for holiness. One gets up like a lion in the morning to serve God, not just to work or play. The morning blessings remind us that the entire body should be engaged in the service of God.

Body Prayers

"Praised are You, Adonai our God, Ruler of the Universe, who has formed the human being with wisdom, and has created in us a multitude of openings and cavities. It is obvious and known before Your glorious throne that if but one of these were open (that should be closed), or one were closed (that should be open), we would be unable to stay alive and stand before You. Praised are You, Adonai, who heals all flesh and does wonders!"

Each morning at 6:00 A.M., I get out of bed and go to the bathroom. As I sit, I reflect on the words of the prayer known as the *Asher Yatzar*. I reflect on the living miracle that is my body's plumbing, its "openings and cavities." Thank God for the little things, for the things that we take for granted, like digestion and elimination, like thirst and urination, like our heartbeat and our breathing. So simple but so necessary, so ordinary yet so holy. For without the body functioning according to its miraculous design, I would be unable to stay alive and stand before God. I would be unable to do good deeds *(gemilut chasadim)*. I would be unable to help repair the world *(tikkun olam)*.

After the bathroom, I tiptoe quietly to the next room where I unroll my yoga mat, open the miniblinds, and begin my morning ritual of postures and prostrations to the forms of the Hebrew *aleph-bet* (alphabet). Facing east, I stand with my feet together and my arms by my sides in *tadasana*, the yoga mountain pose. As I stand slowly and deeply fill and empty my lungs, I form the letter *vav,* which in Hebrew means "and." *And* implies that something will follow. *And* leads us to the next moment, to the future.

Next, I raise my arms until they are parallel to the floor, fingers pointed down, and roll up onto the balls of my feet, forming the letter *zayin* with my body. In yoga this is called the rooster pose. I stretch my arms as wide as I can, lifting up through the crown of my head. I am awake like a rooster at 6:00 A.M. May I be ready to go forward in the new day to fight for what is right.

A few breaths later, I inhale and raise my arms above my head, interlocking my fingers and squeezing my head between my biceps. Lowering my heels to the floor, I exhale and lean my upper body to the left as far as I can to form a *resh* with my body. In Hebrew, *resh* is the symbol for head. In yoga, this is the *nitambasana,* the reed pose. May my head and my body work together so that I may bend but not break.

On I go over the next half an hour, bending and stretching my way through the twenty-seven letter-symbols of the Hebrew *aleph-bet.* Finally, I lay on my back and relax into *savasana,* the corpse pose. I am trying to quiet my mind before the busy day begins, quietly breathing, releasing the grip of muscle on bone.

May God who causes peace to reign in the high heavens, let peace descend on us all, on all Israel, and all the world, and let us say: Amen.

STEVEN A. RAPP

WHO HAS MADE ME ACCORDING TO YOUR WILL

Although Orthodox prayer books contain a blessing that concludes "who did not make me a woman" (for men) and "who made me according to Your will" (for women), a prayer book dating from the fifteenth century from the south of France suggests that women should simply say, "who has made me a woman." The addition of such a blessing may help us to celebrate our uniqueness.

Evening Blessings

Unlike the morning blessings, which focus on gratitude for the workings of the body, the evening blessings are a time for reflection. Some people use the evening blessings as a time for reflecting on whom you need to ask forgiveness from, and to grant forgiveness to people who have hurt you. The following blessing appears in some versions of the evening blessings:

> Ruler of the universe, I hereby forgive everyone who angered me, irked me, or sinned against me. Whether it was against my body or against my possessions, or against my honor or anything that is mine. Whether it was willful or by mistake, intentionally or unintentionally; whether through word or deed or thought. . . . May no one be punished because of me. . . . And, God, may I sin no more, and whatever my sins may be, please erase them.[5]

A first reading of this blessing of forgiveness may lead us to think that it is overly forgiving. We forgive anyone who has sinned against us, even intentionally, without them first asking for forgiveness? It is a very human act to come to the end of the day and to replay in our minds over and over the slights and insults that happened to us during the day. The evening should be a time, though, of ending one day in peace and looking forward to the next, but peace eludes us if we are too wrapped up in the day's insults. So this prayer forces us, in a way, to move past our own human inclination to stew. We simply forgive.

The author of the blessing no doubt recognized that forgiveness can be more complicated than simply a blanket forgiveness for all who have harmed us. However, the blessing is also aware of how much our souls need to experience some complete peace, even if momentarily, before we sleep. In these moments of forgiving everyone and asking for forgiveness, our souls transcend the pettiness that can mark our days and we experience a brief moment of peace with all those around us.

Rabbi Nina Beth Cardin notes that this blessing is not only about our relationship with others, but about our connection with the Divine:

> The prayer seems to say that if we model forgiveness, especially unearned forgiveness, so will we merit unearned forgiveness from God. And perhaps as important, once we learn to forgive others, we can learn to forgive ourselves of those imperfections, those lapses that are part and parcel of our daily lives. This formula for forgiveness leads to a readiness to forgive, and an awareness that helps us avoid the need to be forgiven.

Although the evening blessings are an opportunity for the individual to spend some time reflecting, some use the evening blessings as a way of connecting with their families. If you are a parent of young children, spend time with them before bed; then recite the words of the *Shema* with them. There are a number of melodies for the evening blessings which have been specifically written for parents to use to sing their children to sleep. (See "Recommended Listening," p. 192.) The melodies are soothing, reflective music to calm the spirit before sleep comes.

Bedtime for Micah and Benjamin

My wife and I treasure the bedtime routine that we have established with our boys (Micah, age four, and Benjamin, age one). I suppose our enthusiasm is due to the fact that our nighttime rituals represent a merging of the activities that brought each of us the greatest comfort and joy when we were children. For my wife, Allison, that activity was reading. For me, it was singing. We believe that our kids are enjoying the best of what we both cherished.

We began reading to Micah even before birth, and he quickly demonstrated his mother's love of stories. With every passing birthday, he has insisted on adding one more book to his bedtime reading. Of course, four books can be awfully time-consuming, so we ask him to choose only one long book, as well as a few of his shorter favorites. His bookshelves contain a mixture of Jewish and secular stories that encourage young readers to be confident, sensitive, fun-loving, and spiritual people. We love that he has practically memorized some of his most adored stories, along with the lessons they teach.

After we've finished reading, it's time for bedtime songs. Although reading is often a shared family activity, singing is always special "alone time" for each of our boys. Benjamin, clutching his beloved little blue bear, enjoys being cradled in my arms as I walk in circles around his room, singing *Hashkiveinu* and the *Shema*, the Jewish prayers traditionally recited at bedtime. Micah likes to listen while lying on his stomach, so I cuddle up next to him in bed, stroking his back gently as I sing the prayers. Sometimes, he sings along, although he usually prefers simply to listen. I always sing one or two additional lullabies as well—everything from Debbie Friedman to Tom Chapin to Billy Joel. Micah is rarely awake by the time I finish, but if he is, I give him something happy to think about, along with a blanket of kisses. Minutes later, he is sleeping soundly.

To be sure, our bedtime ritual requires a lot of time. However, Allison and I never regret the extra minutes we devote to Micah and Benjamin at the end of the day. Bedtime provides us with so many precious opportunities: to help our boys lose themselves in the worlds of story and song; to guide them in becoming more well-rounded and deeply spiritual people; to instill in them a sense of safety amid the darkness of night; to open their hearts to our love—and God's love—for them. Most of all, our bedtime ritual affords us the privilege of watching our sons' eyes grow heavier and heavier until they drop off to sleep, with our wonder-struck glances and gentle voices filling the final moments of the day. It is nothing less than sacred—indescribably tender, each and every day.

KEN CHASEN

WHERE AM I TODAY AND WHERE AM I PLANNING ON BEING TOMORROW?

Today I recite morning blessings from the prayer book as part of my prebreakfast praying in my sunny dining room, facing east. Often, I race through the list of blessings, and my mind wanders to the business of the day ahead as I utter the ancient Hebrew words. Sometimes I am distracted by the other noises and activity in the house. On more days than not, however, I can be "mentally present" as I speak the traditional prayers thanking God for blessing me with a soul, for creating my body with wisdom, for making me a Jew. I breathe deeply, and, even if just for one moment, I appreciate the miraculous gift that is my soul. As I come to each prayer, I listen to my heart's beating, feel the emptiness in my hungry stomach, stretch my spine up straight, or stamp my feet on the solid ground, and I thank God that my organs work relatively well and that my body functions as it should. Most of all, I am reminded of how fragile life is, how precarious is my existence, and how fortunate I am to face a new day.

WHERE TO START AND HOW TO CONTINUE

Morning Blessings

The focus of the morning blessings is gratitude for being awake and aware. Before getting out of bed, pause and consider the blessings you have in your life.

As you come to full consciousness, focus your attention on the parts of your body. As you start to do this exercise look at the list of morning blessings and recite the blessing that is appropriate for that part of your body.

Consider attaching the text for the *Asher Yatzar* blessing to a wall outside your bathroom door to recite it after having used the bathroom first thing in the morning.

Rabbi Ed Feinstein makes this suggestion: The tradition teaches that one should pray every day. Begin the day with a few moments of meditation and reflection, as he does. Recollect the passions that brought you to this point in life. Reconnect with your deepest values. Evaluate where you are in life and where you are going. Listen to the voice of the soul. Stand for a few minutes in the presence of God before sitting on the freeway ramp for half an hour.

He also suggests that each word of the blessing is uniquely precious and deserving of its own *kavanah,* its own intense concentration. Say each word and stay there, until you have internalized that word. Fully realize the power and depth of each word. There's no hurry to get on to the next. It may take some time to finish the whole blessing, but you'll be transformed in the process.

Rabbi Rachel Cowan recommends that you begin each day sitting quietly for about twenty minutes, facing Jerusalem, with your eyes closed—just as she does. Pay attention to the sounds that come from the outside and to your own breath. Take notice when your thoughts have carried you off into anxiety, longing, planning, self-criticism, judgment, anger, regret, and then come back gently and un–self-critically to your breath. Then you can begin your morning prayers, or just your day.

Rabbi David Cooper advises us to develop a list of our own blessings to be used in the morning: "The idea is to have a list of acknowledgements and affirmations that you can say daily as a morning routine. Over time that process of offering blessings warms the heart and opens the pathways to the soul."[6] Here is a suggestion from his own list:

> I am thankful to be free to choose my life's path, to go where I wish, to speak my mind and to live in peace. Thank you, Source of Life, Essence of Awareness, and Fountain of Peace. [As you say this blessing consider the following physical movement.]
>
> Walking slowly, notice your body movements; notice all the visual and aural stimuli; be completely present in the moment. End the series of morning blessings with an affirmation to try to stay awake and present as much as possible this day—in a continual state of thankfulness and a deep sense of inner peace.[7]

For those of us who are not great at constructing meaningful language in the early morning, the Rabbis have helped us out, urging us to recite these words upon rising: *Modeh* [fem., *modah*] *ani lifanekha melekh chai vekayam, shehechazarta bi nishmati bechemla raba emunatekha* (I am grateful to You, the living Sovereign, for returning my soul to me as a result of Your overwhelming compassion for me). You may want to whisper these words to yourself. Or you may want to try to recite them over and over as a *kavanah,* a sacred mantra. Or perhaps softly sing them to yourself, allowing your voice to increase in its volume as you regain your strength and become fully awake, repeating them throughout the day. You may want to read a selection from Olitzky and Forman's *Sacred Intentions: Daily Inspiration to Strengthen the Spirit, Based on Jewish Wisdom* (Jewish Lights) (see "Recommended Reading," p. 192) before or after you say your morning prayers.

Evening Blessings

Spend some moments reflecting on your day, specifically considering people in your life whom you may have wronged during the day. Recite the blessing for forgiveness (see p. 186).

As you say the blessing that invokes the angels for protection, let your mind wander to those in your life and in the world who need protection. Envision the angels' protection over all of those people.

Allow yourself to end the day with some absolute quiet. Focus on the words of the *Shema* as a meditation to help you remove yourself from the day, to ease yourself towards relaxation and sleep.

If you have children, consider learning a Jewish song to be sung at bedtime, and say the *Shema* with them.

You may want to read a selection from Olitzky and Forman's *Restful Reflections: Nighttime Inspiration to Calm the Soul, Based on Jewish Wisdom* (Jewish Lights) (see "Recommended Reading," p. 192) before or after you say your nighttime prayers.

RECOMMENDED READING

Cooper, David A. *The Handbook of Jewish Meditation Practices: A Guide for Enriching the Sabbath and Other Days of Your Life.* Woodstock, Vt.: Jewish Lights Publishing, 2000.

Frankiel, Tamar, and Judy Greenfield. *Entering the Temple of Dreams: Jewish Prayers, Movements, and Meditations for the End of the Day.* Woodstock, Vt.: Jewish Lights Publishing, 2000.

———. *Minding the Temple of the Soul: Balancing Body, Mind, and Spirit through Traditional Jewish Prayer, Movement, and Meditation.* Woodstock, Vt.: Jewish Lights Publishing, 1997.

Green, Arthur, and Barry Holtz, eds. *Your Word Is Fire: The Hasidic Masters on Contemplative Prayer.* Woodstock, Vt.: Jewish Lights Publishing, 1993.

Hoffman, Lawrence, ed. *My People's Prayer Book.* Vol. 5: *Birchot Hashachar (The Morning Blessings).* Woodstock, Vt.: Jewish Lights Publishing, 2001.

Olitzky, Kerry M., and Lori Forman. *Restful Reflections: Nighttime Inspiration to Calm the Soul, Based on Jewish Wisdom.* Woodstock, Vt.: Jewish Lights Publishing, 2001.

———. *Sacred Intentions: Daily Inspiration to Strengthen the Spirit, Based on Jewish Wisdom.* Woodstock, Vt.: Jewish Lights Publishing, 1999.

Rapp, Steven A. *Aleph-Bet Yoga: Embodying the Hebrew Letters for Physical and Spiritual Well-Being.* Woodstock, Vt.: Jewish Lights Publishing, 2002.

RECOMMENDED LISTENING

Mah Tovu [Ken Chasen, Joshua Zweibeck, Steven Brodsky]. *Days of Wonder, Nights of Peace: Family Prayers in Song for Morning and Bedtime.* Springfield, N.J.: Behrman House, 2001. A book and CD of melodies for the morning and evening blessings.

SELECTED PRAYER BOOKS

Reform

On the Doorposts of Your House, pp. 3–6. New York: Central Conference of American Rabbis, 1994.

Gates of Prayer: The New Union Prayer Book, pp. 51–54. New York: Central Conference of American Rabbis, 1975.

Conservative

Siddur Sim Shalom, pp. 2–12 and 244–249. Edited by Rabbi Jules Harlow. New York: Rabbinical Assembly and United Synagogue of America, 1985.

Daily Prayer Book: Ha-Siddur Ha-Shalem, pp. 2–17, and 846–855. Translated by Philip Birnbaum. New York: Hebrew Publishing Company, 1969.

Orthodox

The Complete Artscroll Siddur, pp. 2–20 and 288–295. Translated by Rabbi Nosson Scherman. Brooklyn: Mesorah Publications, 1984.

Reconstructionist

Kol HaNeshamah: Shabbat Vehagim, pp. 140–171. Philadelphia: Reconstructionist Press, 1995.

10

וצונו על הטבילה

Mikvah

DEBRA NUSSBAUM COHEN

THE BASICS OF *MIKVAH*

Into the dangerous, cold swirling ocean waters Dianne plunged naked, one night shortly before she got married in her hometown on the New Jersey shore. She was accompanied by about a dozen close female friends; the two strongest swimmers joined her in the rough Atlantic water while the rest waited on shore. "There's something about the power and majesty of the ocean at night," says Dianne. "It was untamed and dangerous and exciting. It was very primal," as an experience tied into themes of birth, transition, and rebirth.

Dianne, a liberal Jew, immersed that night in the Atlantic as a *mikvah,* joining the long chain of generations of Jewish women who have immersed in a ritual bath. Her groom, Larry, was doing the same thing with a group of his friends farther down the beach. "I am definitely not a spiritual-type person," he said later, but he found that immersing himself in the ocean as a rite of transition was "very positive. It was purging and cleansing and purifying."

Observing *mikvah* refers to the act of fully submerging oneself in water, either in a ritual bath constructed to hold a combination of "living water" from rain or another natural source (like a stream) and tap water, or in a moving body of water (like the ocean or a river). Ritual immersion is a mitzvah, or obligation, for traditionally observant Jewish women and is discussed extensively in the Torah. Archaeologists have confirmed it as an important Jewish practice in ancient times, proven by the discovery of a number of *mikvaot* in the Old City of Jerusalem and atop the mountain of Masada.

Although some men participate in *mikvah,* before getting married or before holy days, the ritual is associated primarily with women. According to traditional Jewish law, married women enter a *mikvah* seven days after the end of their menstrual period. This twelve-day (or so) period is called *niddah.* They enter the *mikvah* in a state of "ritual impurity," *tumah,* and leave it in a state of "ritual purity," *taharah.* During the period of *tumah,* traditional women and their husbands do not touch in any way; after immersing they reconnect physically. As a result of the link to a woman's monthly cycle, *mikvah* is strongly tied to fertility and sexuality. Because Jewish tradition frames the time of a woman's menstrual period as one of "ritual impurity," some liberal Jews regard *mikvah* negatively.

At the same time, many liberal Jews are reclaiming this observance and reconceptualizing it as something consonant with their contemporary sensibilities. Some immerse in a *mikvah* to mark the transition into or out of a special or challenging time in their lives: marriage, divorce, the end of chemotherapy, the beginning of fertility treatments, recovery from rape. A smaller number of women are observing the mitzvah in a traditional way but reframing the separation of the sexes in a more egalitarian fashion. Some men, inspired by the mystical aspects of *mikvah,* immerse before each Shabbat and prior to the High Holidays. For them, as for women on a monthly basis, immersion can be a way to mark the passage and elevation from one spiritual state into another and sanctify the moment ahead. *Mikvah* is also used for men and women as the final step in their conversion to Judaism. This is a requirement of conversions under Orthodox and Conservative auspices and is being used increasingly under Reform.

The typical *mikvah* is a simple tiled square pool large enough for one person at a time. Steps lead down into it, and its water generally rises only about chest high. The attendant—a woman who is present only to make sure that the person immersing has done it completely (allowing water to cover the entire body) and to answer any questions—stands in the room but outside the *mikvah* pool.

MY FIRST ENCOUNTER WITH *MIKVAH*

The first time I went to the *mikvah* was exactly when most other Jewish women do—one evening shortly before my wedding. I went to the *mikvah* in Crown Heights, Brooklyn. I was taken by my soon-to-be mother-in-law, who is a member of the Lubavitch community there. The first time, I went to honor her and to honor Jewish tradition, by which I felt alternately attracted and repelled.

Today, eleven years later, I go each month. Now I do not go for the sake of my mother-in-law, nor for Jewish tradition, nor even for the sake of my husband or marriage. I go for myself. Over time, it has become a very meaningful, healing practice, one that I fully embrace both as a feminist-egalitarian Jew and as one who regards Jewish tradition as a precious inheritance.

Before my wedding, I also went to the *mikvah* out of curiosity. I'd read about the Crown Heights *mikvah* in Liz Harris's book *Holy Days,* an account of the traditional Jewish community that first appeared in the *New Yorker* magazine. Based on her description, I expected the *mikvah* to look something like a spa, all white tile and Spartan chic. I was wrong.

In its heyday the Crown Heights *mikvah* was something special—large and relatively spacious, and far more modern than anything the Hasidic community had previously enjoyed.

When I entered it in 1990, it looked much as it does today: a bit rundown, its wallpaper curling at the seams, with rather ordinary, worn fixtures in the preparation rooms. Upon entering, you are asked to pay $10 ($18 if you're a bride and going for the first time), then pick up a plastic comb and a small bar of motel-style wrapped soap. The attendant hands each woman a frayed but clean terrycloth robe and ushers her into an expanded bathroom where she bathes, shaves (if she usually does), and combs her hair as part of the pre-*mikvah* preparation. The *mikvah* is not used for personal hygiene, like a bath or shower. Its waters are meant to effect a spiritual cleansing rather than a physical one. Rigorous pre-use cleaning, including removing all nail polish and trimming long nails, is done so that the waters of the *mikvah* will touch the entire body in its pure form.

My mother-in-law-handed me over to the *mikvah* attendant that first night, who showed me into the *kallah* room (bride's room), the bathroom given to brides because it's a little bit bigger than the others, and I prepared according to the list posted on the wall, which detailed the parts of my body that needed cleaning and checking, before I rang the intercom to tell the *mikvah* lady (the attendant) that I was ready.

After taking me into the room with the *mikvah* pool, the attendant asked me to remove my robe so that she could check my body for anything that might present an impediment to the *mikvah* water connecting with every inch of me. She looked me over in a way that seemed at once careful and impersonal. Although I was relieved when she was quickly done, she didn't make me feel like she was secretly calculating my percentage of body fat.

Then I walked into the tepid water, and, following her instructions for immersion, recited the blessing word-for-word after her, before immersing again. I had anticipated some charged spiritual experience under the water, but it just didn't happen. The whole thing felt like an anticlimax. So for a time after my wedding I didn't go back.

MY SECOND VISIT TO THE *MIKVAH*

Three years into my marriage, I had our first child. After an induced, painful, and failed labor, the baby was born by cesarean section. When he was placed on my chest and I looked into his eyes for the first time, I realized—I mean really felt—that there is a Creator. I'd never before really believed in God. Now, without premeditation or expectation, I saw. I understood that my husband and I could not have created this new life, this whole and unique human being, by ourselves. I saw firsthand the Talmud's teaching that three are three partners in creation: man, woman, and the Shekhinah.

A couple of months later, after postpartum bleeding had ended and my doctor had approved my full return back into the physical aspects of life, I was thinking about how dramatically life had changed since my son's birth.

Of course, now it was focused on formula and diapers, and like most new parents I was exhausted and exhilarated. Most of all, I was in awe of what had emerged from my body. He was of me and yet his own person, deeply connected to me and yet unequivocally separate.

Becoming a mother had been a profound experience—physically, emotionally, and spiritually. I wanted to mark the end of this transformative childbearing year in a way that felt significant and spiritual. After thinking about it, and despite the disappointment of my first immersion experience, I realized that the perfect thing to do was to go to *mikvah*.

This time it was to the Upper West Side *mikvah* in Manhattan. Apprehensive about going, I didn't remember the blessing and had forgotten what else was involved. I was so nervous that when the busy *mikvah* lady asked me rather tersely, "Shower or bath?" I just blurted out, "Shower." (Later I learned that if a woman thoroughly prepares at home, she can just shower before entering the *mikvah,* but when the full preparation is done at the *mikvah,* a bath is recommended.)

When I came up from the *mikvah*'s water and shared with her that I'd just had my first child, she offered an uninspired *mazal tov* and ushered me out. Like the first time, I had no great spiritual revelation while underwater. I didn't feel God's presence while immersed any more or less than I did anywhere else. In fact, caught up in the concern about doing it right, my mind wasn't focused on the Creator at all.

Nevertheless, walking down Broadway in the warm spring night air, my body and hair still wet with the *mikvah*'s water, I felt something special. I felt happy and renewed. It felt good to have closed this incredible year of my life in a Jewish—and uniquely, inherently female—way.

SUBSEQUENT VISITS

In the months that followed, I went sometimes and skipped other times, when the demands of the day were too great. When we were ready to have another baby, however, I went every month, aware that the time of the month when women go to the *mikvah* is about the time that most women ovulate, the prime time to conceive. Going to *mikvah* also allowed me to keep focused on the holiness of our efforts.

It took a long time to get pregnant this time, and going to the *mikvah* helped me experience and move past my worry. Each month I would be disappointed when my period arrived. Each month, while preparing at the *mikvah,* I would lie back in the bathtub and indulge my sadness. When I walked out of the *mikvah* pool, I would be filled with hope and anticipation. I'd leave my sadness at the *mikvah* and return home feeling ready to begin a new cycle.

When I finally did get pregnant, it didn't last long. Miscarrying at the end of the first trimester, I hemorrhaged and was rushed to the hospital for an emergency procedure to stop the bleeding. It took me many days to feel physically right again, after the blood loss, the general anesthesia, and being engulfed in sadness and fear that we would not be able to have another child.

I dwelt in that place for two weeks. I mourned the loss of the pregnancy and my dashed hopes, and I let my body heal. When it was then time to go the *mikvah*, I felt oddly open and unusually vulnerable, both emotionally and physically.

While I lay in the bath preparing, I cried. When I went into the *mikvah* and was submerged in its water, I prayed to be able to move forward. When I emerged from the *mikvah,* I was ready to begin again, and I went home with my tears dried and my heart full with hope.

ACHIEVING A REGULAR RHYTHM OF RITUAL

Nine months later I gave birth to my first daughter. Feeling even more connected with *mikvah* now than before, I have gone each month since then. I am grateful for this ritual that belongs to me as a Jewish woman, although it is not without its intellectual and emotional challenges.

Some friends have expressed distaste when I've confided my *mikvah* observance to them. They see it as a tradition borne of the patriarchy that oppresses female sexuality. I've grappled with these issues, and I can't say that they're completely wrong. (See "Wrestling with Tradition," p. 208.)

I've also heard people say that it feels too much like Christian baptism for them. I remind them that Christianity adapted it from Jewish tradition.

Confronting and thinking through these objections has only deepened the feeling that *mikvah* belongs to me. As a Jewish woman, I own it, and its uniqueness in the canon of Jewish law makes it more dear to me.

THE UNIQUENESS OF *MIKVAH*

Mikvah is unique among the commandments. Three of the 613 commandments are considered special women's mitzvot: baking and separating challah, lighting Shabbat candles, and going to the *mikvah.* Certainly men can and do bake challah and light Shabbat candles, particularly when there is no woman present, but no man can immerse in a *mikvah* to sanctify fertility and the cycle of nature that only women experience. Its uniqueness, its woman-centricity in a tradition that often seems to banish women to the margins of religious

practice, makes it even more precious. Going to the *mikvah* has provided me with a way to give a Jewish structure to time and emotion.
For me it is about separation and sanctification.

After my second daughter was born, I decided to treat myself to
a visit to the new, beautiful, and lavishly decorated *mikvah* closer to
my home, as a way to celebrate the end of the year spent bringing her
into the world. There the walls are clothed in elegant wallpaper, and
the solid cherry doors are adorned with cut-crystal knobs. The carpet
is thick and the waiting room chairs and chaise are lavishly uphol-
stered. The preparation rooms alone are worthy of a spread in
Architectural Digest. Rosy pink marble floors and wall tile as well as
gentle lighting provide a backdrop to top-of-the-line Italian and
British porcelain fixtures with polished brass knobs. The sink has
shapely sculpted legs, and the bathtub is luxuriously deep and long.
The towels and robe provided are sparkling white and fluffy, and
every imaginable amenity is laid out.

Still, it's the *mikvah* itself that is the centerpiece. The walls of the
room are clad with Jerusalem stone, and the pool is lined in deep teal
tile. Above it is a small dome set into the ceiling, which is surrounded
by gold leaf and painted with airy, light clouds. The water is clear and
warm. At this *mikvah,* immersion has become a sensual, luxurious
experience.

At home, I have only a couple of minutes to shower at the start
of each hectic day; often one of my children calls for me or comes into
the bathroom unannounced. Preparing at the *mikvah,* I can take my
time. No one is going to intrude, and I luxuriate in the reflective solitude. In the *mikvah* itself, the hectic world of my everyday life feels
miles away, and I take as much time as I wish to meditate and
immerse.

When I emerge to go home, I feel peaceful and renewed, ready
to meet my husband with happiness and warmth no matter how
sharp the argument or grueling our day may have been. It's not about
sex; it's about separation—the separation between one interval of
time and another, the separation between one mood and another. The
truth is that my husband doesn't much care whether I go to the *mikvah*

or not. When he left the Hasidic community as a young man, he left behind the restrictions that he believes are embodied in its understanding of observance. So I go each month for myself.

WHY I GO TO THE *MIKVAH*

Some might argue that the solitude I enjoy at the *mikvah* could be experienced at a retreat or through prayer or meditation. Those are different types of experiences. Prayer mostly uses the head and, at its best, also engages the heart. *Mikvah* is a fully embodied experience of sanctification.

In the *mikvah* I am stripped bare, both literally and emotionally, before my Creator. I am suspended in the archetypal womb. I am at once both woman and child, a unique individual and a tiny part of all creation. Even as I am fully present in the moment, I am linked to all the generations of Jewish women before me who have immersed. It helps me to cultivate a consciousness of the Creator's presence in my life.

Although we can, and do, create new rituals that help to fill in the spaces where women's voices have been absent from Jewish religious life, *mikvah* has the added aspect of being rooted in tradition. *Mikvah* immersion is now, and has always been, a place for women to celebrate and sanctify that which makes us female.

HOW *MIKVAH* IS BEING UTILIZED

Religiously liberal Jews are meeting and embracing the idea of *mikvah* in growing numbers. Some women are creating a *simchat chakhmah,* or "celebration of wisdom" ritual to help them move from midlife to later life, often around the time of their sixtieth birthday. These rituals generally include learning Torah, creative readings, some blessings, and testimonials from friends and loved ones. Often there is singing and dancing as well. Some of these women have included in their celebration a visit to the *mikvah,* followed by a festive brunch with their closest women friends.

Women are immersing as a way of healing after physical trauma—like a cancer diagnosis and treatment, or rape—and to add a spiritual dimension to the medically and emotionally draining process of infertility treatments. They are immersing to mark purely joyful developments, to create extended prewedding *mikvah* rituals, and to celebrate rabbinic ordination.

A smaller but still growing group of liberal Jewish women observe the *mikvah* in the traditional manner on a monthly basis. A small number of liberal men are using the *mikvah* in increasing numbers, as well. They use it as preparation for their wedding, for the Jewish holidays, or simply for regular spiritual renewal.

Mini-*mikvahs* are also being used by some parents in the *simchat bat,* or welcoming ceremony, that they hold for their newborn daughters. This idea was developed by Rabbi Michael Strassfeld and Sharon Strassfeld, who welcomed the birth of their daughter this way in 1973. Although some feel that the ritual is reminiscent of a baptism, the *mikvah* is, of course, originally a Jewish rite, from which baptism was later derived. Water is tied to covenant and faith in the Torah, such as when Miriam's faith in God's presence merited the miraculous appearance of a well wherever she journeyed with the Israelites in the desert. The association between the *mikvah*'s "living waters" and the uniquely female nature of cyclical immersion also makes it a rich symbol to use in a welcoming ceremony for a baby girl, a kind of ritual foreshadowing for her life years down the road.

BRINGING GOD BACK INTO INFERTILITY TREATMENT

Adina Kalet and her husband had a son who was conceived without medical intervention. She went to a *mikvah* the first time while undergoing treatment for (medically defined) infertility a few years later, as they tried to have a second child. Kalet went to the *mikvah* after her eggs had been retrieved during her second round of in vitro fertilization (IVF), while they waited to see if the eggs became fertilized.

I started doing IVF about a year into my infertility treatments, and it was hard emotionally and physically; it didn't feel sacred. You get injections, which was mostly annoying even though the meaning of it was so intense. No one was paying attention to what was happening emotionally. It was also really expensive, which made it high stress too.

There are two or three days between egg retrieval and their insertion, and then a couple of weeks to see if the pregnancy test is positive. It's a hard two or three weeks. It's very high-tech and emotionless. I was telling a rabbi friend how hard this was, that it felt like God wasn't involved.

I never even considered *mikvah* before I got married. But I started reading about the imagery of water and fertility, and it gave me something to really focus on. I wanted to recognize those two or three days of waiting to see if embryos developed, when it's usually such a mysterious process (when it happens within the body). I also thought that this was a good time to prepare to receive back that which was taken from me.

I wrote a poem, and we [her sister-in-law, a cantor, and her friend, a female rabbi] said a couple of prayers. I asked each of them to choose something. I talked a little bit about the meaning of it for me, in the waiting room of the *mikvah*. We sat there, in front of the *mikvah* lady who was about six months pregnant and thought we were weird, and then I went in. They were behind a sheet while I immersed.

It felt really meaningful. I was attending to my spirit, trying to take care of myself in a way that the doctors and nurses weren't doing for me. It felt really comforting and very much my own. I had no rules and regulations associated with it. It felt like a physical thing that I had to do.

Kalet went during three rounds of IVF, but not in the last cycle, which she says "reflected my hopelessness." Precisely a year after her last solo *mikvah* immersion, she went again: this time, with her husband, son, and their new daughter, Sara, who had been adopted from a Colombian orphanage. They had brought Sara to the *mikvah* to have her converted and become a member of the Jewish people.

MEN AND *MIKVAH*

Although the *mikvah* is associated primarily with women, there are some traditional Jewish communities where men use the *mikvah* as part of regular spiritual practice. Some liberal Jewish men are now renewing this practice. Jerry Raik, a Hebrew school director, began going to the Lower East Side (of New York) *mikvah* in the 1970s, to keep his friend, the late writer Paul Cowan, company. Cowan went at the behest of a Hasidic rabbi with whom he was close. The first time, they went before Yom Kippur.

> There have been some years when I've gone way more often than just before Yom Kippur and other years when I haven't gone at all. We liked it and used to go, the two of us and sometimes some other people, on Friday afternoons.
>
> Men go in one at a time, with no *shomer* because there's no mitzvah. It's just a rite of purification, and its very dicey whether you have that sense of it or not. When I felt stuff, it would be, like, the day after. You either dunk once in every direction, or if you're from a certain group of Hasidim or other mystically inclined people, you might dunk four times in every direction.
>
> More recently when I've gone, it's been on the Upper West Side [of Manhattan]. At [Congregation] Ansche Chesed, I fitfully once or twice started something called the AC Men's *Mikvah* Club. A few of us went a few times, then nothing happened for a long time. Now I've been talking about it again and a few people are interested.
>
> For us it was a very strange thing to be doing, but at the same time it turned out to be quite comfortable. I feel it's like when I've been in synagogue [one day;] the next day I catch myself realizing that I'm praying differently than I usually do, with more of a heightened consciousness, with a greater focus.

A Man and His Stepson Experience the *Mikvah*

On a late Friday afternoon at Elat Chayyim, a Jewish retreat center in Woodstock, New York, fifteen men, my fourteen-year-old stepson (Elia), and myself gather together. As we sit in a circle, Rabbi Jeff Roth works his way through a Hasidic tale, using it as an invitation to us to let go of our preoccupations with the week that has passed and prepare for the potential for holiness that he suggests envelops us when we enter the *mikvah* waters.

We are all undressed and feel emotionally naked as well. We are a mix of body shapes and types, young and old, not much for the makings of a photo shoot. I am surprised about how comfortable Elia is among us. We break into groups of four for this end-of-the-week spiritual "tune-up" as we make our way to the hot tub that doubles as our *mikvah*. Like traditional *mikvaot,* its waters flow from a nearby natural source. However, the natural setting and the familiarity of a Jacuzzi seems to offer a measure of comfort for these men, most of whom have never visited a *mikvah* before. So we immerse three times: once to cleanse our souls of what has transpired during the week just past; once to prepare us for the immediate experience; and once to help prepare us for Shabbat. Suddenly the distant ritual of the past has found an access point in the present.

Elia, two other men, and I occupy the water first, choosing to do all three immersions, one man at a time. While one may seem more comfortable than another in some part of this ritual activity, all of us feel somewhat awkward. For me, perhaps it is because I am experiencing such intimacy with Elia. It is he who helps me to understand the profundity of the sacred ritual we have undertaken together as he verbalizes what he feels with each immersion. I am overwhelmed by his honesty and stunned as he expresses the pressures that he feels from the world around him. So I stay in the tub a little longer than the others, mixing my tears with the warm swirling waters. When I rise slowly—the world feels new again—I am ready to now enter Shabbat.

RABBI SHAWN ISRAEL ZEVIT

Andy Immerses before His *Chuppah*

Andy was naked in front of ten of his closest male friends. He stood on the banks of the Potomac River at 6:00 A.M. the day of his wedding, and he did what most men do when encountered with unusual nakedness: he made jokes about it. Soon Andy started moving into the waters, and as the joking stopped and the quietness of the still morning enveloped the group, he took a deep breath, immersed himself in the Potomac, said a blessing thanking God for having reached this moment in his life, and immersed once more. He came back to shore where his friends were singing wedding songs, picked up his clothes, and hightailed it back to the car before the early morning kayakers got a surprise.

RABBI DANIEL JUDSON

WRESTLING WITH TRADITION:
CONCEPTS OF PURITY AND IMPURITY

Embracing the idea of *mikvah,* for a contemporary Jewish woman, can be intellectually challenging. Bound up with the idea of immersion are the concepts of *tumah* and *taharah* from Leviticus. The Bible appears unequivocal: "Do not come near a woman during her period of uncleanness to uncover her nakedness" (Lev. 18:19). "If a man lies with a woman in her infirmity and uncovers her nakedness, he has laid bare her flow and she has exposed her blood flow; both of them shall be cut off from among their people" (Lev. 20:18).

It was customary in ancient times for married Jews to abstain from sexual relations during the days that a woman was menstruating. Later the Rabbis of the Talmud extended the prohibition for a week after the period ended, and constructed layers of law around it by prohibiting all physical contact between husband and wife for that twelve- to fourteen-day interval.

Mikvah immersion is the apex of the complex set of Jewish laws called *taharat hamishpachah,* or "family purity," observed today primarily by Orthodox Jews. These laws dictate sexual interaction between married Jews. They forbid a husband and wife to sleep in the same bed, to sit close to each other, or even to pass a glass to each other lest they become overcome by desire and transgress the prohibition on sex at this time. I appreciate how distance can sharpen desire during the two weeks of separation, but I believe that we are able to keep our urges in check without such statutory control. From my perspective, the practice of complete separation also brings with it the sense that a menstruating woman is tainted, that she is dangerously impure. It objectifies her into something from which a man must shrink back almost in fear.

Susan Handelman, in the book *Total Immersion,* writes: "The laws of *tumah* and *taharah* are suprarational, 'above' reason. And it is precisely because they are of such a high spiritual level, beyond what intellect can comprehend, that they affect an elevated part of the soul, a part of the soul that transcends reason entirely." She also writes: "If we strip the words 'pure' and 'impure' of their physical connotations, and perceive their true spiritual meaning, we see that what they really signify is the presence or absence of holiness." I don't feel less capable of holiness when menstruating. However, I do understand menstruation on a spiritual level as the potential for life, and that it is a time of shedding and preparation for renewal, an autumn and a winter of the body's monthly cycle.

Rachel Adler is one of the few Jewish feminist theologians to have thoroughly confronted the concepts of ritual impurity and purity. In the *First Jewish Catalogue,* Adler, who then identified as an Orthodox Jew, wrote:

> *Tumah* is the result of our confrontation with the fact of our own mortality. It is the going down into darkness. *Taharah* is the result of our reaffirmation of our own mortality. It is the reentry into light. *Tumah* is evil or frightening only when there is no further life. Otherwise, *tumah* is simply part of the human cycle. To be *tameh* is not wrong or bad. Often it is necessary and sometimes it is mandatory.
>
> The *mikvah* simulates the original living water, the primal sea from which all life comes, the womb of the world, the amniotic tide on which the unborn child is rocked. To be reborn, one must reenter this womb and "drown" in living water. . . . We emerge from the *mikvah* *tahor,* having confronted and experienced our own death and resurrection. *Taharah* is the end beyond the end, which constitutes a beginning, just as the Messianic "end of days" is in actuality the beginning of days.

A few years ago Adler—who now identifies with the Reform movement—wrote another essay, published in *Lifecycles, Vol. 2: Jewish Women on Biblical Themes in Contemporary Life* (Jewish Lights), retracting her earlier view and now terming it a "theology for the despised." While in earlier eras of Jewish history men could be rendered ritually impure by seminal emission or contact with a human or animal corpse (and theoretically still can), they no longer ritually transform themselves into a spiritually pure state. This ritual transformation has been left only for women, Adler wrote, and in every way the idea of menstrual impurity has been used to oppress women. She goes on to applaud the idea of salvaging the *mikvah* for new rituals thanking God for renewed life but says that the traditional concepts of ritual purity and impurity, as they apply to women, are unjust.

The Rabbis of the Talmud certainly had ambivalent feelings about women. We are described as light-headed *(rosh kalah)* creatures on the one hand, and the very foundation of Jewish life on the other. The Rabbis may have been imbued with great wisdom, but they were also men of their time and place, and our record of what they discussed reflects that.

There are many things stated in the Torah that all Jews today— even those of us who understand it to be written by the Creator and therefore inerrant—do not follow literally, or have rabbinically reinterpreted in order to accommodate various attitudes borne of modernity. Therefore I do not integrate into my own thinking the statements and implications from the Torah and the Talmud that I know are incorrect. Nevertheless, I am not willing to discard the entirety of this part of Judaism just because of the limited ways in which the authors viewed women. However they may have defined its role, I know that *mikvah* reaches back into the earliest days of our tribe, when women bathed at the end of their menstrual cycle and, in so doing, acknowledged the power and potential of the female cycle.

As Rabbi Rachel Sabath puts it:

> If the waters of the *mikvah* represent the waters of Eden, where all humanity was first created, then immersing in the *mikvah* is the closest I can get to that place where we first encountered God. It is a monthly reconnection to the physical experience of the body that

God created. It is an opportunity to acknowledge and praise the infinite wisdom and rhythm of the female body.

I embrace *mikvah* not because I walk into it in any way tainted and emerge somehow purified, but for the other ways in which it transforms me and enables me to move fully from one part of my month and my life into the next, in the enduring cycle of which I am but one part.

DIVING—TENTATIVELY—INTO *MIKVAH*

No one in this Conservative movement–affiliated woman's family had ever before gone to the *mikvah*. She went the first time before she got married and continues the practice each month, generally in her local *mikvah*, but most recently in the ocean near the beach where she and her husband were vacationing. Out of her sense of modesty, at her request, I have not included her name.

The first time my soon-to-be husband ever suggested I go to the *mikvah* I thought he was out of his mind. I thought it was archaic and misogynist. Then I started to learn about it, started reading about it, and I realized that I didn't have to do it as prescribed by the Rabbis.

I could do it as something that was renewing. It was an opportunity to look at it as the waters of life, and it felt really powerful as someone entering into marriage with the hope of creating life.

I go each month because it's really healthy for our marriage, to be apart and come back together, and I have a husband who feels that it's honoring the family, that it's a way of bringing blessing into the home.

No way do we separate from touching, but we don't have sex. I also go the day after my period stops, but I did wait the whole two weeks when I was trying to get pregnant.

WHERE TO START AND HOW TO CONTINUE

The first thing to do is to find a *mikvah* where you feel comfortable. If you have a friend who has gone, she will probably be happy to accompany you the first time.

Because a growing number of Conservative, and a few Reform, congregations have *mikvaot,* there may be one under liberal auspices in your community. If not, there are *mikvaot* in most Orthodox communities. A good place to ask is a local Orthodox synagogue or a Chabad house. Many Jewish newspapers issue an annual magazine or supplement that is a guide to the local Jewish community and often lists local *mikvaot.*

If there is no *mikvah* nearby, consider immersing in a natural body of water—a lake or ocean. It is a different kind of experience, and a very powerful one, that fulfills the mitzvah to immerse.

Mark the days of your period on a calendar and the seven days after it ends, as long as you see no blood. Observant women check internally each evening with special white squares called *bedikah* cloths, which can be purchased for a nominal sum at any *mikvah.*

After seven postmenstrual days have passed, you are ready to go. Call ahead to the *mikvah* to make sure that it is open. Most *mikvaot* open to women just before it gets dark, because you can start preparing before sunset, and stay open for a few hours. The custom of women going only after dark is rooted in a desire to preserve their privacy, since presumably any woman exiting a *mikvah* is going straight into her husband's arms.

Mikvaot provide towels and washcloths, shampoo and soap, flip-flops or paper slippers, and a robe to wear; most provide things like clean combs, toothpaste, and new toothbrushes, as well as cotton swabs, rubbing alcohol, a pumice stone, and dental floss. You may want to take your own toiletries and grooming aids with you. I always bring cuticle snippers, a razor and gel, my own hairbrush and toothbrush and makeup, and fresh underwear.

You will pay the *mikvah*'s fee as you enter—which can be $10 or $18 or more, depending on the *mikvah.* If it is your first visit, let the *mikvah* lady know that you are unfamiliar with *mikvah*-related procedures, and she will help to introduce you to this mitzvah and explain what to do.

Then you'll spend between half an hour and an hour preparing. The things to do are usually listed on a piece of paper on the bathroom wall.

You will bathe, remove your nail polish, comb every hair on your body, shave those hairs which you usually remove, buff down calluses, and thoroughly clean every nook and cranny of your body. You will floss between your teeth and scrub between your toes and ears, pare your nails and clean under them, remove scabs, clean out ear piercings and your belly button with a cotton swab.

The idea is to be free of anything that might impede the *mikvah* water from touching every part of your body. Once ready, you'll put on the robe and alert the *mikvah* lady.

When the *mikvah* room itself is empty of other women, the attendant will usher you in from the preparation room.

She will tell you to turn your back to her and take your robe off so that she can check your back for any obstructions (scabs, etc.) that you may not have been able to see. Then you'll turn around and she will cursorily check you from head to toe.

Being naked and looked over by a *mikvah* lady is an idea with which many women are uncomfortable. The truth is that *mikvah* attendants behave in a businesslike manner. The mitzvah of immersion is your commitment alone. Her role is that of an assistant, helping you to immerse without obstruction, not that of a judge.

A good *mikvah* lady doesn't make *mikvah* visitors self-conscious. These women see everybody—the fit and fabulous, and the rest of us, as well—naked, and so they aren't going to be shocked by a less than toned body.

In fact, the regular attendant at the *mikvah* I often visit—a sweet, grandmotherly woman—says "Kosher!" with happiness in her voice after I've immersed in the required manner. Then, as I wrap my robe around me after coming out, she generally says to me (as she surely does to all the women she attends), "Mazal tov! May you have much mazal!" Her tone and attitude are so joyously infectious that I feel as if I'm going out into the world armed with this wonderful woman's blessing.

Back to the immersion procedure: The *mikvah* lady will tell you to enter the *mikvah*. You'll walk down the stairs until you're standing in the middle of the small square pool, where the water will usually reach about chest high.

Standing with legs slightly apart, arms extended with fingers loosely spread, you take a deep breath, bend down, and raise your feet so that you are suspended in the water, every part including your hair completely covered by the *mikvah*'s living waters. Standing up again, you recite the blessing.

Most *mikvaot* have a laminated card with the blessing in Hebrew and in transliteration right at eyelevel on the edge of the *mikvah*. If you're unsure of the blessing, tell the *mikvah* lady and she will have you repeat it after her.

Then you dunk a second time without blessing, and then generally a third time and more, as you wish.

Tell the *mikvah* lady if you want to take a few moments in the *mikvah* to pray or think about something special.

Until recently I immersed the conventional three times, but lately I have felt confident enough to add to it, and have begun immersing a total of six times: once before the blessing and once after, and then once for each of my children and my marriage. Just before and during each of those immersions I think of each of my children and ask the Creator to keep him or her in good health and protected from all harm. I also ask for help in making our home peaceful and loving.

I feel that being in the *mikvah* is kind of like being under the wedding canopy where, our sages say, the heavens are especially open to you.

EASY STEPS

The traditional ritual is simple. It involves two immersions, going completely beneath the surface with arms and legs spread, fingers loosely held apart, so that the *mikvah* water touches every part of you. Following the first immersion, one comes up and says this simple blessing: *Barukh ata Adonai Elohenu Melekh ha-olam asher kidshanu bemitzvotav vetzivanu al-tevillah.* (Praised are You, Adonai our God, Sovereign of the universe, who has made us holy with mitzvot and instructed us concerning immersion.)

The second immersion is done without a blessing. It is a common practice for women today to immerse a third time; some immerse even more times, while they pray or petition God to guard those whom they love.

FOR A BRIDE GOING TO *MIKVAH*
Rabbi Rachel T. Sabath

May you find life in
Immersion in these
Living waters of Eden.
May they connect
You to the moment
Of creation, of perfection;
To the waters of
Our ancestors from Sinai to New York
And to your descendants.

In these living waters
May you feel inside
The presence of the
Force of life and
The power of ritual.

As you emerge,
May you feel the
Comforting presence
Of the *Shekhinah*
May you be embraced and ready to move
through the next transition of your life.

May these living waters of *Mikvah*
Be with you, purifying you,
Bringing you closer to the Garden of Eden.
As you stand beneath the *Chuppah,*
May these waters be a safe womb-like place
To which you can return
Throughout all the transitions of your life.

May all of these moments be filled,
As the sea is filled with water,
With overflowing blessings of life.

RECOMMENDED READING

Abramov, Tehilla. *The Secret of Jewish Femininity: Insights into the Practice of Taharat HaMishpacha.* Southfield, Mich.: Targum Press, 1988.

Adler, Rachel. "*Tumah* and *Taharah:* Ends and Beginnings." In *The Jewish Woman,* edited by Elizabeth Koltun. New York: Schocken Press, 1976.

––––––. "'In Your Blood, Live': Re-visions of a Theology of Purity." In *Lifecycles Volume 2: Jewish Women on Biblical Themes in Contemporary Life,* edited by Debra Orenstein and Jane Litman. Woodstock, Vt.: Jewish Lights Publishing, 1997.

Cohen, Shaye J. D. "Purity and Piety: The Separation of Menstruants from the Sancta." In *Daughters of the King: Women and the Synagogue,* edited by Susan Grossman and Rivka Haut, Philadelphia: Jewish Publication Society, 1992.

Kaplan, Aryeh. *Waters of Eden: The Mystery of the Mikveh.* New York: Orthodox Union, 1993.

Lamm, Norman. *A Hedge of Roses: Jewish Insights into Marriage and Married Life.* New York: Feldheim, 1966.

Slonim, Rivkah, ed., *Total Immersion: A Mikvah Anthology.* Northvale, N.J.: Jason Aronson, 1996.

Wasserfall, Rahel. "Menstrual Blood into Jewish Blood." In *Women and Water: Menstruation in Jewish Life and Law.* Hanover, N.H.: Brandeis University Press, 1999.

Notes

PP. IX–XVIII
FOREWORD

1. Barbara Kirschenblatt-Gimblett, "Performance of Precepts/Precepts of Performance: Hasidic Celebration of Purim in Brooklyn," in *By Means of Performance,* edited by Richard Schechner and Will Appell (Cambridge: Cambridge University Press, 1997), p. 109.
2. Ibid.
3. Ibid.
4. See, for example, an anthropological perspective on the Jewish customs of death and mourning: Samuel C. Heilman, *When a Jew Dies* (Berkeley: University of California Press, 2001).

PP. 23–40
TALLIT AND *TALLIT KATAN*

1. From the online presentation of *Women and Tallit,* Reform Synagogues of Great Britain, 1987. Reprinted with permission.
2. Irwin Kula and Vanessa L. Ochs, *The Book of Sacred Jewish Practices: CLAL's Guide to Holiday and Everyday Rituals and Blessings* (Woodstock, Vt.: Jewish Lights Publishing, 2001.)
3. From www.ohevshalom.com. Reprinted with permission.

PP. 41–60
THE BROAD SPECTRUM OF KASHRUT

1. Unless otherwise noted, all biblical quotations in this chapter are adapted from *The Five Books of Moses* translated by Everett Fox (New York: Schocken Books, 1995).
2. Babylonian Talmud, *Baba Kamma* 91b.
3. Babylonian Talmud, *Chullin* 84a.
4. Moses Maimonides, *The Guide of the Perplexed,* vol. 2, translated by Shlomo Pines (Chicago: University of Chicago Press, 1963), p. 599.
5. Ibid., p. 600.
6. Quoted in Isaac Klein, *A Guide to Jewish Religious Practice* (New York: Jewish Theological Seminary, 1992), p. 303.
7. This means "nonsacred" (i.e., nonsacrificial) meat.
8. For a brilliant analysis of how all of our journeys are really four journeys, see Ken Wilber, *Sex, Ecology, Spirituality: The Spirit of Evolution* (Boston: Shambhala Publications, 1995). Wilber draws his main idea, the theory of holons, from the writings of the Jewish thinker Arthur Koestler (1905–1983).

9. See Rabbi Rami Shapiro's website www.SimplyJewish.com.
10. Arthur Waskow, "And the Earth Is Filled with the Breath of Life." Available online at http://users.erols.com/jsblevins/waskow.htm.
11. Babylonian Talmud, *Chullin* 103b.
12. Babylonian Talmud, *Chullin* 113b. Because the Talmud is not specific, various customs have emerged regarding the time required to wait after a meat meal before eating anything made with milk. Customs range from waiting periods of six hours to three hours to one hour. Only a very brief time, about half an hour, is required after a milk meal before eating meat.
13. Babylonian Talmud, *Avot* 4b.
14. *Pirkei Avot* 4:2.
15. Samuel Dresner, *The Jewish Dietary Laws: Their Meaning for Our Time* (New York: Rabbinical Assembly, 1982), p. 41.

PP. 61–85
ENTERING SHABBAT

1. This selection originally appeared in Kerry M. Olitzky, *From Your Father's House: Reflections for Modern Jewish Men* (Philadelphia: Jewish Publication Society, 1999), pp.83–84. Used with permission.

PP. 87–104
DAILY PRAYER

1. Hayim Halevy Donin, *To Pray as a Jew: A Guide to the Prayer Book and Synagogue Service,* United Synagogue of America: Basic Books, 1980, p. 3.
2. Adapted from Tracee Rosen, "Prayers for Each Stage of Life," a sermon delivered at Valley Beth Shalom, Encino, Calif., 2000.
3. Avram Davis, ed., *Meditation from the Heart of Judaism: Today's Teachers Share Their Practices, Techniques, and Faith* (Woodstock, Vt.: Jewish Lights Publishing, 1997), p. 84.
4. Shefa Gold, in Ibid., pp. 131–138.

PP. 105–128
TORAH STUDY

1. Translation from Lawrence Kushner and Kerry M. Olitzky, *Sparks beneath the Surface* (Northvale, N.J.: Jason Aronson, 1993), pp. 107–108.
2. Translation from Barry Holtz, ed. "On Reading Jewish Texts," in *Back to the Sources* (New York: Summit Books, 1994), p. 29.

PP. 129–150
BLESSINGS THROUGHOUT THE DAY

1. Abraham Joshua Heschel, *Man's Quest for God* (New York: Macmillan Publishing, 1954), p. 5.
2. *Mishneh Torah, Hilkhot Berakhot* 1:3 and 1:6.
3. Lawrence Kushner, *Honey from the Rock: An Introduction to Jewish Mysticism* (Woodstock, Vt.: Jewish Lights Publishing, 2000), pp. 51–52.
4. Gregory J. Davis, "A *Kavannah* for Rendering an Opinion in Court," *Sh'ma* 28, no. 542 (Nov. 28, 1997): 8.
5. Babylonian Talmud, *Berakhot* 28b.
6. Chava Weissler, *Jewish Spirituality: The Traditional Piety of Ashkenazic Women*, vol. 2 (New York: Crossroad Publishers, 1987), p. 256.
7. Norman Tarnor, *A Book of Jewish Women's Prayers* (Northvale, N.J.: Jason Aronson, 1995), p. 17.
8. Adapted from Nina Beth Cardin, *Out of the Depths I Call to You* (Northvale, N.J.: Jason Aronson, 1992), p. 86.

PP. 169–193
UPON RISING AND GOING TO BED

1. Martin Buber, *Tales of the Hasidim: Early Masters* (New York: Schocken, 1947), p. 235.
2. *Bereshit Rabbah* 12:6.
3. *Mishnah Berurah* 1:1.
4. Psalm 111:10.
5. Translated by Rabbi Nina Beth Cardin.
6. David A. Cooper, *The Handbook of Jewish Meditation Practices: A Guide for Enriching the Sabbath and Other Days of Your Life* (Woodstock, Vt.: Jewish Lights Publishing, 2000), pp. 26–27.
7. Ibid, p. 29.

Glossary

aliyah: Being called up to the Torah to make the blessings before and after the Torah reading at the synagogue services.

Amidah: The "standing prayer" also known as the *Shemoneh Esreh.* Central prayer of the three daily services, named as such because it is said while standing.

Asher Yatzar: Literally, "who has created." The name of the prayer recited after using the bathroom.

atarah: Embroidered neckband or collar of the *tallit gadol,* often containing the blessing for putting on the tallit.

Barkhu: The call to prayer recited in *Shacharit* and *Maariv.*

bayit: The box of each tefillin that contains the prayer parchments.

bedikah: A check or inspection.

Birkat Hamazon: Grace after meals.

Birkot Hashachar: Literally, "blessings of the dawn." The name for the prayers said in the morning as you arise.

challah: Twisted egg bread used for Shabbat and holidays.

chevrutah: Literally "companion"; study buddy.

Chumash: The Hebrew name for the printed edition of the first five books of the Bible.

chuppah: Marriage canopy.

fleishig: Yiddish for "meat."

gartl: A thick black cord or belt that is worn during praying. It is usually long, and one wraps the midsection of the body two or three times, then knots the cord. Commonly worn by Hasidim, the *gartl* is thought by some to divide the spiritual and upper half of the body (heart and mind) from the more physical and lower half of the body.

gematria: Jewish numerology.

hashkamah minyan: Early morning prayer service, usually at dawn.

Hashkiveinu: Literally, "cause us to lie us down." The name for the prayer that is recited as part of the bedtime *Shema* ritual. This prayer asks God to "lay us down in peace, and raise us up, O Sovereign, to life."

havdalah: A brief ritual that marks the transition from Shabbat to the rest of the week.

hekhsher: "Validation"; a symbol certifying that a food product is kosher.

hiddur mitzvah: A concept known as "beautifying the mitzvah" (or ritual object), thus using silver boxes to cover the tefillin.

kasher: To make fit or proper.

kashrut: Fitness or propriety; the dietary laws.

kavanah: Concentration, focus, or attention; a meditation said preceding an action, designed to heighten our awareness of and appreciation for the act we are about to do; it also refers to spontaneous (as opposed to fixed) prayer.

kesher: Tefillin knot.

keva: The set or fixed text of prayer.

kiddush: From the Hebrew word *kadosh,* to make holy. It is the prayer said over wine to help usher in the Sabbath day.

kipah seruga: A colorful knitted *kipah.*

kohanim: The priestly caste.

kosher: Fit or proper.

laying tefillin: Yiddish for "putting on" tefillin.

maabarta: Protruding piece of leather on the tefillin strap.

Maariv: The evening service.

marit ayin: Literally, "appearance to the eye," the prohibition of doing something that would give the wrong impression to other people.

mashgiach: Kosher overseer or supervisor.

mechitzah: A partition in a synagogue that separates men and women.

midrash: Literally "to seek." It has a broad meaning of any interpretation of the Torah, but more often it refers to a type of interpretation that is in the form of a story.

Mikraot Gedolot: The Hebrew Bible with Aramaic translation and commentary.

mikvah (pl. *mikvaot*): Jewish ritual bath.

milchig: Yiddish for milk.

Minchah: The afternoon service.

minyan: A quorum of ten or more adult Jews for prayer. (In Orthodox Judaism, it must be ten male Jews.)

mitzvah: Commandment, divine instruction, sacred teaching.

motzi: Hebrew for "who brings forth," the main line in the blessing said over bread that initiates a meal.

Musaf: An additional service (parallel to the additional Temple sacrifice) on the Sabbath, festivals, and Rosh Chodesh. In Reform liturgy this service is omitted.

niddah: Menstruation. In Jewish law, the days of the menstrual period itself plus seven more days.

pareve: Yiddish for neutral, neither milk nor meat.

parshat hashavua: The weekly Torah portion.

Pentateuch: The Greek name for the printed edition of the first five books of the Bible.

phylacteries: The generally accepted English translation for tefillin.

ratzuah: Tefillin strap.

sefirot: God's emanations, according to Jewish mysticism.

Shabbat: Hebrew for Sabbath, sometimes pronounced *Shabbes,* the Ashkenazi Hebrew and Yiddish form of the same word.

seudah shlishit: The third meal on Shabbat.

Shacharit: The morning service.

Shaddai: Almighty God.

shechitah: Ritual slaughter.

sheitl: A wig worn by Orthodox women.

Shekhinah: The feminine aspect of God in Judaism. It refers to God's immanence. Also known as the Divine Presence.

Shema: The creed in Judaism proclaiming God as one (Deut. 6:4). Added to it are three paragraphs that focus on the commandments and the Exodus from Egypt (Deut. 6:5–9, Deut. 11:13–21, and Num. 15:37–41).

Shema she-al hamitah: Literally, "the *Shema* on the bed." The name for the group of prayers said before going to sleep.

Shemoneh Esreh: Literally means "eighteen," referring to the blessings of the *Amidah,* although today it consists of nineteen blessings.

shiva minyan: Referring to the community created for the sake of mourners so that they might be supported to say Kaddish, the mourner's prayer.

shomer (fem. *shomeret*): Literally, "guard"; a person who watches another immerse to ensure that it is done correctly. The term is also used in Jewish sources to refer to the woman herself, in watching over her cycle in this way, and to a person who stays with a corpse until it is buried (a requirement of Jewish law).

shtibel: A Yiddish word for a small synagogue.

shtreiml: A fur hat worn primarily by Hasidic ultra-Orthodox men.

shul: The Yiddish term for synagogue.

Shulchan Arukh: Literally, "the prepared table." A traditional code of Jewish law and practice, attributed to Joseph Karo in 1565 C.E., that became authoritative for traditional Judaism.

sukkah: The wooden outdoor booth constructed for the week of the fall holiday of Sukkot. Jews are instructed to dwell in the sukkah during the holiday in remembrance of the booths that the Israelites lived in during the wandering in the wilderness.

taharah: Ritually pure.

tallit: Prayer shawl.

tallit gadol: A large tallit or prayer shawl.

tallit katan: A small tallit, a four-cornered undergarment; sometimes called *arba kanfot* (literally, four corners).

tallitot: Plural of tallit (*tallesim* in Yiddish, or the Ashkenazi pronunciation of Hebrew).

Tanakh: The Hebrew Bible. An acronym for the three major divisions of the Bible: Torah, *Neviim* (Prophets), and *Ketuvim* (Writings).

techinah: Petitionary prayer usually used to refer to women's personal Yiddish prayers.

tefillah: The Hebrew word for prayer. It is also the term used in rabbinic literature that refers to the *Shemoneh Esreh* when used with the definite article *ha.*

tefillin: Prayer boxes, from the Hebrew word for prayer; the plural form comes from Mishnaic Hebrew.

tefillin shel rosh: Head tefillin.

tefillin shel yad: Arm tefillin.

Torah: The law or the teaching. This term could refer to the Torah scroll itself or to the printed version of the scroll, or to any kind of Jewish religious teaching.

treyf: "Torn"; Yiddish for not kosher; in Hebrew, *trefah.*

tumah: Ritual impurity.

tzitziot: Plural of *tzitzit,* although both words are used as the plural.

tzitzit: Fringes on the corners of the tallit, sometimes referred to as *tzitzis* in the Ashkenazi Hebrew form as well as in Yiddish; some people consider *tzitzit* as a Jewish form of macramé; sometimes called *arba kanfot.*

yarmulke: Yiddish for *kipah.*

yirat shemayim: Literally, "awe of heaven," a traditional notion that suggests that one should be in awe of God and therefore fearful of the Divine.

Zohar: A thirteenth-century Jewish mystical classic, known in English as "The Book of Splendor." The *Zohar* was written by Moses de Leon in the fourteenth century but was attributed to Shimon Bar Yochai, a figure from the mid-second century.

Suggestions for Further Reading

Cohen, Norman J. *The Way Into Torah*. Woodstock, Vt.: Jewish Lights Publishing, 2000.

Donin, Hayyim Halevy. *To Be a Jew*. New York: Basic Books, 1972.

Gillman, Neil. *The Way Into Encountering God In Judaism*. Woodstock, Vt.: Jewish Lights Publishing, 2001.

Green, Arthur. *These Are the Words: A Vocabulary of Jewish Spiritual Life*. Woodstock, Vt.: Jewish Lights Publishing, 2000.

Hoffman, Lawrence A., ed. *My People's Prayer Book: Traditional Prayers, Modern Commentaries*. 8 vols. Woodstock, Vt.: Jewish Lights Publishing, 1997–.

Hoffman, Lawrence A. *The Way Into Jewish Prayer*. Woodstock, Vt.: Jewish Lights Publishing, 2000.

Klein, Isaac. *A Guide to Jewish Religious Practice*. New York: Jewish Theological Seminary of America, 1992.

Kula, Irwin and Vanessa L. Ochs. *The Book of Jewish Sacred Practices: CLAL's Guide to Everyday and Holiday Rituals and Blessings*. Woodstock, Vt.: Jewish Lights Publishing, 2001.

Kushner, Lawrence. *The Way Into Jewish Mystical Tradition*. Woodstock, Vt.: Jewish Lights Publishing, 2001.

Matlins, Stuart M., ed. *The Jewish Lights Spirituality Handbook: A Guide to Understanding, Exploring and Living a Spiritual Life*. Woodstock, Vt.: Jewish Lights Publishing, 2001.

Olitzky, Kerry M., and Ronald Isaacs. *The "How to" Handbooks for Jewish Living*, 3 vols. Hoboken, N.J.: KTAV, 1993–2002.

Orenstein, Debra, ed. *Lifecycles, Volume 1: Jewish Women on Life Passages and Personal Milestones*. Woodstock, Vt.: Jewish Lights Publishing, 1994.

Siegel, Richard, Michael Strassfeld, and Sharon Strassfeld. *The Jewish Catalogue*. 2 vols. Philadelphia: Jewish Publication Society, 1973, 1976.

Wolfson, Ron. *Hanukkah,* 2nd ed.: *The Family Guide to Spiritual Celebration.* Woodstock, Vt.: Jewish Lights Publishing, 2001.

Wolfson, Ron. *The Passover Seder.* Woodstock, Vt.: Jewish Lights Publishing, 1999.

Wolfson, Ron. *Shabbat,* 2nd ed.: *The Family Guide to Preparing for and Celebrating the Sabbath.* Woodstock, Vt.: Jewish Lights Publishing, 2002.

About the Contributors

Rabbi Nina Beth Cardin is the director of Jewish life at the JCC of Greater Baltimore. She is an author and teacher whose most recent books are *The Tapestry of Jewish Time: A Spiritual Guide to the Holidays and Lifecycle Events* (Behrman House), and *Tears of Sorrow, Seeds of Hope: A Spiritual Companion to Infertility and Pregnancy Loss* (Jewish Lights Publishing).

Debra Nussbaum Cohen is author of *Celebrating Your New Jewish Daughter: Creating Jewish Ways to Welcome Baby Girls into the Covenant* (Jewish Lights Publishing) and speaks to synagogues, conferences, and Jewish federation groups about how Jewish rituals—new and traditional—can enhance our spiritual lives. She is a religion writer for *New York Jewish Week,* and has written for the *Wall Street Journal, New York* magazine and the *Village Voice,* as well as other Jewish publications.

Rabbi Ruth M. Gais is the director of the New York Kollel: The Center for Adult Jewish Study at Hebrew Union College–Jewish Institute of Religion, where she was ordained. She has a doctorate in classical archaeology from Princeton University. After many years of teaching about the ancient world, she decided to change directions and become a rabbi.

Mark Kligman is associate professor of Jewish musicology at Hebrew Union College–Jewish Institute of Religion, New York, where he teaches in its School of Sacred Music. He received his bachelor's degree at the University of Michigan and his doctorate from New York University. He specializes in the liturgical traditions of Middle Eastern Jewish communities and has published several articles on the liturgy of Syrian Jews. His work also extends to historical trends in the liturgical music of Ashkenazi and Sephardic traditions.

Haviva Ner-David is a writer, activist, and student and teacher of Torah. She is studying for ordination as an Orthodox rabbi and working toward her doctorate in the Philosophy of Halakhah at Bar Ilan University. Her book, *Life on the Fringes: A Feminist Journey toward Traditional Rabbinic Ordination,* chronicles her own spiritual journey, harmonizing her feminist ideology with her love for and commitment to Jewish tradition. She has written many articles, book chapters, and short stories. Ner-David is active in Jewish feminist causes, such as Women of the Wall (struggling for the right of women to pray with a Torah, tallit, and in song at the Western Wall) and Mevoi Satum (fighting for the rights of women whose husbands refuse to give them a Jewish divorce). She lives in Jerusalem.

Vanessa L. Ochs is the Ida and Nathan Kolodiz Director of Jewish Studies at the University of Virginia and associate professor in its Department of Religious Studies. She is the author of *Words on Fire: One Woman's Journey into the Sacred* (Westview) and *Safe and Sound: Protecting Your Child in an*

Unpredictable World (Penguin), and co-editor of *The Book of Sacred Jewish Practices: CLAL's Guide to Holiday and Everyday Rituals and Blessings* (Jewish Lights Publishing). She has a doctorate degree and was awarded a Creative Writing Fellowship by the National Endowment for the Arts for her writing.

Rabbi Mark Sameth is the spiritual leader of Pleasantville Community Synagogue in Pleasantville, New York. An essay on his return to Judaism appears in Sid Schwarz, *Finding a Spiritual Home: How a New Generation of Jews Can Transform the American Synagogue.* Before his ordination, he was a rabbinical intern and keyboardist at Congregation B'nai Jeshurun in New York City. A former award-winning country and western songwriter, his songs have been recorded by Loretta Lynn, Ed Bruce, Dickie Lee, and others.

Rabbi Andrew Vogel is assistant rabbi at Temple Shir Tikva in Wayland, Massachusetts. Ordained at the Hebrew Union College–Jewish Institute of Religion in New York, he has also served as rabbi at Temple Kol Emeth in Marietta, Georgia. He lives with his wife, Martha Hausman, and their daughter, Rosa, in the Boston area.

Credits

Notes

Notes

Notes

About JEWISH LIGHTS Publishing

People of all faiths and backgrounds yearn for books that attract, engage, educate, and spiritually inspire.

Our principal goal is to stimulate thought and help all people learn about who the Jewish People are, where they come from, and what the future can be made to hold. While people of our diverse Jewish heritage are the primary audience, our books speak to people in the Christian world as well and will broaden their understanding of Judaism and the roots of their own faith.

We bring to you authors who are at the forefront of spiritual thought and experience. While each has something different to say, they all say it in a voice that you can hear.

Our books are designed to welcome you and then to engage, stimulate, and inspire. We judge our success not only by whether or not our books are beautiful and commercially successful, but by whether or not they make a difference in your life.

We at Jewish Lights take great care to produce beautiful books that present meaningful spiritual content in a form that reflects the art of making high quality books. Therefore, we want to acknowledge those who contributed to the production of this book.

Stuart M. Matlins, Publisher

PRODUCTION
Tim Holtz, Martha McKinney & Bridgett Taylor

EDITORIAL
Amanda Dupuis, Polly Short Mahoney,
Lauren Seidman & Emily Wichland

COVER DESIGN
Tim Holtz

TYPESETTING
Susan Ramundo, SR Desktop Services, Ridge, New York

JACKET / TEXT PRINTING & BINDING
Lake Book, Melrose Park, Illinois

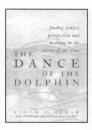 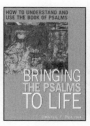   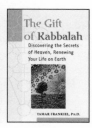

Spirituality

My People's Prayer Book: *Traditional Prayers, Modern Commentaries*
Ed. by *Dr. Lawrence A. Hoffman*

Provides a diverse and exciting commentary to the traditional liturgy, helping modern men and women find new wisdom in Jewish prayer, and bring liturgy into their lives. Each book includes Hebrew text, modern translation, and commentaries *from all perspectives* of the Jewish world.

Vol. 1—*The Sh'ma and Its Blessings*, 7 x 10, 168 pp, HC, ISBN 1-879045-79-6 **$23.95**
Vol. 2—*The Amidah*, 7 x 10, 240 pp, HC, ISBN 1-879045-80-X **$23.95**
Vol. 3—*P'sukei D'zimrah* (Morning Psalms), 7 x 10, 240 pp, HC, ISBN 1-879045-81-8 **$24.95**
Vol. 4—*Seder K'riat Hatorah* (The Torah Service), 7 x 10, 264 pp, HC, ISBN 1-879045-82-6 **$23.95**
Vol. 5—*Birkhot Hashachar* (Morning Blessings), 7 x 10, 240 pp, HC, ISBN 1-879045-83-4 **$24.95**

Six Jewish Spiritual Paths: *A Rationalist Looks at Spirituality*
by Rabbi Rifat Sonsino 6 x 9, 208 pp, HC, ISBN 1-58023-095-4 **$21.95**

Becoming a Congregation of Learners
Learning as a Key to Revitalizing Congregational Life by Isa Aron, Ph.D.;
Foreword by Rabbi Lawrence A. Hoffman, Co-Developer, Synagogue 2000
6 x 9, 304 pp, Quality PB, ISBN 1-58023-089-X **$19.95**

Self, Struggle & Change
Family Conflict Stories in Genesis and Their Healing Insights for Our Lives
by Dr. Norman J. Cohen 6 x 9, 224 pp, Quality PB, ISBN 1-879045-66-4 **$16.95**

Voices from Genesis: *Guiding Us through the Stages of Life*
by Dr. Norman J. Cohen 6 x 9, 192 pp, Quality PB, ISBN 1-58023-118-7 **$16.95**

Ancient Secrets: *Using the Stories of the Bible to Improve Our Everyday Lives*
by Rabbi Levi Meier, Ph.D. 5½ x 8½, 288 pp, Quality PB, ISBN 1-58023-064-4 **$16.95**

The Business Bible: *10 New Commandments for Bringing Spirituality &*
Ethical Values into the Workplace
by Rabbi Wayne Dosick 5½ x 8½, 208 pp, Quality PB, ISBN 1-58023-101-2 **$14.95**

Being God's Partner: *How to Find the Hidden Link Between Spirituality and Your Work*
by Rabbi Jeffrey K. Salkin; Intro. by Norman Lear **AWARD WINNER!**
6 x 9, 192 pp, Quality PB, ISBN 1-879045-65-6 **$16.95**; HC, ISBN 1-879045-37-0 **$19.95**

God & the Big Bang
Discovering Harmony Between Science & Spirituality **AWARD WINNER!**
by Daniel C. Matt 6 x 9, 224 pp, Quality PB, ISBN 1-879045-89-3 **$16.95**

Soul Judaism: *Dancing with God into a New Era*
by Rabbi Wayne Dosick 5½ x 8½, 304 pp, Quality PB, ISBN 1-58023-053-9 **$16.95**

Finding Joy: *A Practical Spiritual Guide to Happiness* **AWARD WINNER!**
by Rabbi Dannel I. Schwartz with Mark Hass
6 x 9, 192 pp, Quality PB, ISBN 1-58023-009-1 **$14.95**; HC, ISBN 1-879045-53-2 **$19.95**

Life Cycle/Grief

Against the Dying of the Light
A Parent's Story of Love, Loss and Hope
by *Leonard Fein*

The sudden death of a child. A personal tragedy beyond description. Rage and despair deeper than sorrow. What can come from it? Raw wisdom and defiant hope. In this unusual exploration of heartbreak and healing, Fein chronicles the sudden death of his 30-year-old daughter and reveals what the progression of grief can teach each one of us.

5½ x 8½, 176 pp, HC, ISBN 1-58023-110-1 **$19.95**

Mourning & Mitzvah, 2nd Ed.: *A Guided Journal for Walking the Mourner's Path through Grief to Healing with Over 60 Guided Exercises*
by *Anne Brener, L.C.S.W.*

For those who mourn a death, for those who would help them, for those who face a loss of any kind, Brener teaches us the power and strength available to us in the fully experienced mourning process. Revised and expanded. 7½ x 9, 304 pp, Quality PB, ISBN 1-58023-113-6 **$19.95**

Grief in Our Seasons: *A Mourner's Kaddish Companion*
by *Rabbi Kerry M. Olitzky*

A wise and inspiring selection of sacred Jewish writings and a simple, powerful ancient ritual for mourners to read each day, to help hold the memory of their loved ones in their hearts. Offers a comforting, step-by-step daily link to saying Kaddish.

4½ x 6½, 448 pp, Quality PB, ISBN 1-879045-55-9 **$15.95**

 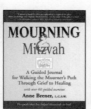   

Tears of Sorrow, Seeds of Hope
A Jewish Spiritual Companion for Infertility and Pregnancy Loss
by Rabbi Nina Beth Cardin   6 x 9, 192 pp, HC, ISBN 1-58023-017-2 **$19.95**

A Time to Mourn, A Time to Comfort
A Guide to Jewish Bereavement and Comfort
by Dr. Ron Wolfson   7 x 9, 336 pp, Quality PB, ISBN 1-879045-96-6 **$18.95**

When a Grandparent Dies
A Kid's Own Remembering Workbook for Dealing with Shiva and the Year Beyond
by Nechama Liss-Levinson, Ph.D.
8 x 10, 48 pp, HC, Illus., 2-color text, ISBN 1-879045-44-3 **$15.95**   For ages 7–13

Spirituality—The Kushner Series
Books by Lawrence Kushner

The Way Into Jewish Mystical Tradition

Explains the principles of Jewish mystical thinking, their religious and spiritual significance, and how they relate to our lives. A book that allows us to experience and understand the Jewish mystical approach to our place in the world.

6 x 9, 224 pp, HC, ISBN 1-58023-029-6 **$21.95**

Jewish Spirituality: *A Brief Introduction for Christians*

Addresses Christian's questions, revealing the essence of Judaism in a way that people whose own tradition traces its roots to Judaism can understand and appreciate.

5½ x 8½, 112 pp, Quality PB, ISBN 1-58023-150-0 **$12.95**

Eyes Remade for Wonder: *The Way of Jewish Mysticism and Sacred Living*
A Lawrence Kushner Reader Intro. by *Thomas Moore*

Whether you are new to Kushner or a devoted fan, you'll find inspiration here. With samplings from each of Kushner's works, and a generous amount of new material, this book is to be read and reread, each time discovering deeper layers of meaning in our lives.

6 x 9, 240 pp, Quality PB, ISBN 1-58023-042-3 **$16.95**; HC, ISBN 1-58023-014-8 **$23.95**

   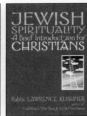 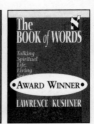

Invisible Lines of Connection: *Sacred Stories of the Ordinary* AWARD WINNER!
5½ x 8½, 160 pp, Quality PB, ISBN 1-879045-98-2 **$15.95**

Honey from the Rock: *An Introduction to Jewish Mysticism* SPECIAL ANNIVERSARY EDITION
6 x 9, 176 pp, Quality PB, ISBN 1-58023-073-3 **$15.95**

The Book of Letters: *A Mystical Hebrew Alphabet* AWARD WINNER!
Popular HC Edition, 6 x 9, 80 pp, 2-color text, ISBN 1-879045-00-1 **$24.95**; *Deluxe Gift Edition,* 9 x 12, 80 pp, HC, 4-color text, ornamentation, slipcase, ISBN 1-879045-01-X **$79.95**; *Collector's Limited Edition,* 9 x 12, 80 pp, HC, gold-embossed pages, hand-assembled slipcase. With silkscreened print. Limited to 500 signed and numbered copies, ISBN 1-879045-04-4 **$349.00**

The Book of Words: *Talking Spiritual Life, Living Spiritual Talk* AWARD WINNER!
6 x 9, 160 pp, Quality PB, 2-color text, ISBN 1-58023-020-2 **$16.95**; HC, ISBN 1-879045-35-4 **$21.95**

God Was in This Place & I, i Did Not Know: *Finding Self, Spirituality and Ultimate Meaning*
6 x 9, 192 pp, Quality PB, ISBN 1-879045-33-8 **$16.95**

The River of Light: *Jewish Mystical Awareness* SPECIAL ANNIVERSARY EDITION
6 x 9, 192 pp, Quality PB, ISBN 1-58023-096-2 **$16.95**

Because Nothing Looks Like God
by Lawrence and Karen Kushner; Full-color illus. by Dawn W. Majewski
11 x 8½, 32 pp, HC, Full-color illus., ISBN 1-58023-092-X **$16.95**   **For ages 4 & up**

Children's Spirituality

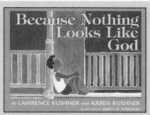

Because Nothing Looks Like God
by *Lawrence and Karen Kushner*
Full-color illus. by *Dawn W. Majewski*

For ages 4 & up

MULTICULTURAL, NONDENOMINATIONAL, NONSECTARIAN

What is God like? The first collaborative work by husband-and-wife team Lawrence and Karen Kushner introduces children to the possibilities of spiritual life. Real-life examples of happiness and sadness—from goodnight stories, to the hope and fear felt the first time at bat, to the closing moments of life—invite us to explore, together with our children, the questions we all have about God, no matter what our age.
11 x 8½, 32 pp, HC, Full-color illus., ISBN 1-58023-092-X **$16.95**

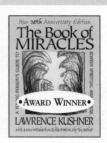

Where Is God?
What Does God Look Like?
How Does God Make Things Happen? (Board Books)

For ages 0–4

by *Lawrence and Karen Kushner*; Full-color illus. by *Dawn W. Majewski*

Gently invites children to become aware of God's presence all around them. Three board books abridged from *Because Nothing Looks Like God* by Lawrence and Karen Kushner.
Each 5 x 5, 24 pp, Board, Full-color illus. **$7.95**   SKYLIGHT PATHS Books

Sharing Blessings
Children's Stories for Exploring the Spirit of the Jewish Holidays

For ages 6 & up

by *Rahel Musleah* and *Rabbi Michael Klayman*; Full-color illus.

What is the spiritual message of each of the Jewish holidays? How do we teach it to our children? Through stories about one family's life, *Sharing Blessings* explores ways to get into the *spirit* of thirteen different holidays.
8½ x 11, 64 pp, HC, Full-color illus., ISBN 1-879045-71-0 **$18.95**

The Book of Miracles   AWARD WINNER!
A Young Person's Guide to Jewish Spiritual Awareness

For ages 9 & up

by *Lawrence Kushner*

Introduces kids to a way of everyday spiritual thinking to last a lifetime. Kushner, whose award-winning books have brought spirituality to life for countless adults, now shows young people how to use Judaism as a foundation on which to build their lives.
6 x 9, 96 pp, HC, 2-color illus., ISBN 1-879045-78-8 **$16.95**

Children's Spirituality

In Our Image
God's First Creatures   AWARD WINNER!
by *Nancy Sohn Swartz*
Full-color illus. by *Melanie Hall*

For ages
4 & up

A playful new twist on the Creation story—from the perspective of the animals. Celebrates the interconnectedness of nature and the harmony of all living things. "The vibrantly colored illustrations nearly leap off the page in this delightful interpretation." —*School Library Journal*
9 x 12, 32 pp, HC, Full-color illus., ISBN 1-879045-99-0 **$16.95**

 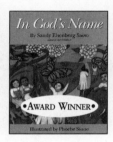 

God's Paintbrush   AWARD WINNER!
by *Sandy Eisenberg Sasso*; Full-color illus. by *Annette Compton*

For ages
4 & up

Invites children of all faiths and backgrounds to encounter God openly in their own lives. Wonderfully interactive; provides questions adult and child can explore together at the end of each episode. 11 x 8½, 32 pp, HC, Full-color illus., ISBN 1-879045-22-2 **$16.95**

Also available: A Teacher's Guide: **A Guide for Jewish & Christian Educators and Parents**
8½ x 11, 32 pp, PB, ISBN 1-879045-57-5 **$8.95**

God's Paintbrush Celebration Kit 9½ x 12, HC, Includes 5 sessions/40 full-color Activity Sheets and Teacher Folder with complete instructions, ISBN 1-58023-050-4 **$21.95**

In God's Name   AWARD WINNER!
by *Sandy Eisenberg Sasso*; Full-color illus. by *Phoebe Stone*

For ages
4 & up

Like an ancient myth in its poetic text and vibrant illustrations, this award-winning modern fable about the search for God's name celebrates the diversity and, at the same time, the unity of all people. 9 x 12, 32 pp, HC, Full-color illus., ISBN 1-879045-26-5 **$16.95**

What Is God's Name? (A Board Book)

For ages
0–4

An abridged board book version of award-winning *In God's Name*.
5 x 5, 24 pp, Board, Full-color illus., ISBN 1-893361-10-1 **$7.95** A SKYLIGHT PATHS Book

The 11th Commandment: *Wisdom from Our Children*
by *The Children of America*   AWARD WINNER!

For
all ages

"If there were an Eleventh Commandment, what would it be?" Children of many religious denominations across America answer this question—in their own drawings and words. "A rare book of spiritual celebration for all people, of all ages, for all time."—*Bookviews*
8 x 10, 48 pp, HC, Full-color illus., ISBN 1-879045-46-X **$16.95**

Children's Spirituality

Cain & Abel   AWARD WINNER!
Finding the Fruits of Peace

For ages 5 & up

by *Sandy Eisenberg Sasso*
Full-color illus. by *Joani Keller Rothenberg*

A sensitive recasting of the ancient tale shows we have the power to deal with anger in positive ways. Provides questions for kids and adults to explore together. "Editor's Choice"—American Library Association's *Booklist*

9 x 12, 32 pp, HC, Full-color illus., ISBN 1-58023-123-3 **$16.95**

For Heaven's Sake   AWARD WINNER!

For ages 4 & up

by *Sandy Eisenberg Sasso*; Full-color illus. by *Kathryn Kunz Finney*
Everyone talked about heaven, but no one would say what heaven was or how to find it. So Isaiah decides to find out. 9 x 12, 32 pp, HC, Full-color illus., ISBN 1-58023-054-7 **$16.95**

God Said Amen   AWARD WINNER!

For ages 4 & up

by *Sandy Eisenberg Sasso*; Full-color illus. by *Avi Katz*
Inspiring tale of two kingdoms: one overflowing with water but without oil to light its lamps; the other blessed with oil but no water to grow its gardens. The kingdoms' rulers ask God for help but are too stubborn to ask each other. Shows that we need only reach out to each other to find God's answer to our prayers. 9 x 12, 32 pp, HC, Full-color illus., ISBN 1-58023-080-6 **$16.95**

God in Between   AWARD WINNER!

For ages 4 & up

by *Sandy Eisenberg Sasso*; Full-color illus. by *Sally Sweetland*
If you wanted to find God, where would you look? This magical, mythical tale teaches that God can be found where we are: within all of us and the relationships between us.
9 x 12, 32 pp, HC, Full-color illus., ISBN 1-879045-86-9 **$16.95**

A Prayer for the Earth: *The Story of Naamah, Noah's Wife*

For ages 4 & up

by *Sandy Eisenberg Sasso*; Full-color illus. by *Bethanne Andersen*   AWARD WINNER!
Opens religious imaginations to new ideas about the story of the Flood. When God tells Noah to bring the animals onto the ark, God also calls on Naamah, Noah's wife, to save each plant on Earth. 9 x 12, 32 pp, HC, Full-color illus., ISBN 1-879045-60-5 **$16.95**

But God Remembered   AWARD WINNER!
Stories of Women from Creation to the Promised Land

For ages 8 & up

by *Sandy Eisenberg Sasso*; Full-color illus. by *Bethanne Andersen*
Vibrantly brings to life four stories of courageous and strong women from ancient tradition; all teach important values through their actions and faith.
9 x 12, 32 pp, HC, Full-color illus., ISBN 1-879045-43-5 **$16.95**

Healing/Wellness/Recovery

Jewish Paths toward Healing and Wholeness
A Personal Guide to Dealing with Suffering
by *Rabbi Kerry M. Olitzky*; Foreword by *Debbie Friedman*

Why me? Why do we suffer? How can we heal? Grounded in personal experience with illness and Jewish spiritual traditions, this book provides healing rituals, psalms and prayers that help readers initiate a dialogue with God, to guide them along the complicated path of healing and wholeness. 6 x 9, 192 pp, Quality PB, ISBN 1-58023-068-7 **$15.95**

Healing of Soul, Healing of Body
Spiritual Leaders Unfold the Strength & Solace in Psalms
Ed. by *Rabbi Simkha Y. Weintraub, CSW,* for The National Center for Jewish Healing

For those who are facing illness and those who care for them. Inspiring commentaries on ten psalms for healing by eminent spiritual leaders reflecting all Jewish movements make the power of the psalms accessible to all.
6 x 9, 128 pp, Quality PB, Illus., 2-color text, ISBN 1-879045-31-1 **$14.95**

Jewish Pastoral Care
A Practical Handbook from Traditional and Contemporary Sources
Ed. by *Rabbi Dayle A. Friedman*

Gives today's Jewish pastoral counselors practical guidelines based in the Jewish tradition.
6 x 9, 464 pp, HC, ISBN 1-58023-078-4 **$35.00**

Twelve Jewish Steps to Recovery: *A Personal Guide to Turning from Alcoholism & Other Addictions . . . Drugs, Food, Gambling, Sex . . .* by Rabbi Kerry M. Olitzky & Stuart A. Copans, M.D. Preface by Abraham J. Twerski, M.D.; "Getting Help" by JACS Foundation 6 x 9, 144 pp, Quality PB, ISBN 1-879045-09-5 **$13.95**

One Hundred Blessings Every Day: *Daily Twelve Step Recovery Affirmations, Exercises for Personal Growth & Renewal Reflecting Seasons of the Jewish Year* by Rabbi Kerry M. Olitzky 4½ x 6½, 432 pp, Quality PB, ISBN 1-879045-30-3 **$14.95**

Recovery from Codependence: *A Jewish Twelve Steps Guide to Healing Your Soul* by Rabbi Kerry M. Olitzky 6 x 9, 160 pp, Quality PB, ISBN 1-879045-32-X **$13.95**

Renewed Each Day: *Daily Twelve Step Recovery Meditations Based on the Bible* by Rabbi Kerry M. Olitzky & Aaron Z. *Vol. I: Genesis & Exodus*; *Vol. II: Leviticus, Numbers and Deuteronomy*
Vol. I: 6 x 9, 224 pp, Quality PB, ISBN 1-879045-12-5 **$14.95**
Vol. II: 6 x 9, 280 pp, Quality PB, ISBN 1-879045-13-3 **$14.95**

Spirituality/Jewish Meditation

Aleph-Bet Yoga
Embodying the Hebrew Letters for Physical and Spiritual Well-Being
by *Steven A. Rapp*

Foreword by *Tamar Frankiel* and *Judy Greenfeld*; Preface by *Hart Lazer*

Blends aspects of hatha yoga and the shapes of the Hebrew letters. Connects yoga practice with Jewish spiritual life. Easy-to-follow instructions, b/w photos.
7 x 10, 128 pp, Quality PB, b/w photos, ISBN 1-58023-162-4 **$16.95**

Discovering Jewish Meditation
Instruction & Guidance for Learning an Ancient Spiritual Practice
by *Nan Fink Gefen*

Gives readers of any level of understanding the tools to learn the practice of Jewish meditation on their own. 6 x 9, 208 pp, Quality PB, ISBN 1-58023-067-9 **$16.95**

One God Clapping: *The Spiritual Path of a Zen Rabbi* AWARD WINNER!
by *Alan Lew* with *Sherril Jaffe*

A fascinating personal story of a Jewish meditation expert's roundabout spiritual journey from Zen Buddhist practitioner to rabbi. 5½ x 8½, 336 pp, Quality PB, ISBN 1-58023-115-2 **$16.95**

 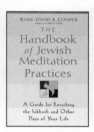   

The Handbook of Jewish Meditation Practices
A Guide for Enriching the Sabbath and Other Days of Your Life
by *Rabbi David A. Cooper*

Jewish practices and traditions, easy-to-use meditation exercises, and contemplative study of Jewish sacred texts. 6 x 9, 208 pp, Quality PB, ISBN 1-58023-102-0 **$16.95**

Stepping Stones to Jewish Spiritual Living: *Walking the Path Morning, Noon, and Night*
by Rabbi James L. Mirel & Karen Bonnell Werth
6 x 9, 240 pp, Quality PB, ISBN 1-58023-074-1 **$16.95**; HC, ISBN 1-58023-003-2 **$21.95**

Meditation from the Heart of Judaism: *Today's Teachers Share Their Practices, Techniques, and Faith* Ed. by Avram Davis
6 x 9, 256 pp, Quality PB, ISBN 1-58023-049-0 **$16.95**; HC, ISBN 1-879045-77-X **$21.95**

The Way of Flame: *A Guide to the Forgotten Mystical Tradition of Jewish Meditation*
by Avram Davis 4½ x 8, 176 pp, Quality PB, ISBN 1-58023-060-1 **$15.95**

Minding the Temple of the Soul: *Balancing Body, Mind, and Spirit through Traditional Jewish Prayer, Movement, and Meditation* by Tamar Frankiel and Judy Greenfeld
7 x 10, 184 pp, Quality PB, Illus., ISBN 1-879045-64-8 **$16.95**

Entering the Temple of Dreams: *Jewish Prayers, Movements, and Meditations for the End of the Day* by Tamar Frankiel and Judy Greenfeld
7 x 10, 192 pp, Illus., Quality PB, ISBN 1-58023-079-2 **$16.95**

Spirituality & More

The Jewish Lights Spirituality Handbook
A Guide to Understanding, Exploring & Living a Spiritual Life
Ed. by *Stuart M. Matlins, Editor-in-Chief, Jewish Lights Publishing*

Rich, creative material from over fifty spiritual leaders on every aspect of Jewish spirituality today: prayer, meditation, mysticism, study, rituals, special days, the everyday, and more.
6 x 9, 456 pp, Quality PB, ISBN 1-58023-093-8 **$18.95**; HC, ISBN 1-58023-100-4 **$24.95**

The Story of the Jews: *A 4,000-Year Adventure—A Graphic History Book*
Written and illustrated by *Stan Mack*

Through witty cartoons and accurate narrative, illustrates the major characters and events that have shaped the Jewish people and culture. For all ages.
6 x 9, 304 pp, Quality PB, Illus., ISBN 1-58023-155-1 **$16.95**

The Jewish Prophet: *Visionary Words from Moses and Miriam to Henrietta Szold and A. J. Heschel*
by *Rabbi Dr. Michael J. Shire*

This beautifully illustrated collection of Jewish prophecy features the lives and teachings of thirty men and women, from biblical times to modern day. Provides an inspiring and informative description of the role each played in their own time, and an explanation of why we should know about them in our time. Illustrated with illuminations from medieval Hebrew manuscripts.
6½ x 8½, 128 pp, HC, 123 full-color illus., ISBN 1-58023-168-3 **$25.00**

The Enneagram and Kabbalah: *Reading Your Soul*
by Rabbi Howard A. Addison 6 x 9, 176 pp, Quality PB, ISBN 1-58023-001-6 **$15.95**

Cast in God's Image: *Discover Your Personality Type Using the Enneagram and Kabbalah*
by Rabbi Howard A. Addison 7 x 9, 176 pp, Quality PB, ISBN 1-58023-124-1 **$16.95**

Mystery Midrash: *An Anthology of Jewish Mystery & Detective Fiction* AWARD WINNER!
Ed. by Lawrence W. Raphael 6 x 9, 304 pp, Quality PB, ISBN 1-58023-055-5 **$16.95**

Criminal Kabbalah: *An Intriguing Anthology of Jewish Mystery & Detective Fiction*
Ed. by Lawrence W. Raphael; Foreword by Laurie R. King
6 x 9, 256 pp, Quality PB, ISBN 1-58023-109-8 **$16.95**

Sacred Intentions: *Daily Inspiration to Strengthen the Spirit, Based on Jewish Wisdom*
by Rabbi Kerry M. Olitzky & Rabbi Lori Forman
4½ x 6½, 448 pp, Quality PB, ISBN 1-58023-061-X **$15.95**

Restful Reflections: *Nighttime Inspiration to Calm the Soul, Based on Jewish Wisdom*
by Rabbi Kerry M. Olitzky & Rabbi Lori Forman
4½ x 6½, 448 pp, Quality PB, ISBN 1-58023-091-1 **$15.95**

Embracing the Covenant: *Converts to Judaism Talk About Why & How* Ed. by Rabbi Allan Berkowitz & Patti Moskovitz 6 x 9, 192 pp, Quality PB, ISBN 1-879045-50-8 **$16.95**

Wandering Stars: *An Anthology of Jewish Fantasy & Science Fiction* Ed. by Jack Dann; Intro. by Isaac Asimov 6 x 9, 272 pp, Quality PB, ISBN 1-58023-005-9 **$16.95**

Israel—A Spiritual Travel Guide: *A Companion for the Modern Jewish Pilgrim* AWARD WINNER!
by Rabbi Lawrence A. Hoffman 4¾ x 10, 256 pp, Quality PB, ISBN 1-879045-56-7 **$18.95**

Women's Spirituality

The Women's Torah Commentary: *New Insights from Women Rabbis on the 54 Weekly Torah Portions* Ed. by *Rabbi Elyse Goldstein*

For the first time, women rabbis provide a commentary on the entire Five Books of Moses. More than twenty-five years after the first woman was ordained a rabbi in America, these inspiring teachers bring their rich perspectives to bear on the biblical text. In a week-by-week format; a perfect gift for others, or for yourself. 6 x 9, 496 pp, HC, ISBN 1-58023-076-8 **$34.95**

Moonbeams: *A Hadassah Rosh Hodesh Guide* Ed. by *Carol Diament, Ph.D.*

This hands-on "idea book" focuses on *Rosh Hodesh*, the festival of the new moon, as a source of spiritual growth for Jewish women. A complete sourcebook that will initiate or rejuvenate women's study groups, it is also perfect for women preparing for *bat mitzvah*, or for anyone interested in learning more about *Rosh Hodesh* observance and what it has to offer. 8½ x 11, 240 pp, Quality PB, ISBN 1-58023-099-7 **$20.00**

 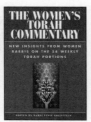   

Lifecycles In Two Volumes **AWARD WINNERS!**
V. 1: *Jewish Women on Life Passages & Personal Milestones*
Ed. and with Intros. by Rabbi Debra Orenstein
V. 2: *Jewish Women on Biblical Themes in Contemporary Life*
Ed. and with Intros. by Rabbi Debra Orenstein and Rabbi Jane Rachel Litman
V. 1: 6 x 9, 480 pp, Quality PB, ISBN 1-58023-018-0 **$19.95**
V. 2: 6 x 9, 464 pp, Quality PB, ISBN 1-58023-019-9 **$19.95**

ReVisions: *Seeing Torah through a Feminist Lens* **AWARD WINNER!**
by Rabbi Elyse Goldstein 5½ x 8½, 224 pp, Quality PB, ISBN 1-58023-117-9 **$16.95**;
208 pp, HC, ISBN 1-58023-047-4 **$19.95**

The Year Mom Got Religion: *One Woman's Midlife Journey into Judaism*
by Lee Meyerhoff Hendler 6 x 9, 208 pp, Quality PB, ISBN 1-58023-070-9 **$15.95**

Ecology

Torah of the Earth: *Exploring 4,000 Years of Ecology in Jewish Thought*
In 2 Volumes Ed. by *Rabbi Arthur Waskow*

An invaluable key to understanding the intersection of ecology and Judaism. Leading scholars provide a guided tour of Jewish ecological thought.
Vol. 1: *Biblical Israel & Rabbinic Judaism,* 6 x 9, 272 pp, Quality PB, ISBN 1-58023-086-5 **$19.95**
Vol. 2: *Zionism & Eco-Judaism,* 6 x 9, 336 pp, Quality PB, ISBN 1-58023-087-3 **$19.95**

Ecology & the Jewish Spirit: *Where Nature & the Sacred Meet* Ed. and with Intros.
by Ellen Bernstein 6 x 9, 288 pp, Quality PB, ISBN 1-58023-082-2 **$16.95**

The Jewish Gardening Cookbook: *Growing Plants & Cooking for Holidays & Festivals*
by Michael Brown 6 x 9, 224 pp, Illus., Quality PB, ISBN 1-58023-116-0 **$16.95**;
HC, ISBN 1-58023-004-0 **$21.95**

Theology/Philosophy

Love and Terror in the God Encounter: *The Theological Legacy of Rabbi Joseph B. Soloveitchik*
by *Dr. David Hartman*

Renowned scholar David Hartman explores the sometimes surprising intersection of Soloveitchik's rootedness in halakhic tradition with his genuine responsiveness to modern Western theology. An engaging look at one of the most important Jewish thinkers of the twentieth century.
6 x 9, 240 pp, HC, ISBN 1-58023-112-8 **$25.00**

These Are the Words: *A Vocabulary of Jewish Spiritual Life*
by *Arthur Green*

What are the most essential ideas, concepts and terms that an educated person needs to know about Judaism? From *Adonai* (My Lord) to *zekhut* (merit), this enlightening and entertaining journey through Judaism teaches us the 149 core Hebrew words that constitute the basic vocabulary of Jewish spiritual life. 6 x 9, 304 pp, Quality PB, ISBN 1-58023-107-1 **$18.95**

Broken Tablets: *Restoring the Ten Commandments and Ourselves*
Ed. by *Rabbi Rachel S. Mikva*; Intro. by *Rabbi Lawrence Kushner* AWARD WINNER!

Twelve outstanding spiritual leaders each share profound and personal thoughts about these biblical commands and why they have such a special hold on us.
6 x 9, 192 pp, Quality PB, ISBN 1-58023-158-6 **$16.95**; HC, ISBN 1-58023-066-0 **$21.95**

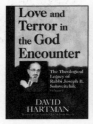   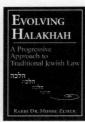 

A Heart of Many Rooms: *Celebrating the Many Voices within Judaism* AWARD WINNER!
by Dr. David Hartman 6 x 9, 352 pp, Quality PB, ISBN 1-58023-156-X **$19.95**;
HC, ISBN 1-58023-048-2 **$24.95**

A Living Covenant: *The Innovative Spirit in Traditional Judaism* AWARD WINNER!
by Dr. David Hartman 6 x 9, 368 pp, Quality PB, ISBN 1-58023-011-3 **$18.95**

Evolving Halakhah: *A Progressive Approach to Traditional Jewish Law*
by Rabbi Dr. Moshe Zemer 6 x 9, 480 pp, HC, ISBN 1-58023-002-4 **$40.00**

The Death of Death: *Resurrection and Immortality in Jewish Thought* AWARD WINNER!
by Dr. Neil Gillman 6 x 9, 336 pp, Quality PB, ISBN 1-58023-081-4 **$18.95**

The Last Trial: *On the Legends and Lore of the Command to Abraham to Offer Isaac as a Sacrifice* by Shalom Spiegel 6 x 9, 208 pp, Quality PB, ISBN 1-879045-29-X **$17.95**

Tormented Master: *The Life and Spiritual Quest of Rabbi Nahman of Bratslav*
by Dr. Arthur Green 6 x 9, 416 pp, Quality PB, ISBN 1-879045-11-7 **$18.95**

The Earth Is the Lord's: *The Inner World of the Jew in Eastern Europe*
by Abraham Joshua Heschel 5½ x 8, 128 pp, Quality PB, ISBN 1-879045-42-7 **$14.95**

A Passion for Truth: *Despair and Hope in Hasidism* by Abraham Joshua Heschel
5½ x 8, 352 pp, Quality PB, ISBN 1-879045-41-9 **$18.95**

Your Word Is Fire: *The Hasidic Masters on Contemplative Prayer* Ed. by Dr. Arthur Green and Dr. Barry W. Holtz 6 x 9, 160 pp, Quality PB, ISBN 1-879045-25-7 **$15.95**

Life Cycle & Holidays

The Jewish Family Fun Book: *Holiday Projects, Everyday Activities, and Travel Ideas with Jewish Themes*
by *Danielle Dardashti* and *Roni Sarig;* Illustrated by *Avi Katz*

With almost 100 easy-to-do activities to re-invigorate age-old Jewish customs and make them fun for the whole family, this complete sourcebook details activities for fun at home and away from home, including meaningful everyday and holiday crafts, recipes, travel guides, enriching entertainment and much, much more. Illustrated.
6 x 9, 288 pp, Quality PB, Illus., ISBN 1-58023-171-3 **$18.95**

The Book of Jewish Sacred Practices
CLAL's Guide to Everyday & Holiday Rituals & Blessings
Ed. by *Rabbi Irwin Kula* & *Vanessa L. Ochs, Ph.D.*

A meditation, blessing, profound Jewish teaching, and ritual for more than one hundred everyday events and holidays. 6 x 9, 368 pp, Quality PB, ISBN 1-58023-152-7 **$18.95**

Celebrating Your New Jewish Daughter: *Creating Jewish Ways to Welcome Baby Girls into the Covenant—New and Traditional Ceremonies*
by Debra Nussbaum Cohen; Foreword by Rabbi Sandy Eisenberg Sasso
6 x 9, 272 pp, Quality PB, ISBN 1-58023-090-3 **$18.95**

The New Jewish Baby Book AWARD WINNER!
Names, Ceremonies & Customs—A Guide for Today's Families
by Anita Diamant 6 x 9, 336 pp, Quality PB, ISBN 1-879045-28-1 **$18.95**

Parenting As a Spiritual Journey
Deepening Ordinary & Extraordinary Events into Sacred Occasions
by Rabbi Nancy Fuchs-Kreimer 6 x 9, 224 pp, Quality PB, ISBN 1-58023-016-4 **$16.95**

Putting God on the Guest List, 2nd Ed. AWARD WINNER!
How to Reclaim the Spiritual Meaning of Your Child's Bar or Bat Mitzvah
by Rabbi Jeffrey K. Salkin 6 x 9, 224 pp, Quality PB, ISBN 1-879045-59-1 **$16.95**

The Bar/Bat Mitzvah Memory Book: *An Album for Treasuring the Spiritual Celebration* by Rabbi Jeffrey K. Salkin and Nina Salkin
8 x 10, 48 pp, Deluxe HC, 2-color text, ribbon marker, ISBN 1-58023-111-X **$19.95**

For Kids—Putting God on Your Guest List
How to Claim the Spiritual Meaning of Your Bar or Bat Mitzvah
by Rabbi Jeffrey K. Salkin 6 x 9, 144 pp, Quality PB, ISBN 1-58023-015-6 **$14.95**

Bar/Bat Mitzvah Basics, 2nd Ed.: *A Practical Family Guide to Coming of Age Together*
Ed. by Cantor Helen Leneman 6 x 9, 240 pp, Quality PB, ISBN 1-58023-151-9 **$18.95**

Hanukkah, 2nd Ed.: *The Family Guide to Spiritual Celebration*—The Art of Jewish Living
by Dr. Ron Wolfson 7 x 9, 240 pp, Quality PB, Illus., ISBN 1-58023-122-5 **$18.95**

Shabbat, 2nd Ed.: *Preparing for and Celebrating the Sabbath*—The Art of Jewish Living
by Dr. Ron Wolfson 7 x 9, 320 pp, Quality PB, Illus., ISBN 1-58023-164-0 **$19.95**

The Passover Seder—The Art of Jewish Living
by Dr. Ron Wolfson 7 x 9, 352 pp, Quality PB, Illus., ISBN 1-879045-93-1 **$16.95**

   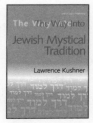